FOR MY NAME'S SAKE

Books by RONALD SETH

BALTIC CORNER: TRAVEL IN ESTONIA
(*Methuen*)

A SPY HAS NO FRIENDS
(*André Deutsch*)

THE PATRIOT

SPIES AT WORK: A HISTORY OF ESPIONAGE

THE ART OF SPYING
(*Peter Owen*)

A NEW PROSE TRANSLATION OF OVID'S ART OF LOVE
(*Spearman*)

LION WITH BLUE WINGS: THE STORY OF THE GLIDER PILOT
REGIMENT

SECRET SERVANTS: THE STORY OF JAPANESE ESPIONAGE
(*Gollancz*)

THE UNDAUNTED: THE STORY OF RESISTANCE IN WESTERN EUROPE
(*Frederick Muller*)

Juveniles

OPERATION RETRIEVER

OPERATION LAMA

THE TRUE BOOK ABOUT THE SECRET SERVICE
(*Frederick Muller*)

OPERATION ORMER

HOW SPIES WORK

THE SPY AND THE ATOM-GUN
(*Geoffrey Bles*)

FOR MY NAME'S SAKE

A brief account of the struggle of the Roman Catholic
Church against the Nazis in Western Europe
and against Communist persecution
in Eastern Europe

by

RONALD SETH

LONDON
GEOFFREY BLES

Printed in Great Britain by
Richard Clay & Co Ltd Bungay
for the publishers
Geoffrey Bles Ltd
52 Doughty Street, London, WC1

© RONALD SETH 1958

". . . they shall lay their hands on you, and persecute you, delivering you . . . into prisons, being brought before kings and rulers for my name's sake."

(Luke 21 v. 12)

Foreword

IN WRITING this very brief account of the response of the Roman Catholic Church to the sufferings inflicted upon it, first by the Nazis and then by the new Communist régimes of Europe, I have attempted to record in simple form a chapter of history which we tend to forget.

The War is now a long way off and except for personal experiences we are daily becoming less and less interested in the events in Europe between 1939 and 1945. The new Communist countries are distant in space, and not only distant, but shut off from us so effectively that the ordinary man knows little or nothing of what goes on in them. What the eye does not see, nor the ear hear, we are not likely to grieve over.

What happened to the Churches under the Nazis, what has happened and is still happening to the Churches under the Communists, while calling up our grief, should, by the token of the courage and fortitude of the servants of the Churches, call up our admiration, and above all our humility, an emotion which has almost been suffocated out of our experience by the all-embracing materialism of our times.

The plan of my account needs, perhaps, a word of explanation. First, I have omitted the Nazi persecution of the Roman Catholic Church in Germany proper. This is too complicated a subject to be dealt with within the limits at my disposal, and in any case, has special features which do not fall within my general scheme. Second, I have dealt with Nazi persecution only in the occupied countries of Western Europe, because it is not possible to obtain in these days the relevant information from the countries of East Europe, and the documentation is scanty.

But if the Nazi persecution of the Church in Eastern Europe is omitted, I believe this is more than compensated by my account of the Communist persecution in those countries. For this persecution continues with increasing severity to this day; it is actual; and for this reason has a greater call upon our sympathy than what is over and done with and cannot be changed. We could if we would, I believe, do something to help, though the moral courage and the moral strength needed for the effort may at first sight daunt us.

Many people have helped me in the compilation of this book, so many that I dare not begin to name them, lest I should leave some out. But all who read this I would assure once more of my deep gratitude.

I am not a Roman Catholic, but I make no apology for writing this book. I was inspired by the subject, and for me that is sufficient reason. I have tried to be as scrupulously fair as my natural failings would let me be. I hope, too, that I offend no Catholic by the maladroitness of my language. If I have erred against rank or title or the accepted ecclesiastical phrase, I ask to be forgiven and my ignorance excused.

RONALD SETH

Contents

FOREWORD   vii

PART ONE

The Church and the Crooked Cross

Chapter I.	HOLLAND	3
Chapter II.	BELGIUM	23
Chapter III.	OCCUPIED FRANCE	68
Chapter IV.	AUSTRIA	76
Chapter V.	ITALY	93
Chapter VI.	DACHAU	104

PART TWO

The Church's Struggle Against Communist Persecution

Chapter VII.	THE NEW THREAT	113
Chapter VIII.	THE BALTIC STATES	117
Chapter IX.	YUGOSLAVIA	125
Chapter X.	BULGARIA	139
Chapter XI.	ALBANIA	143
Chapter XII.	THE GERMAN PEOPLE'S REPUBLIC	149
Chapter XIII	HUNGARY	161
Chapter XIV.	POLAND	183
Chapter XV.	RUMANIA	202
Chapter XVI.	CZECHO-SLOVAKIA	215
Chapter XVII.	THE TECHNIQUE	232
	CHART SHOWING MAIN DEVELOPMENTS IN TECHNIQUE OF PERSECUTION	244
	BIBLIOGRAPHY	245

PART ONE

The Church and the Crooked Cross

CHAPTER I

Holland

UNTIL THE advent of National Socialism in Germany, persecution of the Roman Catholic Church had been unknown in western Europe for many, many years. The paganism of Nazi philosophy made it clear, however, that sooner or later the Church in Germany must come into collision with the temporal power in the Third Reich. When this happened, it might bow before the storm and sign its own death-warrant, or resist and suffer martyrdom. As the war-clouds began to gather, it looked very much as if the former course might be adopted, though no one can say with certainty what time might have effected; but it was plain that the Church in any other country which should happen to come under the Nazi sway would be faced with the same crisis, for never was Christianity so incompatible with the doctrines of any ideology as it was with National Socialism, except, of course, Communism.

In his conversations with Rauschnig, as recorded in *Hitler Speaks*, in the chapter headed 'Anti-Christ', the Führer made quite clear his attitude towards Christianity. Though he dismissed the Protestant Churches with contempt, the Roman Catholic Church he looked upon as a great and powerful institution. It was, however, an institution that was already an anachronism. As such it could have no place in a National Socialist State, and he proposed, therefore, to get rid of it, though with as little fuss as possible. He insisted upon the latter, because persecution might prolong its life, since martyrs are notoriously long-lived, if not in the flesh, at least in the spirit. He would eliminate it step by step, and so slowly that its passing would be as imperceptible to itself as to spectators. As he saw Christianity, the only use it had, in any of its forms, was the consolation of the sick and aged, and in this rôle he would tolerate it, provided that it did not prevent or hinder the spread of his own pagan religion. Reduced to this, time would do the rest, for with the rising generations brought up to

3

worship the new idols, the adherents of Christianity would eventually die off, and all the Churches of "the Jewish swindle" would automatically disappear. In the meantime, however, the Church must confine itself to its purely religious functions, must be set apart from the State, and must shun all political activity.

It was a cold-blooded, ruthless, and, for his sinister purposes, an entirely sound psychological approach to his problem. Most men are apt to be lax in their religious observance, so long as neither they nor their religion is subjected to violence. But open persecution calls up a latent obstinacy in adherence to principles which come to the surface of consciousness only under the threat of torture, prison, and death. A quietly executed, almost secret, campaign would be much more efficacious than anti-religious restrictions and dire punishments for failure to observe them.

The history of the Third Reich tends to show how right Hitler was in his appreciation of the situation. The attitudes of the Catholic Church in Germany towards the Nazis creates something of a puzzle to laymen, and, indeed, to many clerics. It is not intended to deal with the question here. True, there were prelates, like Cardinal von Galen, Bishop of Munster, who set themselves actively to oppose Nazi paganism, and there were simple priests and laymen prepared to face death rather than bow down to false idols. But taken all in all, it appears at first sight that the Church was prepared to be quiescent rather than militant; to fall back, rather than stand firm before the new Anti-Christ.

Perhaps Hitler and his henchmen expected that the Church in other countries on which it was his ambition to impose the benefits of the New Order would act in much the same way. But they had overlooked three things: one, that until the War was over a régime of occupation would have to be administered in the new territories, and that occupations almost always generate resistance; two, that until hostilities ended, consolidation of the New Order could not be effected in the unreal and somewhat fluctuating conditions of occupation; and three, that they might be defeated, and that until this proved not to be the case, the occupied peoples would not only take heart from the hope, but would behave as though it were a foregone conclusion. The actual circumstances, then, fostered a militant attitude in the occupied peoples, and in such an atmosphere the Church had a duty which it had to perform or perish. In many cases, the Church rallied the people by setting an example in leadership, restoring strength to minds and limbs at the same time that it reawakened spirits. It is suggested that it was the lack of similar circumstances in Germany that produced a different reaction from the Church there. After all, the Government of the Third Reich was German, as were the clergy and Faithful of the Church. It was not a question of a *foreign* power attempting to force its will on an unwilling people. For these, and other, reasons, especially the fact of the consolidated power of the Nazi Reich, it is unwise to be critical of the Catholic Church in Germany during the reign of Hitler.

In every country occupied by their armies, the Nazis came into open conflict with the Church, and nowhere can be found a more remarkable example of a firm, unwavering stand taken against Nazism by the hierarchy of the Catholic Church than in Holland, though, as we shall see, it is closely rivalled by Belgium.

Two initial factors must be appreciated in order to give the opposition of the Dutch Catholic Church its proper perspective. First, though it was not the State Church, its members numbered no fewer than 36·4 per cent of the population. The remaining 47·8 per cent of Dutchmen registered as members of Christian communities were Protestants; but since these were divided among a number of denominations, the Catholics were the most numerous single religious body, and at the same time, the strongest. They were politically organised and formed the most numerous parliamentary party; they had their own schools, colleges and universities; they owned a powerful Press and a radio station; and they had their own Trade Unions. Second, the Dutch Nazi Party was among the earliest National Socialist movements, modelled completely on the German pattern, to be formed abroad.

From the first appearance of National Socialism on the Dutch scene, the Catholic Church took the strongest stand. In 1934 the Archbishop and Bishops declared membership of the Nazi Party to be incompatible with membership of the Church, and threatened to refuse the Sacraments to all those Catholics who joined or supported the Party. From this firm stand there could be no retreat when the Führer's troops took possession of the country.

As in every other country overrun by Germany, the first weeks and months of occupation produced a confusion and a numbness of mind and spirit, which Seyss-Inquart, the Reichskommissar, did nothing to dispel when he declared at his installation ceremony that it was Germany's intention to respect the Dutch national character and to refrain from forcing on the country an ideology foreign to the people. The Dutch and Germans are closely related in their ancestry, and the Nazi cry was that the big German brother wished only to protect the smaller nation from its enemies and to bestow on it all the benefits of the New Order. The Germans hoped that the Dutch would appreciate this, and co-operate to the full in the great work that lay ahead.

It was not long, however, before the real intentions of the Nazis became apparent and Seyss-Inquart began the process of nazification, the first moves towards which were restrictions against the Jews. The campaign against the Jews, which began in October 1940, was instituted earlier in Holland than in any other occupied country.

It is strange how badly informed the Nazis were about the Dutch character and their way of thinking, and even their way of life itself. They clearly expected that the Dutch would not intervene in any attack made on the Jews, provided that the Gentiles were not touched in any way. This expectation shows more clearly, perhaps, than anything else the Nazi ignorance of their Dutch victims.

Jews had first come to the country in the seventeenth century as refugees from the persecution of their race in Spain and Portugal. Since the Dutch were themselves victims of Spain, from whose yoke they were attempting to free themselves at this time, they gave a friendly welcome to the Jewish immigrants. For their part, the Jews showed their gratitude for the kindness by throwing themselves whole-heartedly into the building up of the new Dutch Republic, which was soon to experience a most phenomenal prosperity. The Dutch recognised the contribution which the Jews had made to the development of their country and gave this recognition concrete form by granting the Jews full and equal rights of citizenship. The Jews were, therefore, regarded—as they had always been since these times—as an integral part of the nation, and, this being so, any attack on them was looked upon by the Dutch Gentile population as an attack on the whole nation.

The Nazi restrictive measures against the Jews brought a response from the whole nation before which anyone less obstin-

ately pig-headed or less blinded by racial hatred would have retreated. But not Seyss-Inquart! Instead, the process of elimination
was speeded up, and within a short time large numbers of Jews
were being arrested and deported to concentration camps, and the
whole Jewish community was in a state of the most acute distress.

Though, unlike the Dutch Reformed Church, the Dutch
Catholic Church did not in the beginning protest against the
attack on the Jews, this is not to say that it did not feel as strongly
about what was happening as any other section of the nation.
The Catholics and Jews had always been on most friendly terms,
and in the last twenty years the mission among the Jews had been
the object of ever-widening interest. The mission in Holland may
not have won many converts to Catholic Christianity, but it had
strengthened the bonds of friendship between the Catholics and
Jews. But even if this had not been so, the anti-semitism of the
Nazis would have made it impossible for the most militant of all
anti-Nazi forces in Holland to stand by acquiescently.

If the Church did not join in direct protest against what was
going on so early as did the Protestants, it was because the time was
not considered ripe. The Church had its plan of defence against the
Nazis, and when the right time came it would go into action. The
time came early in 1942.

Such fantastic proportions had been reached in the Nazi deportation of the Dutch Jews that, if it continued at the present
rate, by the end of 1942 nearly half the Jewish population of
Holland would have vanished. In a few months more what the
Nazis referred to as "the final solution", that is, the complete extermination of the Jews, would have been achieved, at least as far
as Holland was concerned.

Now, the Dutch Protestants had vigorously attacked the anti-
Jewish measures from the very first, and had become so vociferous
that they had attracted the attention of Seyss-Inquart to themselves. To teach them a lesson not to interfere, the Reichskommissar hurried forward the plan which he had for the eventual extermination of the Churches as a power in Holland. He had good
reason to do this, for such was the strength of the Churches that,
by this time, they had come to be looked upon as a powerful
element in the national leadership. With the proclaimed support
of the Churches, the people had begun to resist vigorously in
many fields of existence.

On 17th February, 1942, a delegation of the Reformed and Catholic Churches called upon Seyss-Inquart, who received them personally. They handed to the Reichskommissar a protest against "the almost complete lawlessness" under which thousands of men and women were sent to camps or elsewhere without being charged with or tried for any crime. The protest had no effect upon Seyss-Inquart except perhaps to make him intensify all measures designed to bring all sections of the population to heel in the speediest possible time.

It must not be thought, however, that if protests had no effect upon the Germans, they were entirely ineffective. There can have been no greater boost to the morale of the nation than these courageous and unambiguous condemnations of tyranny. Had the Church remained silent, the Faithful would have been perplexed, and in their perplexity lost heart and presently their souls, which corporately represented the soul of the nation. In the circumstances the nation would have been utterly destroyed.

The protest which the Church presented to Seyss-Inquart, though the first direct approach to the Germans, was not the first pronouncement it had uttered, a warning clear in meaning and implication, a declaration of the position the Church intended to take up. In a Pastoral Letter which was read in all Catholic Churches on 10th November, 1940, the Bishops warned of the threat from a materialist outlook "in which there is no place for Christ", and stated categorically that the Faithful would have to fight to preserve their "spiritual goods", particularly their Catholic schools.

Now, while the Nazis professed, at the beginning, that they had no desire to change the Dutch way of life except for the better, and hoped co-operation between the Dutch and themselves would be fruitful of results in this connection, unfortunately the military position was such—as the Dutch themselves surely appreciated—that restrictions had to be placed on certain public organs, the chief of which were, of course, the Press and radio. The Catholic Press refused to abide by the German directives, and in the spring of 1941 it was liquidated, except for one or two small weeklies, but not before it had played its part in showing the way to the Faithful, disseminating the warnings of the Bishops, and sounding their call to battle. Nevertheless, without its newspapers, the Church was deprived of a formidable weapon.

8

The early months of spring 1941 found tension high in all the occupied countries. The people had completely thrown off the numbing shock of defeat and occupation; the Germans had lost the battle for Britain permanently, and would clearly not attempt an immediate invasion of England. So hopes were running high, and courage just as high, and in these months resistance reached its first peak.

It was in these conditions that in March the Bishops issued another Pastoral Letter in which they repeated the ban on the admission to the Sacraments of all Catholics "who are known to support the National Socialist idea to an important extent". It would seem that the repetition of this ban was necessary because in the changed circumstances many of the clergy and Faithful were in doubt as to its continued validity. The effect of this Pastoral Letter was greater, perhaps, than that of almost any other issued by the Bishops during the occupation. In the moral field, all Dutch Catholics were assured of the full support of the Church in their opposition to German corruption. In the spiritual field, it united all Dutch Catholics in their defence of the moral doctrines of Catholicism. It also brought suffering and martyrdom to the priesthood, for from this time on all Dutch Nazis and their open sympathisers were barred from the Holy Table, were refused burial in consecrated ground, were refused marriage if one or both were Nazis, and, later, no member of the Dutch Catholic Church who fell fighting on the Russian front could have sung for him a requiem for the repose of his soul.

The Dutch Nazis were furious at the intrepid insistence of the clergy on carrying out the instructions of their Bishops, and issued threats, which, with the support of the Germans, were all too often put into effect. In increasing numbers the priests were arrested and sent to forced-labour or to concentration camps, where they were brutally treated or even killed. But no matter what humiliations and sufferings were heaped upon them, the clergy would not allow themselves to compromise the stand their Church had taken.

When Hitler attacked Russia, the Nazis hoped that now, at all events, the Churches would shift their position, especially the Catholic Church. For how could a Church which had denounced Communism not regard a war against Communism as a holy crusade? It was, indeed, a difficult situation in which the Church found itself. But a broadcast by the Queen to the nation over Radio Orange, from London, showed the way. She welcomed Russia as an ally, without any reservations, and with this lead, the Church's mind was settled. In the struggle against Nazi paganism there must be a single-mindedness of purpose. If the Russians were fighting to destroy this paganism, then they must be supported, no matter what their own ideology might be.

The German anger in the face of this disappointment of their hopes was intense. All pretence of peaceful co-operation was now cast aside, and the campaign to nazify the country was speeded up. The first move in this campaign, as it affected the Church, was Seyss-Inquart's decree for the formation of a Labour Front on the German pattern. As has already been mentioned, the confessional Trade Union movement was one of the main bases of Christian social life in Holland, and if these Trade Unions were to become members of a Nazi organisation, the ground on which the Churches had taken up their stand against the Nazis would be knocked from under their feet. This was particularly true with regard to the Catholic Church.

So, on 3rd August, 1941, the Archbishop of Utrecht and the four Bishops caused to be read from all the pulpits in the country a Pastoral Letter condemning the interference of the Germans with the Catholic Trade Unions. It was not possible, they said, after recounting the many injustices inflicted on Catholics by the Germans, for Catholics to be under the control of people "whose spiritual outlook was in flat contradiction to the Catholic outlook". Since the Catholic Workers' Union had been compelled against its will to enter the service of the Nazis, Catholics could no longer remain members. Up to this time, though membership of organisations affiliated to National Socialism was prohibited, it did not actually carry exclusion from the Sacraments. Now, however, "membership in these affiliated bodies must be considered just as inadmissible as membership of the National Socialist movement. Therefore, the Sacraments must be refused to those who remained members of one of the organisations affiliated with the Worker's Union in its new form and all other bodies affiliated with the National Socialist Party". This meant, of course, the extermination of the Catholic Trade Union movement, which had a membership of 200,000, and which had rendered a tremendous service in the social and religious fields. "Openly and loudly we raise our voice against the injustice done to these tens of thousands by robbing them of their social status," said the Bishops. "We protest against the moral constraint and the attempt to force upon them a conception of life conflicting with their religious convictions."

Once again the Nazis had illustrated their complete misunderstanding of the Dutch character. In Germany the denominational Trade Unions had not resisted, and the Church had not protested. But one must repeat that the circumstances differed; that while the duly elected Government in Germany issued the decrees, here in Holland it was a foreign occupying power. Because the mass of German people were uninterested in the type of régime they had, it did not follow that the Dutch should be equally uninterested. The Nazis did not appreciate this any more than did many others.

As the second half of 1941 worked its way out, the perceptive became convinced that what had happened in the past would be nothing compared with what must come. Sooner or later the Dutch and their Nazi tyrants must become locked in a fearful struggle; nor would this struggle be long delayed.

The mounting anti-Jewish campaign has already been noted. It was to be intensified even more as the year ended and 1942 broke. But it must not be thought that all German efforts were concentrated on achieving "the final solution". Simultaneously, Dutch life and Dutch institutions were attacked with an almost equal hostility.

For example, after killing the denominational Trade Union movements, the Nazis turned their attention to education, the intention being to destroy Christian education and to bring up the youth on the principles of Nazism. To this end the order went forth that the curriculum in primary, secondary and high schools was to be "brought up to date". Jewish and Gentile children could no longer attend the same schools. German control of Leyden and Delft universities was tightened. Though the denominational schools were not, as yet, directly attacked, the Secretary General of Education was given the power to close such schools and dismiss or suspend their staffs if he believed such action to be warranted. In fact, the schools were allowed to remain open only so long as—in the words of the Secretary General—their curricula were "propelled in such directions that the younger generation could obtain a sound knowledge of the ideals of our times".

In this year of 1942, the Germans were to see the tide of war turn against them, and with each backward step they took, the more ferociously did they attack the defenceless people of the occupied countries. Men and women were seized and drafted into Germany's war industries. Much of what little food there was, was snatched from the near-starving peoples and put on the trains for Germany. The natural resources were bled white to provide the essentials for the Nazi war-machine.

Until now the Nazis had been content to wreak their vengeance on the simple clergy and the Faithful. They had not dared openly to attack the Church leadership physically, believing, it would seem, that if they did so they would forfeit any hope they still had of exterminating the Church according to Hitler's technique, and that the effect on the Faithful might goad them to even greater excesses of active resistance. Now, however, they seemed to realise that so long as the Church leaders felt they had nothing to fear physically, they would never be muzzled, but would continue to inspire anti-Nazi activity. They were growing alarmed, too, at the obvious preparations for open revolt which were becoming more and more apparent. So they turned on the leaders, and arrested scholars and churchmen of outstanding reputation. Among the Catholics arrested were the famous Carmelite father, Dr Titus Brandsma, a professor at the Catholic University of Nijmegen, who was imprisoned in Germany; Dr Hein Hoeber, a director of the International Catholic Press Bureau, who died as the result of torture and ill-treatment in a concentration camp; and another Carmelite, Father F. van der Mey, who was also sent to a concentration camp in Germany.

When the leaders of the Churches handed to Seyss-Inquart their protest against the treatment of the Jews, on 17th February, they protested at the same time, "their emphatic and most serious objections to the present development of events", and begged the Reichskommissar to remember the promises he had made at his installation to "leave the foundations of Dutch life untouched", and to "recognise in the name of God, the spiritual distress of the Netherlands people and to avoid doing further harm". "Without entering into politics (the Churches) must yet raise their voices where the principles of justice and charity are being denied. They would be forsaking their duty towards the authorities if they, representing the majority of the population, did not express their anxiety about the feeling of tension that is increasing among all classes of the Dutch people."

In making their protest the Catholic leaders had been under no illusion that their pleas would have any effect on Seyss-Inquart. In their joint Lenten Pastoral, which was read in all Churches on 22nd February, the Bishops exhorted the Faithful "to be ready, armed with truth, justice and responsiveness to the Gospel of Peace" against a threat which "becomes stronger as the pressure on us increases". The Letter concluded with these words: "Only Christianity, with its faith in a personal God, with its firm moral law as sanctioned by God, and with its urgent commands of justice and charity, possesses the guarantee for a healthy social order."

In the campaign against the schools, the Catholic authorities steadfastly refused to permit the introduction of Nazi educational principles. When a certain chief inspector of schools in the two mainly Catholic southern provinces instructed his inspectors to demand complete co-operation in training for the New Order, only one of them agreed to do so. The other sixteen replied that they were Catholics, and had taken an oath to the Constitution to which they intended to remain loyal; they could never do anything which would conflict with their Catholic convictions.

In the late spring of 1942 the Germans concentrated their attention on the Dutch medical profession. For some time they had attempted to interfere with the doctors' professional code, by instructing them to supply to the authorities information about their patients. The doctors resisted strongly and formed themselves into a secret organisation known as *Medisch Contact*, by means of which they united practically all members of the profession in concerted resistance. Now the Germans insisted that all doctors must join what they called the Netherlands Union of Health Insurance Physicians, which was an off-shoot of their Netherlands Chamber of Physicians, an organisation shunned by all Dutch doctors except the few who had Nazi leanings. The *Medisch Contact* immediately issued an appeal to all doctors to boycott the Union, and to this appeal the Archbishop of Utrecht added his own strong plea. The Union, he said, "would be used to infiltrate Nazi principles into the spheres of medicine and public health".

On 1st April the Germans issued a decree ordering all men between the ages of eighteen and twenty-four to register for "voluntary" labour service. They took this step because the number of Dutchmen who had joined the labour service truly of their own free will was so small that they were of little assistance to the German war-machine. In addition to this age-group, all men who were unemployed, or not usefully employed, and students who had no professional training were called up for this service.

The Church at once issued a warning. In a Pastoral Letter read in all churches in May, the Bishops declared: "The labour service promised that no one would be prevented from practising religion, but officially it is stated that the labour service can only be National Socialist. This fills us with regret and concern. The views of National Socialism are in direct conflict with Christianity and are the most serious threat to Christian faith and morals. That is why a labour service with Nazi aims is a great danger to youth." For this reason they warned the Faithful to disobey the orders of the occupation authorities, no matter what the consequences might be.

The German reactions to such pronouncements can be imagined. A campaign of terror, directed chiefly against the lower clergy, was instituted, and to those who had already been sent to prisons and concentration camps were added hundreds more. The hierarchy was also given a taste of Nazi anger. The Bishop of Roermond, Monsignor J. H. G. Lemmens, always vocal in his consistent opposition to the Nazi tyranny, was turned out of several rooms in the episcopal residence, which were then used as petrol stores by the Germans. The Rector, Chancellor and one of the professors of the Catholic University of Nijmegen were imprisoned for their flat refusal to allow the Germans to interfere with the administration of the University, and subsequently the University was permitted to remain open only on payment of approximately 183,750 dollars and by accepting strict German supervision of its curriculum.

The Germans now began to fear the Pastoral Letter as a formidable weapon turned against them, and made repeated attempts to prevent copies of the Letters from reaching the presbyteries. The Church countered these moves by sending copies to some responsible parishioner as well as to the presbyteries; then when the presbytery copy was seized, and the Germans believed they had nipped the Bishops' latest warning in the bud, they were surprised when the Letter was still read in all the churches on the following Sunday. There is no record of a Pastoral Letter ever having been suppressed by the Germans.

The "final solution" of the Jewish problem had been planned by Himmler to be achieved by 1st July, 1943. In July 1942 an intensification of the deportation of the Jews was instituted which, for its ferociousness, outstripped all former similar campaigns. Within a short time of the new measures being promulgated many Dutchmen received from an unknown source—afterwards known to be the Dutch Churches acting in unison—a letter which they were asked to send to the German Military Commander, Luftwaffe General Christiansen. Christiansen was chosen as the recipient rather than Seyss-Inquart because it was still believed that a sense of honour and chivalry still existed among German officers. It was a remarkable letter, as the excerpts below illustrate.

"The deportation of our Jewish fellow-countrymen to Silesia and the Protectorate (of Bohemia and Moravia) deepens the gulf between your people and ours to such an extent that it can never be bridged again. . . . We feel the maltreatment of our Jewish fellow-citizens as our own. But suffering will not break us. . . . We therefore call upon you for your intervention, in the name of justice and of Christian love, for the sake of our Jewish fellow-countrymen and for the future of Europe. It is not to our shame that we are sending you this letter anonymously. It is the fault of those who punish every utterance of insulted humanity and injured national dignity with execution, concentration camp, or prison."

The Churches had been mistaken in their belief that Christiansen's sense of honour and chivalry would respond to the appeal. On 2nd August, Seyss-Inquart's deputy declared in a speech: "The Roman Catholic Church and the Protestant Churches have addressed to the Military Commander, General Christiansen, a request for the better treatment of the Jews. The Jews are Germany's most dangerous enemies. Dutchmen cannot actively defend themselves against them while looking through the spectacles of stupid humanitarian sentiment. Owing to the passivity of the Dutch, we Germans have taken over the solution of the Jewish question, and have started to send the Jews to the east. . . . In the Catholic

Churches a document was read criticising the anti-Jewish measures taken to safeguard our struggle. . . . Because of this the Germans must consider the 'Roman Catholic Jews' their worst enemies and arrange for their quickest possible removal to the east. . . ."

When the Dutch Church leaders gave their support to Russia, as we have seen, the anger of the Nazis was vehement, and much more so against the Catholics, from whom they had expected more sympathy. As a bribe, however, to win over Catholic opinion, the Nazis offered the Bishops the use of the German-controlled Radio Hilversum for broadcasting religious services. Immediately he heard of the offer, the Archbishop of Utrecht repeated his instruction that, since all German-controlled radio stations were constantly broadcasting attacks on Christian principles and on the Churches, no Dutch Catholic might co-operate with such a station. This was a rebuff to the Nazis almost equal to that administered by the Bishops' refusal to admit Nazis to the Sacraments, which only a short time before had been underlined by an incident which quickly became generally known to the population.

In Broesbeck, a small border town near Nijmegen, a Catholic had one day collapsed from heart-failure in the street, and the parish priest had administered Extreme Unction. After the man's death the priest learned that he had been a member of the Dutch Nazi Party, and refused to bury him. The Nazis then tried to get a German priest from over the border to carry out the last rites, but though a priest was found who was willing to come, the German Bishops ordered him not to.

This makes an interesting incident in itself. For though in Germany the Church did not forbid the Sacraments to Nazis, the Bishops had issued a ruling that no German priest, unless he were a Service chaplain, might officiate anywhere outside the frontiers of the Reich. In making this ruling, the German Bishops recognised the jurisdiction of the non-German Bishops; but perhaps it had a deeper significance—that the German Bishops were conscious at last of the evil which had developed in their country as a result of their weakness *vis-à-vis* the Nazis.

The Germans did not take the Archbishop of Utrecht's refusal to accept their offer of broadcasting facilities quietly. First of all they suppressed the Catholic *Pro Deo* movement, arresting four of its leaders, including the Vicar-General of 's Hertogenbosch, Monsignor F. N. J. Hendriks, who had caused anti-Nazi pamphlets to be distributed. A few months later the Bishop of 's Hertogenbosch died, and his Coadjutor, Monsignor Mussaerts, was appointed to succeed him. Monsignor Mussaerts immediately appointed Monsignor Hendriks to be his Vicar-General, though he was still in a concentration camp in Germany, where the Director of *Pro Deo*, the Rector Roovackers, was also interned.

The Germans also reopened their campaign against the religious Orders, brothers and nuns being evicted from their houses and missions. Among them were the Society of St Joseph for Foreign Missions at Rosendaal, which had to move to the Society's house at Tilburg; the Sparrendal Mission at Vucht, whose house the Germans commandeered; the brothers of the Sacred Heart at Bergen-op-Zoom, who were driven from their house; the Maris Stella Hospital at Scheveningen, which was ordered to move to the east of the country; and convents in Hilvarenbeek, Jutland and 's Hertogenbosch, which were evacuated.

That the Church did not retreat in the face of this persecution is best seen in some remarks made in a broadcast speech over Hilversum on National Socialist Day, 30th January, 1943, by Seyss-Inquart. "I can only say that it is intolerable that organisations exist which are trying to endanger the safety of this territory in the rear of the men who are fighting in the East. We must be hard and we shall become harder. The Churches should understand the significance of our struggle. All denominations can practise fully their faith under National Socialist occupation and are even able to express their viewpoint regarding measures taken by the occupying Power. I believe, therefore, that they are under the moral obligation at least, not to hinder the German prosecution of the War."

The Reichskommissar's threat: "We shall become harder", was no idle one. The Russian victory at Stalingrad, the steadily increasing raids by the Royal Air Force on west German cities and Churchill's hints at a new turn in the war, brought a fresh surge of hope, a new strength to resist to the Dutch, as they did to all other occupied peoples. The Germans, too, saw the writing on the wall, though they pretended not to; and their actions now became those of men terrified by the looming prospect of defeat.

Early in the year they intensified the measures with regard to the call-up for forced-labour. All former measures had failed, because vast numbers of those declared eligible immediately went into hiding, and were so well protected by those who hid them that they were not found. Collective fines, the arrest and deportation of relatives of the missing men, or "divers" as they were referred to in the Dutch vernacular—*Onderduikers*—added to the out-and-out reign of terror. In the middle of the previous year—August 1942—the first hostages had been shot. These executions now increased in number, the victims being chosen from prisoners especially set aside to act as hostages, and macabrely called *Todeskandidaten*—Candidates for Death.

As the terror increased, so did the resistance of the Dutch people. The tension in all sections of the community was such that only a small incident was needed to touch off open revolt. Typically the Germans chose a large incident as the fuse.

It was Himmler's idea to re-intern 300,000 men of the Dutch Armed Forces, an idea which Hitler also strongly favoured. Neither Seyss-Inquart nor Fischböck, the General Commissar for Finance and Economic Affairs, was enthusiastic; and being on the spot, and thus able to judge the situation, they were completely justified in their reluctance to put Himmler's orders into effect.

The wily Himmler, with his usual sense of self-preservation, persuaded Hitler to draft the Proclamation himself, and it was with this Proclamation that General Christiansen lit the fuse when he published it on 29th April, 1943. To a people already made nervous by other events, the re-internment of so great a number of their menfolk seemed an overwhelming blow. But when the initial numbness had passed, it was felt that some action was essential. The action chosen was a "general" strike; and for the second time since the occupation began the Dutch people used this formidable weapon. But the strike was by no means general, and the Germans took most vigorous action, with mass arrests and the shooting of many hostages. During the state of emergency, which the Germans kept in force until 7th May, no fewer than 145 executions were carried out.

Though on the surface the strikes may have seemed a failure they were in reality the turning-point of Dutch Resistance. Up to this time Resistance had been spasmodic and sectional. The strikes taught the people, once and for all, the dangers inherent in being insufficiently organised. They also acquired a new will to resist. They had come to know one another better, and had become bound more closely together.

New oppressive measures followed the strikes. Forced-labour was made openly compulsory; all radio sets were confiscated; the deportation of the Jews was intensified; more and more people were executed. In response, Resistance, in all its forms, became more and more active.

Much of the responsibility for the strikes was placed by the Germans on the Church. The Dutch S.S. journal *Storm* declared: "The strikers were mostly sheep of the Roman Catholic Church. Why have the Bishops exhorted to resistance against the German occupation in all their Pastoral Letters? It would be ridiculous to answer: Because of Dutch interests. The Roman Catholic clergy and Dutch interests are as implacable enemies as fire and water. Just as they tried to cause unrest with hate-sowing pamphlets when anti-Jewish measures were taken, they exhorted to sabotage some Sundays ago, because Dutch labourers must give man-power for the fight against a world revolution of God-hating Bolshevism. They, the Bishops, priests and clergy, are responsible, and the S.S. considers it no more than reasonable and logical that those who drive the Dutch workers against German rifles must be punished more than their victims. Professors and physicians who strike are no less punishable than labourers and farmers. We demand one punishment: the bullet for all those brutes serving the Jewish-Bolshevist cause."

In the month before the strikes, on 21st February, 1943, the Bishops caused a Pastoral Letter to be read in all the churches, in which they quoted in full their latest protest to Seyss-Inquart. The second half of this protest read as follows:

"Now to all this, is added the hunting down, as if they were slaves, the arrest and deportation, of thousands of young people.

"In all these actions the Divine Law has been violated in increasing measure.

"The Churches preach against hate and the spirit of vengeance in the hearts of our people, and raise their voice against manifestations of these vices. According to the Word of God no one can be his own judge. But in the same measure the Churches also have the duty, by their calling, to preach this word of God: 'Obey God rather than men.' This serves as the ruling in all conflicts of conscience, even in those arising from the measures in

19

question. By virtue of Divine Law no one may offer the slightest collaboration in acts of injustice, because, in so doing, he shares the guilt of the injustice itself.

"Herr Reichskommissar, it is in obedience to the Lord that the Churches are obliged to address this letter to you; they pray that God may lead you in His way, that you may restore the right so grievously violated in the exercise of your power."

The "all this" referred to in the first sentence of our quotation was the number of measures against which the Church had previously protested; the lack of justice; the persecution and execution of Jewish fellow-citizens; the imposition of a conception of life and of the world that "was contradictory to the Gospel of Jesus Christ"; forced-labour service as an institution of National Socialist education; the violation of the freedom of Christian instruction; the imposition of forced-labour in Germany on Dutch workers; the execution of hostages; the arrest and imprisonment of persons, among them ecclesiastical dignitaries, "under such conditions that a very considerable number have already made the sacrifice of their lives in concentration camps". It was a formidable list.

After the strikes the Bishops issued another Pastoral Letter. In it they said: "Now the limit has been reached. All able-bodied men who are available will be deported, a deportation on a scale such as the Christian world has never known. To find something comparable one has to go back to the time of the Babylonian captivity, when God's people were taken into exile, which moved the prophet Jeremiah to exclaim: 'A voice has been heard on the heights; a voice of lamentation, of mourning and of tears, which is the voice of Rachel, weeping for her children' (Jeremiah xxxi, 15).

"What revolts us is not only the deportation itself, but also the horrible injustice, contrary to all human and divine laws. As shepherds of your souls we cannot keep silent on what is done to our people. Posterity would stigmatise us with eternal shame if we witnessed this injustice in silence. It is the task of the Bishops to defend justice, and to condemn evil as such; if not, they would forsake their duty. . . . Today our country is not only usurped, but a large part of its population has been carried away by force. Our men are forced to work for the enemy.

"At first it was said that Dutchmen had to work abroad because here there was neither work nor bread for them. Today, as has been explicitly stated, they must work for Germany in order to assure a German victory. This is where our conscience is aroused. . . . Today we may not do anything for our country; we are even compelled under the threat of heavy penalties to assist the enemy.

"This is where the injustice lies against which we raise our voice. Although we are told that it is the duty of all Christians to fight Bolshevism, this is only a trap. Whoever really wishes to fight 'atheistic Bolshevism', so severely condemned by the Pope, should not suppress Christianity by all possible means, as is being done by Nazism, which it is true, does not persecute it in a bloody way but throttles its vitality. Nazis in power do not even hesitate to prevent the Church from caring for the souls of her own children. . . . No, dearly beloved brethren, the only means to fight Communism is not Nazism but Christianity. . . ."

These courageous protests only served to inflame the Germans more, and by the beginning of 1944 there was little new for them to wreak upon the Dutch. All they could do was to increase the ferocity of the measures they had already instituted, and this they did.

Resistance met the terror of seizures, reprisal executions and all the horrors of existence under the frantic Germans with increased activity. As the year progressed the Nazis had more and more reason to be frantic. The invasion of the Continent brought about the co-ordination of all Dutch Resistance, and early in September, just before the Allies liberated southern Holland, a Resistance was formed under the leadership of Prince Bernhard.

The winter of 1944-45 brought to the Dutch of the German-held northern part of the country the greatest suffering of the whole occupation. As a result of the freeing of the south, there was a severe shortage of fuel, gas and electricity, and the Germans, as a reprisal for the railway strike which had started on the day of the Arnhem operation and continued right up to the German surrender, began to confiscate inland water vessels, which led to a complete breakdown of food supplies in western Holland. On top of this, the weather produced the severest winter in Holland in living memory. Food became so scarce that a dire state of famine was added to the other hardships of the Dutch.

During this time the Church in German-held Holland continued to comfort the Faithful and to assist in every practical way it could. Thus, from the arrival of the Germans up to the surrender, the Church was, in the words of the then Archbishop of Canterbury, "an active focus of resistance against Nazi tyranny". By becoming the conscience of the nation, it gave to the Dutch, in an hour of extreme need, a sense of direction, from which stemmed the will to resist the Nazi evil. The resistance of the Dutch people is an epic scarcely excelled by the history of resistance in any other occupied country. By the prominent and courageous rôle which it played in encouraging this resistance, the Church remained not only true to itself, but true also to the mandate of Christ.

And while the Archbishop and Bishops stood firm and immovable against the evil in their midst, to the south their brothers in Belgium were also uttering defiance to a like evil.

CHAPTER II

Belgium

As Cardinal van Roey, Primate of Belgium, came from a service of confirmation at Etterbeek on 7th May, he was met by the Apostolic Nuncio in Brussels, who told him that according to information just received from the Vatican, the Nazis were about to invade Belgium.

Throughout the period of the "phoney war", the Cardinal, who supported the Belgian policy of neutrality, had not ceased to urge the people to prayer, to exhort them to preserve calm and strength of spirit, to place all confidence in King and Government.

But however he might extol the wisdom of keeping Belgium aloof from the struggle, the Cardinal did not lose sight of reality. Again and again he made his attitude clear, in words similar to those which he spoke in his sermon at the Pontifical High Mass on 29th October, 1939, the Feast of Christ the King, in the presence of King Leopold III, and members of the Government: "All these motives clearly dictate to our country her duty: to maintain peace at all costs; and to do one's duty is always honourable. It would be a crime against the fatherland to become embroiled in the gigantic contest—except in the case of absolute, extreme and unavoidable necessity, that is to say, except in the case where the existence of the country would be directly threatened."

As the uncertain weeks went by, this sense of reality encouraged the Cardinal, early in February 1940, to draw up a list of instructions for priests in the event of the civil population being evacuated from certain parts of the country for reasons of military expediency. If a parish were completely evacuated, the priest was to go with his flock; if the people were scattered, he was to go with the majority. If the evacuation was partial, and the priest had no assistant, he was to stay in the parish, but if there were two priests, one would go and one would stay. Each parish priest was to decide on a place of safe-keeping for any works of art his church might possess. Nor was he to think only of articles of great intrinsic value, but equally of those which had great practical importance. Such objects and documents of value as were not essential to the everyday practice of religion and administration were to be stored in a safe place, preferably in a large town or city, while places must be chosen beforehand for those in daily use. This foresight was to be very amply rewarded.

From Etterbeek on 7th May the Cardinal returned to his archiepiscopal palace at Malines, and was there when the Germans invaded the country three days later. Malines was one of the targets of the Luftwaffe, who encountered no opposition from the Belgian air force in their constant attacks on the city. But the almost continuous state of alert, and the necessity of spending night after night in the cellars of the palace, which had been transformed into air-raid shelters, only seemed to strengthen his intention to remain in Malines unless and until the military should oblige him to leave.

These early days of the war were terrible days for the great majority of the Belgian people. Some days before the capitulation, the Government left Brussels, having delegated powers of administration to the Secretaries-General of Departments. But not all of these officials could find the courage to remain at their posts, and several fled. With them went many other leaders in most walks of public life.

Deprived of example, encouragement and the security of discipline, hundreds of thousands of ordinary men and women attempted to evade the approaching terror. So to the confusion in high places was added the physical confusion of roads blocked by refugees, homeless and hungry, not knowing what was to happen to them, bewildered and despairing.

In these conditions the steadfastness of the Cardinal was to prove a beacon light, a rallying point. The few leaders who stayed at their posts, themselves looked to him for guidance, as we shall see.

On 16th May the Cardinal sent his secretary, Canon E. Leclef, to Brussels to try to obtain permission from Delfosse, Minister of Communications, for a train to be sent to Malines to evacuate 300 sick and old people. This was the first contact which the Cardinal had had with the Government since 10th May; it was also the only one, for later on the same day the Government left Brussels.

The Cardinal had requested his Vicars-General and Secretaries to join him in Malines, and they had done so. Almost all the civilian population, however, had fled from the city, which was on one of the principal military defence lines. At eight o'clock on 17th May the army began their retreat, and at ten o'clock the German General-Major Criebbel arrived at the town hall with an escort to take command of the city. He assured the Burgomaster that the remaining inhabitants had no cause for fear if they kept calm, but added, so that there should be no misunderstanding, that if a single German soldier was killed he would give the order to shoot, and, if necessary, would seize hostages.

For the next ten days the Cardinal remained immured in his palace. He would have liked to have driven about the city, so that his presence might hearten the people, but the Germans withheld permission for him to do so until 27th May. Then his first visits were to the Grand Séminaire, where there were large numbers of sick and old people, and to the Petit Séminaire, which had been seriously damaged by a German shell. Most of the Religious had stayed in their convents, and these, too, he visited and cheered.

During these days Malines was to all intents and purposes cut off from the outside world, for the telephone and radio systems had broken down. The city was also without gas, electricity and running water. The Cardinal was visited, however, by the Apostolic Nuncio, who arrived with the United States Ambassador, John Cudahy, and two attachés from the Spanish Embassy, who came to offer their services.

Electricity was restored on 23rd May, and for the first time the Cardinal was able to gain news of the events which were rapidly drawing to their tragic close. When, on 28th May, the French Prime Minister made his broadcast announcing the Belgian intention to capitulate, it was to the Cardinal that everyone came for confirmation and explanation, and, when he could not give either, whom they pressed to take steps to discover what was truly happening or had happened.

The next day the Apostolic Nuncio and a former Minister, Albert Janssen, came to the palace shortly before midday. The Nuncio had learned that the King was at a chateau in Flanders, held by the Germans as a prisoner of war. No one had been allowed near him, not even the Italian Ambassador, who had been trying to get news for the King's sister, the Princess of Piedmont. The Nuncio also told the Cardinal that the Government officials who were still in Brussels were meeting the civic authorities to try to decide what attitude to take towards the King.

On hearing this, the Cardinal at once gave it as his opinion that nothing in this connection should be decided until there was fuller and reliable information concerning the whole affair. He also asked the Nuncio to approach the Germans to obtain permission for him to see the King.

That same afternoon M. Janssen and a small party of judicial and Government officials returned to Malines to tell the Cardinal that the Secretaries-General and the civic authorities placed their full confidence in the King. But since they wished to back their support with justification, should they be called upon to do so, they urged the Cardinal to see the King as soon as it could be arranged.

The Cardinal at once left for Brussels, but as the King had not yet been brought to the royal palace at Laeken, it was not possible for the Cardinal to meet him. On 30th May the Italian Ambassador was granted permission to visit Leopold, and when he told the King of the Cardinal's lively desire to see him, the King responded with equal eagerness.

In the mid-afternoon of the following day Colonel van Caubergh, one of the King's equerries, called for the Cardinal and took him to Laeken. At the conclusion of an interview lasting an hour and a half, the Cardinal was convinced that the King had done nothing contrary to honour or conscience. He at once returned to Malines, where he composed a Pastoral Letter setting out the events as related by the King. A hundred or more copies of this Letter were sent out early the following morning to the high officials and dignitaries remaining in Brussels and Anvers. At eleven o'clock the Cardinal met the chief officials and described his interview with the King in detail, with the result that the Court of Cassation announced that justice would continue to be dispensed in "the name of the King", despite the attitude taken by the Government-in-Exile.

In the afternoon of the same day copies of the Pastoral Letter were sent to the Nuncio and to the Spanish and American Ambassadors. Other copies were sent to the Swedish and Swiss Legations with the request that they should be made available to the foreign Press. The next day, Sunday, 2nd June, the Letter was read in all the churches in Brussels and Anvers, and on the following

Sunday in those churches of the diocese which could not be reached quickly, as well as in many churches of the more distant provinces.

In his Letter, the Cardinal, having described precisely the King's reasons for his action in capitulating and his insistence that the Allied commanders had been warned beforehand of his intentions as Commander-in-Chief of the Belgian army, went on: "For our part, we, knowing that we are supported by the sentiments of almost the whole Belgian people, shall continue to give to our King our respect, loyalty and confidence. We request the priests to continue to offer the prayers for the King as prescribed by the liturgy. We earnestly call upon all the Faithful, in their prayers and their communions, unceasingly to recommend to God the cause of the King and the safety of the Fatherland. We would wish all Belgians, conscious of the gravity of the present hour, to stand united around the King, who is the supreme personification of the Fatherland in danger. Finally, let us be sure that at this moment we are witnessing one of the exceptional operations of divine Providence, who manifests His power by tremendous events, in the presence of which we ourselves feel very small. More than ever, then, let us entrust ourselves to the infinite mercy of the Sacred Heart of Jesus, and let us say with the Psalmist: 'Even though we walk in the shadow of death, we will fear no evil, for Thou art with us.'"

The effect of this Pastoral Letter, the first of many which the Cardinal was to issue during the occupation, had a steadying effect upon the morale of the confused and shaken Belgians, not only at home, but also abroad. The capitulation, and the King's part in it, gave rise to much bitter feeling among his subjects. Rumour played a large part, and the more intelligent, knowing that while rumour was prominent in all they heard, did not know how much was rumour, how much truth. The Cardinal's concise statement and his continued support of Leopold cleared away for many all the doubts and much of the shame caused by recent events. Certainly it showed that at least one leader—and he the most powerful moral authority in the country—was prepared to come to the aid of the people in their hour of need, as had his great predecessor, Cardinal Mercier, in 1914. Nor was his leadership to be a mere temporary act, but was to become more and more a guiding star as, with each month, each year that passed, the lowering clouds of Nazi brutality moved darkly over and burst upon the tragic country and its people.

It is difficult to describe briefly and adequately the confusion into which the imminent arrival of the Germans threw the whole country, a chaos so extensive that even the Nazis, greatly though they prided themselves on their ability as organisers and administrators, were momentarily checked. Business could not be conducted on a legal basis in many cities, for the civic authorities had fled; in many areas justice could not be administered, for the magistrates had fled; a state of near anarchy existed in many places, looting was widespread and the public services were at a standstill.

At the end of June the refugees who had fled to a safety in France which was not to materialise, began to return home. Throughout July and August they continued to pour into the country, an endless stream of unhappy, disillusioned people, as confused in mind as they were sore in body. Their return did nothing to alleviate the chaos.

Appointed to the administration of Belgium and northern France, as well as to the control of the military forces of occupation, was General von Falkenhausen, whose uncle, Baron von Falkenhausen, had been Governor-General of Belgium for the last twenty months of the Kaiser's War. To assist him in this quite extensive task Falkenhausen had General Reeder as President of the Military Administration. Under these two men, the Belgian Committee of Secretaries-General were to be responsible for seeing that the wheels were kept turning and the people in a submissive state of mind.

General von Falkenhausen made no attempt to get in touch with the Cardinal. On a visit which he paid to the Apostolic Nuncio he said that he did not believe that the moment was opportune for him to call upon the Cardinal, and would understand if his Eminence did not find it possible to make an approach from his side.[1]

---

[1] Throughout the whole of the occupation the Cardinal had no personal contact whatsoever with the German authorities except for one occasion in 1940 and three in 1941, when he received Oberkriegsverwaltungsrat Thedieck; and two courtesy visits from local commanders at Malines and Anvers in June 1940. All his contacts were either made by letter or, on his behalf, by his secretary Canon Leclef and Canon Van der Elst, a former Army chaplain, then priests of Notre Dame du Rosaire at Uccle.

As soon as conditions allowed, the Cardinal at once began to visit the distressed and wounded, particularly in his own diocese, and to re-establish public worship. He was at first impeded in this work by a German order which forbade the use of motor-cars without special permission. This order was issued on 22nd May, and at once the Apostolic Nuncio approached the German authorities with the request that the Belgian Archbishop Primate and the Bishops should be granted safe-conduct and should be allowed to move freely about their dioceses in the performance of their ecclesiastical duties. In reply to his request he received an immediate assurance that while all political activities directed against the occupying power would be forbidden and suppressed, the movement of the Church authorities in carrying out their ecclesiastical functions would be in no way limited, nor would their motor-cars be commandeered. From May till October, then, the Cardinal was able to make use of his motor-car, but when in the latter month all vehicles of more than eighteen horse-power were forbidden the roads, Falkenhausen's Chief of Staff refused to make an exception of the archiepiscopal motor, and it had to be laid up for the duration of War. A motor-car of only eleven horse-power was, however, immediately placed at the Cardinal's disposal by one of his parishioners, and he used it until the Liberation.

The Cardinal's activities in these confused days brought much comfort to the distressed, and there is no doubt that the rapid re-establishment of the administration of the Faith, which also sprang largely from his leadership, was responsible for the re-emergence of some kind of order in secular affairs. The Germans themselves were quick to recognise the value of the Cardinal's influence, and in June 1940 he received a visit from Captain von Maercker, Commandant of Malines, and later in the month from Colonel Baron von Buttler, Military Commander of Anvers, both of whom asked his Eminence for his assistance in re-establishing normal life. In asking for the Cardinal's support they promised that all the schools and colleges in Malines which had been taken over by the German troops would be freed at once, and so long as the occupation lasted would not again be requisitioned.

At first sight the German order, at the beginning of July, requiring the closing down and departure of all foreign diplomatic missions from Belgium may not seem particularly serious. Its object, of course, was to remove from the country all those neutral observers who might have been constrained to use their influence on behalf of the Belgians when the Germans began to introduce repressive measures. The Apostolic Nuncio was, naturally, included in the diplomats required to leave, and the Cardinal, realising that the Church in Belgium would be entirely cut off from the Holy See by Monsignor Micara's departure, implored the King to intercede with the Germans that he might be allowed to remain. The King did appeal, but without effect, and the Nuncio left before the end of the month. Thereafter all free communication between the Cardinal and the Holy See was forbidden. There were occasions, however, when His Eminence believed it to be essential for His Holiness to be made acquainted with conditions in Belgium, and for him, in return, to receive papal documents without the intervention of the German censorship. This was achieved, but the Germans either learned or surmised what was happening, and many times attempted to discover the Cardinal's secret lines of communication with Rome, though always without success.

The Holy See for its part did not forget the suffering Belgians. Through the Apostolic Nuncio in Berne many millions of francs and quantities of foodstuffs were made available to the Cardinal. The Red Cross also helped with food, and particularly with Swiss condensed milk, which was distributed to the seriously underfed children.

Though two-thirds of Belgium is under cultivation and a fifth of the population is engaged in agriculture, 70 per cent of all food supplies have to be imported. From the very first weeks of the occupation, therefore, the country was faced with conditions of semi-starvation, which as the months and years passed, and the Germans made no attempt to feed their victims, developed into severe famine. In America, the former President, Herbert Hoover, made protracted efforts to obtain permission to send food to Belgium, and the last foreign visitor the Cardinal received until the Liberation was the former American Ambassador, John Cudahy, with whom he discussed the possibility of getting food to the needy Belgians from outside. But neither Hoover's nor Cudahy's efforts met with any success. The help received from the Holy See was thus all the more valuable.

One of the most formidable problems facing Belgium in these early months of occupation was one which, though not entirely peculiar to that country, presented itself to a degree not experienced in any other country. On 10th May, 1940, the Belgian Government had instructed all civilian males aged from sixteen to thirty-five in the provinces of Limburg, Liége, Namur and Belgian Luxembourg to collect at Erquelinnes and Binche, on the Belgian–French frontier. As the Germans advanced, the men of other provinces were given similar instructions, and since all these men formed the reserves of the Belgian armed forces, as soon as the position began to look really desperate they were sent to the south of France.

By the end of May no fewer than 90,000 of the men were concentrated in the three departments of Haute-Garonne, Hérault and Gard. Besides them, there were between 50,000 and 60,000 others who had dropped out on the way whenever they were able to find a place to live and work to do. Nor were these all the Belgian refugees. Hundreds of thousands of men, women and children had fled into France before the advancing Germans, and were now homeless, helpless and practically starving in the western and central provinces of that country. The Belgian Prime Minister, M. Pierlot, who had gone into exile with most of his Government, gave the number of these unfortunates, in a speech at Vichy on 21st July, as two million.

It is not possible for any adequate description to be given of the conditions and sufferings of the great majority of these unhappy people, whose plight was intensified by the great tribulations into which their French hosts themselves were plunged. Those who could find no remunerative work—and those who could were comparatively few—were allowed ten francs a day for food and all other necessities. In those days the exchange rate of the Belgian franc made this sum the equivalent of only a shilling or two, and as the scarcity of food had sent prices soaring, hunger was widespread.

The majority of the sixteens to thirty-fives acting under the instructions of the Belgian Government made the journey together in special trains, and were under the charge of the Belgian army and subject to military discipline. Numbers of them were sent to the fighting areas in France, where they were put to work on digging trenches and other warlike construction; others were sent to work on the farms and in the vineyards; while others, before the French–German armistice, were put into the war factories. But these who could be found work were only a small fraction of the vast total, and the rest were enclosed in veritable concentration camps. Enforced idleness, the hunger caused by an exceptionally poor diet, and the terrible living conditions, laid these youths and young men open to grave moral dangers.

After weeks and months of exposure to this life, the young, especially, presented an extremely serious problem, and the only solution which it seemed might have any efficacy was to return all refugees to Belgium. But how? Those Belgian priests and leaders who had accompanied the exiles were convinced that only efforts emanating from the home-country could make such a plan possible.

Already many parents who had remained in Belgium and had become anxious for the fate of their sons had approached the Cardinal, imploring him to intervene with the authorities. To their entreaties were added written pleas from the leaders of youth organisations and colleges, and finally, between 29th June and 16th July, no fewer than eight prominent men, all connected with youth movements and colleges, visited the Cardinal at Malines and spoke to him in person.

The Cardinal acted at once. He directed the attention of the Red Cross and other relief organisations to the plight of the young Belgians, and made appeals for clothing and shoes to be sent to France. Among his visitors at Malines had been Monsignor Cruysbergh, Chaplain-General of the Flemish Catholic Youth Organisation, and Canon Cardyn, Chaplain-General of the Christian Workers' Youth Organisation, who had experienced the conditions of the exiles at first hand. These two priests he sent back to France, there, in his name, to organise repatriation. He also appealed to the King to use his influence, and the King appointed one of his immediate entourage, Count d'Aspremont-Lynden, to do everything possible to obtain priority for all youths between fifteen and nineteen.

On the last day of July he despatched the Abbé Maes, Director of the Léon XIII Seminary at Louvain, with letters to the Apostolic Nuncio in Vichy and the Spanish Ambassador to France, appealing to them to use their personal influence and the influence of their high positions to speed up the repatriation of the Belgian youth.

The conditions facing the organisers were incredible. Out of the 130,000 to 150,000 men involved, only 90,000 had been enrolled by the military organisation—*Centres de Recrutement de l'Armée Belge*, shortened to CRAB—and the remainder, of whom there were at least 30,000 scattered about the countryside in work which they had found for themselves, were unidentified. Many thousands of them had made their own way north, but those that remained were the cause of great anxiety, for being considered as civilian refugees, since CRAB had no cognisance of them, they could not be included on the special trains carrying the CRABS. Nevertheless, by the middle of September all the young Belgians had been repatriated; and not long afterwards the remaining half-million refugees had all reached home.

The rôle which the Cardinal played in the solution of this tremendous problem was paramount. Had it not been for his firm and rapid action as soon as he had been made aware of the situation, it is quite likely that all Belgian refugees in France would have remained there until the Liberation, in conditions of great suffering, for the French Government, naturally preoccupied with its own serious difficulties, had little time or sympathy for uninvited foreign guests. However, under pressure from the Spanish Ambassador and the Apostolic Nuncio, Vichy found the necessary transportation, and in consequence several hundred thousand Belgians owe to the Cardinal a debt of gratitude that they cannot hope to repay.

So far the Cardinal had not come into direct collision with the German authorities. But the time was soon to arrive when he was to become the champion of all those directly assaulted by the occupying power.

In the middle of July 1940 the Germans issued an order to the effect that all persons holding any public office whatsoever who had fled from Belgium could not be reinstated on their return without the express permission of the Military Commander. This measure was applied to the teaching staff of the Catholic University of Louvain, a special decree being published on 9th September in *Moniteur Belge* by the Secretary-General of the Ministry of Public Instruction to the effect that no matter for what reason they had left Belgium, they must submit a full written statement to a Commission of three setting out where they had been and what they had done while out of the country. If they refused to explain their absence they would be automatically superseded in their posts.

The measure was designed chiefly to remove, with a semblance of justification, all those who might be, or who were known to be, opponents of Nazism. Teachers everywhere, and especially university teachers, are in a position to exert great influence in all directions on their pupils. In England university staffs have very rarely become involved in politics, and university students have even more rarely made any effective impression on a political issue. On the Continent of Europe, on the other hand, university staffs have never hesitated to attempt to influence their pupils in great political issues, and the students have often initiated actions which have fundamentally affected the course of history in their country. The activities of Polish and Hungarian students in recent years are two cases in point.

In the countries occupied by Hitler, from Norway to Greece, it was the university and high-school students who were almost invariably among the first to go over to active resistance. The German authorities were aware of the threat which might develop against them from this quarter, and always attempted very early in the occupation of a country to place a curb on the universities and similar bodies. Once there were vacancies on the teaching staff, no matter how such vacancies might arise, Nazi nominees were put forward to fill them. The chief function of these nominees was not to teach their subject, but to put over propaganda for the New Order. This was now being attempted not only in the Catholic University of Louvain, but in the University of Brussels as well.

Now, the Catholic University of Louvain, like the University of Brussels, had the status of a free university; that is to say, the academic authorities were not required, under the Belgian Constitution, to submit appointments to university posts to the Administration for its approval, and were equally autonomous in respect of courses and regulations. The High Rector of the Catholic University at once refused, therefore, to comply with the order, and permitted the eleven professors involved to resume their work, though they were allowed to submit their statements to the Commission if they wished.

It so happened that there were certain vacancies on the teaching staff of the University caused by death or the continued absence of members abroad, and the Germans also demanded that all nominations to these appointments must be submitted to them for their approval. As soon as he was advised of this, the High Rector, Monsignor van Waeyenbergh, recognised the extremely grave threat which was thus offered to the freedom of the University, and having consulted the Cardinal, who was Chancellor of the University and President of the Administrative Council, he wrote immediately to the Military Administration pointing out the established freedom of the University, and requesting that it should be freed from the effects of the order.

General Reeder, President of the Military Administration, himself replied to the letter. He rejected the High Rector's objections out of hand.

"The Military Administration is well aware," he wrote, "that the University of Louvain, like that of Brussels, has formerly been regarded as a free University. But it is also aware that for some time the two Universities have lost much of their free character on account of the close relations they have maintained with the State. In the opinion of the Military Administration, this is reinforced not only by the equality accorded to the graduates of the two Universities with the graduates of the State Universities, but also by the fact that the State provides them with a great part of their maintenance funds.

"In view of these two facts, the Military Administration is unable, under any hypothesis whatsoever, to be disinterested in the constitution and the teaching of the professorial bodies of the two Universities. The Military Administration already made this point when it declared that the readmission to their posts of those professors who had fled to France, even in the free Universities, should be dependent upon the decision of a Belgian Commission after examining the cases, and upon the approval of the Military Administration. When the Military Administration reserves the right of approving new nominations and new courses, it does so only in logical conformity with the attitude it has previously taken, the basis for which has been debated by the free Universities."

This letter made the Military Administration's intentions perfectly clear. It also made equally clear that any opposition by the University would only lead to its being closed down. The University authorities were, therefore, faced with a grave dilemma. While the free University of Brussels deemed it wise to submit to the German demands, the Cardinal now decided to intervene personally and in the name of the entire Belgian episcopacy on behalf of Louvain.

He presented to the Military Administration a clearly stated and well-argued refutation of General Reeder's points, quoting authorities, and concluded with the warning that if the Germans persisted in their demands, they would find themselves in conflict with the Holy See. The Belgian episcopacy, the University itself and all Belgian Catholics had the outcome of this matter closely at heart, and he did not believe it to be in the interests of the occupying power to wound the vast majority of the Belgian people in this way. Nevertheless, since all Belgians desired to avoid a conflict, if the Germans would say exactly what they wished to obtain from the University of Louvain, provided the principles were fully safeguarded, the University would give the greatest satisfaction it felt to lie within its power.

To this letter Falkenhausen himself replied. He argued that the measure decreed by the Military Administration was necessary for reasons of security, and would not give way on any point.

Falkenhausen's letter resolved the dilemma for the authorities of the University. The Administrative Council, led by the Cardinal, decided that, come what may, they would never submit professorial appointments for the approval of the Germans. For their part, the Germans never once enforced their assumed right of veto. They did, however, make one more attempt to interfere in the affairs of the University.

On 7th November, 1940, the Ministry of Public Instruction, at the behest of the Military Administration, asked the University to invite certain German professors to teach in the University "on exchange". With the agreement of the Cardinal, the Rector replied that though the University recognised the great benefits which would accrue from the exchange of professors, the authorities believed it would be better to postpone such an exchange until a more favourable time. Besides, since September 1939 the University had suspended all exchanges, a decision which had been made known to groups of French, Italian and Spanish professors.

Several of the State Universities had agreed to make such exchanges, and the Germans took Louvain's refusal badly. But though the Rector was approached more than once on the subject, he firmly refused to allow a German professor to teach at Louvain during the whole of the occupation.

As in Norway, Denmark, Holland and elsewhere, so in Belgium, the Nazis declared that they were occupying the country merely to safeguard it from occupation by the Allies. In addition, they declared that they had no hostile feelings towards the Roman Catholic Church. Within a very short time, however, they were making abundantly clear their intention to do everything they could to impede the practice of the Faith.

The first indications came as the Belgian National Day, 21st July, approached. On 2nd July the Cardinal issued the following instructions: "The National Day, Sunday 21st July, will be commemorated with special reverence. The Faithful are asked to offer to the divine Mercy their masses, communions and prayers for the well-being of the Fatherland. With this intention, a solemn mass will be celebrated in all parish churches followed by prayers for the King. All established authorities will be invited to attend this solemn occasion in the principal church. A solemn votive mass may be sung for St Joseph, the Patron Saint of Belgium."

Three days before the festival, however, the Cardinal received from the Feldkommandant at Anvers a letter, issued by the Military Command, forbidding all public buildings and private houses to be decorated with flags; concerts and similar demonstrations to be given in public places and the tolling of church bells were also banned. On the other hand, the Military Command had no objection to the singing of a solemn Te Deum, provided that it was in no way turned into a demonstration. The Cardinal was requested to see that these instructions were rigorously carried out. The Cardinal ignored the letter, and let his own instructions stand.

As each great festival or fast came round, the Germans would find some means of attempting to interfere with its proper performance. It is the custom in Belgium, for example, to put lighted candles on the graves of the departed on All Saints' and All Souls' Days. Falkenhausen ordered that all such candles must be extinguished by half-past five in the evening, and requested the Cardinal to support this measure. Again, 11th November had been set aside by law since 1922 as a national holiday, and it was customary on this day to celebrate a Requiem Mass for the souls of those killed in the War. Consequently, the Cardinal had issued a Pastoral Letter ordaining the singing of this traditional Requiem in all Belgian churches on 11th November, 1940. But as the

Secretaries-General had decided that the day should be an ordinary working day this year, Falkenhausen wrote to the Cardinal requesting him to cancel the singing of the Requiem. On the other hand, said the General, there would be no objection to the patron saint's day of the King, 15th November, being solemnly observed with religious festivities, particularly by the singing of a Te-Deum.

To requests such as these, and they were made regularly during the four years of occupation, the Cardinal made no reply, and took no action, and the people filled the churches to pray for King and country, and to sing the National Anthem.

The people soon began to give a name to this behaviour of Joseph-Ernest Cardinal van Roey, Archbishop of Malines and Primate of Belgium. They called it *josephism*, and it was an indication of their approval and support and admiration of the Cardinal's firm leadership that they did so. Those who are accustomed to think of Resistance in terms of sabotage, a secret Press, the formation of a *maquis*, the organisation of escape-routes and all similar activities, with their attendant risks of torture, imprisonment and death, may regard the Cardinal's refusal to co-operate with the Germans as of small value, but in doing so they would be wrong. Reference has already been made to the confusion which gripped the country and addled men's minds as the result of the events of May 1940. In all the occupied countries in the days and weeks immediately following the defeat the majority of men were numbed into inactivity. In no country is there a record of active, organised Resistance dating from the earliest days. But as the shock wore off, and people were able to measure the intentions of the Germans, there came a reawakening of spirit, an awareness of courage, a restoration of manhood. Belgium was fortunate in having two men like F. J. van de Meulebroeck, Burgomaster of Brussels, and Cardinal van Roey, as, during the occupation of the First World War, she had been fortunate in having Adolphe Max, Burgomaster of Brussels, and Cardinal Mercier as Primate. Burgomaster van de Meulebroeck possessed outstanding courage and stood firm against the Germans in civil matters affecting his great city. His example inspired others to acts which restored their self-respect; and without self-respect any man is lost. Equally, the Cardinal's opposition in spiritual matters had a restorative effect. It worked, however, in a somewhat different way, but in the end proved complementary to other forms of opposition, for from it came a comfort for the spirit; and without a comfort for the spirit a man flounders.

It may be thought that the Cardinal risked little or nothing when he opposed the Germans, since they might hesitate a long time before taking physical action against so eminent a Prince of the Church. Though they had often made plans for the apprehension of that other great Prelate, their own countryman, the Bishop of Munster, at the time that he became more than ordinarily obstreperous, when it came to the point they had always drawn back. In fact, no considerations of this sort would ever have held the Nazis back had they felt that the Cardinal's removal would help them. It can be taken for granted that the risk he ran never occurred to the Cardinal.

As the months passed, the Cardinal was to come more and more into collision with the occupying power, and each occasion carried more and more risk. Yet, as the risk increased, the less, so is seemed, did the Cardinal hesitate before he acted.

In pre-war Belgium there had been two fascist parties: the Rexists, led by Léon Degrelle, and the Vlaamsch National Verbond (VNV), led by De Clercq. Neither party was numerous, but it was sufficiently active not only to make a nuisance of itself, but also to constitute a certain danger. The Belgian authorities arrested these leaders as soon as the situation became threatening, and sent them to France, but when the French collapsed they were set free, and at once hurried back to Belgium.

The Belgian Church, led by the Cardinal and Bishops, had always opposed the Rexists and Flemish Nationalists; and Degrelle and De Clercq recognised in the Church their most constant and redoubtable enemy.

Back in Nazi-occupied Belgium the fascists believed that their hour of triumph had come. Nevertheless, they still feared the influence of the Church, and in order to arrive at some arrangement for a *modus vivendi*, in August Degrelle sought an interview with the Cardinal. The intermediary who approached his Eminence on Degrelle's behalf stated that the events of the War had completely changed the Rexist leader's outlook, and that he was prepared to follow any line which the Cardinal might deem best.

The Cardinal made an appointment for 17th August, but Degrelle failed to keep it, and later informed the Cardinal that he would come to the palace on 3rd September. This time also he did not appear, and the next day a letter from his assistant announced that he would definitely see the Cardinal on the following Friday. The Cardinal now instructed his secretary to write urgently to Degrelle telling him that he could not receive him on that day, and reminding the Rexist leader that he had already waited for him on no fewer than three occasions.

Whether Degrelle received this letter in time is not known. He declared, however, that it had not arrived when he set out for Malines. In the circumstances, the Cardinal agreed to see him.

At this meeting Degrelle informed the Cardinal that he was about to begin the publication once more of the Rexist organ *Le Pays Réel*, and he expressed the wish that, as it was to be both Catholic and Belgian in tone, the Cardinal would not oppose it. He also said that he was proposing to group all Belgian youth into Rexist groups, and asked for the Cardinal's support in this project.

To the first of these points the Cardinal replied: "I cannot judge your publication because I have not yet seen it. But if it is as you say it will be, then I shall not oppose it." To the second he said he would never be able to permit the Catholic youth so to be organised.

Le Pays Réel had appeared only once or twice before its real nature and the true intentions of its editors became apparent. It was to be an organ of pro-Nazi and violently anti-Allied propaganda. As for Degrelle's claim that it would be Catholic in tone, as well as patriotic, in the number which appeared on 6th October, 1940, José Streel launched an attack on the Catholic clergy, accusing them of supporting Free-masons and Jews, and thereby becoming instruments of pro-English agitation. He warned the clergy, and certain Catholic educationalists, to put an end at once to such agitation, and if they did not, Rex would take active steps to persuade them to do so.

Degrelle had sent free copies of *Le Pays Réel* to a very large number of priests. A number of recipients, on seeing the nature of the journal, attacked it in no uncertain terms, and some even wrote to the editors protesting strongly. But Degrelle was impervious to such protests, and in November he sent a letter to a considerable number of parish priests and teachers. In this letter he said that the Belgian clergy had for some time past stopped reading newspapers and magazines, and were therefore ignorant of the world-shattering events that were now an almost daily occurrence. This placed the clergy, who had great moral responsibilities, in a kind of intellectual isolation, which prevented them from giving the assistance to their flocks in these tremendous times that they ought to be able to give. If they read *Le Pays Réel* they would be kept in lively touch with all that was happening.

In his last sentence, Degrelle, hoping no doubt to attract clerical subscribers, made, instead, a bad mistake. He wrote: "In closing, let me add that the Church Authority at Malines sees no obstacle in the way of the clergy and Faithful reading *Le Pays Réel*."

When they read these words, many who had received the letter wrote to the Cardinal asking him to make a public denial that he had ever said this. To all of them the Cardinal replied that since everyone could see what kind of a journal *Le Pays Réel* was, it was not necessary for him to make an official denial of Degrelle's claim, though he was quite willing that it should be made known, by other means, that he did deny it.

It was not long before the contents of the Cardinal's letter reached Degrelle's ears, and in *Le Pays Réel* of 8th December he himself launched an attack on the clergy under the title of "Political Sermons". Even taking into account the violence of the language and the exaggeration and untruthfulness of the charges, the article demonstrated the fear that Degrelle, his followers and their German masters had of the influence of the clergy. After a long tirade in which His Eminence was named, with M. Paul van Zeeland, a former Prime Minister who had escaped to England, as having a personal responsibility for Belgium's current misfortunes, the article concluded: "Instead of mixing themselves up in politics from morning till night, let the clergy occupy themselves rather with bringing about a spiritual revolution within themselves. There is an urgent need for this. The political frenzy of certain priests illustrates only too well their disregard of their religious duties. . . . Let the clergy meditate upon their spiritual mission and devote themselves to that, and they shall have peace. But if they continue their plotting they will find out who is speaking. And do not then let them count on God to get them out of trouble, for God is only on the side of pious priests, and not on the side of the friends of Boerenbond, of Van Zeeland and of Winston Churchill!"

As will be seen later, the threat was no idle one. But neither the Cardinal nor any one of his clergy allowed himself to be deflected by it from his duty. As the occupation extended into months and years, and both Germans and their Rexist and Flemish Nationalist satellites brought increasing pressure to bear on the Church in an attempt to weaken the example of moral strength and courage with which it was encouraging the nation, from the highest prelate to the lowliest curate, not a priest faltered in the determination to stand firm against the evil forces of the New Order.

During the last months of 1940 and the opening months of 1941 it became increasingly clear what the true intention of the Germans was towards the people. Everything and everybody were to be used as German needs dictated, with utter disregard of any suffering which might be caused by increasingly restrictive measures. Hunger was now widespread. All the efforts of neutral sympathisers to get food to the near-starving people were thwarted by the Germans, who, for their part, continued to plunder the totally inadequate stocks to feed their own soldiers. To hunger was added a shortage of coal, brought about by similar means. The Germans ordered the Direction of Mines to supply 410,500 tons a month, 130,000 of which was to be best house-coal to be supplied to the German domestic market, and the remainder supplied to the Wehrmacht, the German State Railways and the industries of Luxembourg, Lorraine and northern France.

Already in the autumn of 1940 the Germans had opened a campaign for recruiting Belgian workers for employment in Germany. They gave the authorities the assurance that only volunteers would be used, and that these would not be employed in the war industries. Now, early in 1941, the Organisation Todt, a leading organisation in the Nazi war-machine though composed of civilians, demanded to be supplied with 10,000 building, metal and textile workers. The fiction of volunteers was kept up. but it was made clear that the work was to be offered to unemployed Belgians, who, if they refused, were to be sent to forced-labour camps.

But resistance to all such demands and to all other restrictive measures was increasingly hardening. In May the miners and metal-workers of Brussels, Liége, Charleroi and Anvers came out on strike in protest against the food situation, declaring that their present rations were inadequate, in view of the hard work expected of them.

The Germans, however, were quite unmoved by such demonstrations and merely increased their demands. They now tried to persuade the Secretary-General for Communications to supply 5,000 Belgian railwaymen for work on the German State Railways. Both the Secretary-General and the Direction of the Belgian State Railways refused to co-operate, but it was not long before Belgian railwaymen were to be among the first to be seized for forced-labour.

During this period there had, of course, been large numbers of Belgians who had been compelled, through one circumstance or another, to volunteer for work in Germany. So that the Church should not appear to encourage "volunteering", the Cardinal, contrary to normal practice, had refused to send chaplains to Germany to minister to the spiritual welfare of the unfortunate men. The situation soon became so acute, however, that several German Bishops grew perturbed, and the Bishop of Berlin wrote to the Cardinal asking if Belgian priests could not be sent. For some time the Cardinal remained resolute, but when the problem became extremely serious he wrote to the Secretary-General for Labour asking him to use his good offices with the Germans to obtain their permission for Belgian priests to be sent to the Reich, particularly to Berlin and Cologne, where the majority of Belgian workers were situated. The Secretary-General complied with this request, but the Germans ignored it, and continued to do so throughout the War.

The remainder of the year 1941 saw the stepping up of restrictive measures against the Belgians, which, as they increased, became progressively harsher. Early in June, as a reprisal for the death of a German soldier in Laeken park, one hundred Laeken men were seized as hostages. Two months later the first Belgians were executed for alleged sabotage, and from this time until the end of the occupation there was scarcely a week in which there were not executions. But the Belgians had regained their spirit and their courage, and were not deterred by any threats or acts from resisting the Germans whenever and wherever resistance could be effective.

The failure of volunteers to come forward in sufficient numbers

43

at last made the Germans drop their masks. Towards the end of September the first compulsory order was issued for 4,000 Belgian railwaymen to be sent to Germany. It was not until 6th March, 1942, however, that Falkenhausen issued an order which revealed that the Germans were prepared to go to the extreme limit. The decree succinctly stated that all Belgians could henceforward be compelled to work for the Germans on certain projects within the territory of the Military Command, and that all private and public enterprises were to be obliged to surrender those nominated. The effect of the order on the Belgians was to send large numbers of those chosen into hiding, and as a reprisal the deportations of innocent men and women to concentration camps was begun.

These events greatly perturbed the Cardinal, but he did not yet feel that he could intervene without being accused of meddling in political matters. Since the first attack on the clergy in 1940 accusing them of doing just this, the Rexists and their fellow-travellers had increased their campaign of vilification, and the Cardinal, to give them no basis of fact for their charges, had been careful to do nothing that could be construed truthfully as political interference. Nevertheless, he had been able to carry this policy to such lengths that in insisting that the Church must refrain from any act that might have a political interpretation, he had, in fact, been able to resist both Nazis and Rexists.

The 20th May, 1941, for example, had been the anniversary of the execution in France of a number of Belgians believed to be dangerous to French security, among whom was Joris Van Severen, founder and leader of the fascist party known as Dinaso (Dietsch Nationaal-Socialist). The members of Dinaso, the Rexists and the VNV proposed holding memorial services for Van Severen and the rest in several churches throughout Belgium.

When this became known, on 13th May, the Cardinal issued a warning to all his clergy.

"It is absolutely essential," he said to the annual Decanal Conference by chance being held on that day, "to avoid all religious services, particularly funeral rites, being made the occasion or pretext for political manifestations. The ecclesiastical Authority does not prohibit prayers for the soul of any deceased whatsoever—contrary to the slanderous claims of certain people—nor to say private masses, nor to celebrate funeral rites in public (except

44

where the deceased is excluded from Christian burial under the Canons 1240 and 1241); but it is not admissible, as certain political parties would wish, to abuse the ceremonies of the Church. If it appears to be the intention of those arranging funeral rites of deceased persons so to abuse the ceremonies of the Church, either by choice of place, or by choice of day, or by any other circumstances, the vicar or rector of the Church is not to celebrate these rites. Funeral services in churches must follow the form and customs approved by the ecclesiastical Authority. A guard of honour at a catafalque, even if covered by any flag whatsoever (except the national flag in certain cases), or the playing of non-liturgical hymns or melodies (as laid down by Decree 185 of the Fifth Provincial Council of Malines) either during or after the mass, or any other things of this kind, are not to be permitted. It is absolutely necessary to see that the funeral rites for soldiers or other meritorious persons, shall be performed discreetly, and not degenerate into a public demonstration. On these occasions there must be no funeral orations."

To assist the implementation of these instructions, the Cardinal also laid it down that unless the deceased was a truly national figure, his funeral rites should be performed in his own parish church. He refused to sanction any deviation from this rule, and throughout the occupation it was a constant source of anger to the Rexists and their friends.

Conforming with these instructions, the priests of many important churches refused to permit the memorial service for Van Severen to be held. The result, naturally, was a renewed out-cry by the Rexists, Dinasos and VNV, who, in their various journals, inveighed against the clergy and the Cardinal with incitements to violence. At Bruges, where the Bishop had flatly refused to permit the celebration of a Requiem Mass for the "victims of Abbéville"—as Van Severen and the rest were called by the Belgian fascists—members of Dinaso marched on the Bishop's palace, tore up the paving-stones and hurled them through the windows. At Malines unknown persons during the night of 23rd/24th May scrawled on the archiepiscopal palace: "We shall avenge Van Severen! Down with the priests!" But these and other incidents only served to harden the resolution of the clergy to obey their Archbishop at all costs.

During the same address to the Decanal Conference from which we have already quoted, the Cardinal also gave the following instruction: "If men or youths belonging to any political party aspire to approach the Holy Table as though they were making a demonstration in so doing—for example, if they come in uniform—Communion can and must be refused them."

The fascist parties were anxious that it should appear to their fellow-countrymen that they were not irreligious, and that the Church demonstrated its approval of them by permitting the wearing of uniforms in church and by celebrating memorial services and funeral services, and they were particularly anxious to communicate corporately in uniform, for these reasons. By enforcing the letter of his instruction that the Church should not be an instrument in any political demonstration of any sort, the Cardinal thus hoist Degrelle and his friends with their own petard.

Priests everywhere, recognising the Cardinal's true motives, applied themselves to carrying out his instructions. Fascists in uniform were refused Communion; no priest would allow any funeral service that did not conform to the rites of the Church to be held in his church; no service that could in any way be classified as a political demonstration was permitted. Later, many priests were to be arrested and deported to one or other of the notorious Nazi concentration camps, for their refusal to disobey their Cardinal, though the charges levelled against them named other supposed crimes.

The outcry made by the Rexists, the VNV and the Dinasos eventually reached such a pitch that Falkenhausen declared himself to be gravely perturbed by the situation, which he believed must terminate in acts of extreme violence against the Church unless it were amicably resolved. By his order, Oberkriegsverwaltungsrat Thedieck called on the Cardinal at Malines to ask His Eminence his reasons for issuing the instructions. The Cardinal explained in detail, and went further by telling Thedieck that in his view the Germans were really responsible for the situation, since it was they who inspired the propaganda in the Press; and besides, their censorship could prevent the publication of anything that did not please them. Thedieck replied to this with the strange assertion that the censorship then in force was not a "preventive censorship", though exactly what he meant by this is not quite clear. He did, however, tell the Cardinal that a very violent article attacking His Eminence and the clergy, which Degrelle proposed to publish in *Le Pays Réel*, had been banned. The banning of this article, however, had no effect at all on the future anti-clerical attacks of the Belgian fascists, though for a time, during the autumn of 1941, their violence of expression was not so extreme as it had been at first.

In February 1942 another incident caused the matter to flare up again. In the autumn of 1941 a number of young Flemish and Walloon fascists had been sent to fight with the Wehrmacht against Russia. Large numbers of them were killed, among them Raymond Tollenaere, Chief of the Black Brigade, who met his death at Leningrad on 21st January, 1942. The VNV wrote to the Cardinal a month later asking him to grant permission to the Vicar of St Cordule at Schoten to hold a memorial service in his church for Tollenaere and all those members of the Black Brigade who had fallen on the Russian front. To this letter the Cardinal replied that he could not, under Canon Law, grant permission for memorial services to be held in any church that was not the parish church of the deceased, and that the attempts of the VNV to obtain his permission could only be interpreted as a political move.

Despite the new access of rage of the fascists, the priests remained firm in their obedience. The Vicar at Châtelet refused to celebrate the obsequies of a soldier killed on the Russian front even though the man was one of his parishioners, for the reason that the Rexists proposed to mount a guard at the catafalque, which was to be covered by a tricolour. The service was held, however, a German Roman Catholic chaplain acting as celebrant. And there were many other similar cases.

It was in the midst of these new attacks that Falkenhausen issued his decree referring to forced-labour, to which mention has already been made, and against which the Cardinal did not feel himself able to protest without inviting a charge of political meddling, which by all his other actions he ostensibly sought to avoid. But another order was issued on 9th April, 1942, which gave the Cardinal the opportunity for which he had been waiting. The order said briefly: "Those working in the coal-mining industry will be obliged to work one Sunday in each month or on feast days, as will be fixed by the Military Administration."

This order clearly violated the liberty of conscience of the workers. The Cardinal saw that he could protest against it on

47

religious grounds and that in so doing he could not be accused of purely political motives. At the same time, however, he attacked the whole process of forced-labour. He called together the six Belgian Bishops, and on 8th May despatched to Falkenhausen a letter remarkable for its outspokenness, signed by them all.

"We have not the habit of protesting against each measure restricting our religious liberties nor against all the other vexations of which our Catholic acts are the object, because we believe that in the sum these measures cause more harm to those who try to impose them than to those on whom they are imposed," wrote the Bishops. "But this time, our responsibility as the Shepherds of Souls prevents us from remaining silent."

They then went on to point out that the freedom to perform their religious observances was a primordial right of all men, and that among Catholics one of the most serious religious duties was the observance of Sundays and feast days. The occupying Power had the obligation to respect this fundamental right of human conscience laid upon it, not only for reasons of humanity, but by the terms of the Hague Convention. The German Authority had no right to compel Belgian workers to disobey their consciences, and least of all by threats of imprisonment, fines and other punishments.

"In the name of our Catholic people," they continued, "we raise our voices to condemn this violation of their consciences and religious liberty. This violation is made worse still by the fact that the work done by the Belgian mine-workers does not, in the main, profit their compatriots. Albeit that Belgium is a producer of coal without equal, we have seen, during this long, hard winter, many families and institutions, particularly among the poor and the workers, deprived of the means of keeping warm, which proves—as, indeed, everybody knows—that our miners are compelled to work for the interests of foreigners. This makes all the more unjust and hateful any restraint upon their religious liberty."

As Catholic Bishops, they declared, it was their mission to come to the defence of the weak. It was with deep pain that they saw the Belgian workers deprived ever more and more of their elemental rights. They had been morally compelled by every possible means to work abroad. The decree of 6th March introduced forced-labour on a legal basis even in work of a military nature, with the threat of deportation for refusal. All these things made the lot of the Belgian workers more and more precarious and distressing, and would certainly inflict a lasting wound in Belgian hearts. If the Germans wished, when peace came at last, to have contact with Belgium, they should not make this contact impossible in advance by measures which deeply wounded the great mass of the population.

A fortnight later Falkenhausen replied in a very long letter, though, he said, the Bishops' letter was not really an appropriate one for the basis of a discussion. In attempting to answer the points raised by the letter of 8th May, the Military Commander, however, made the bad mistake of repeating the well-known Nazi propaganda lines, which need no repetition here.

The Cardinal at once seized on this opportunity to let the Germans know exactly what he thought of their propaganda. Having rejected as unacceptable Falkenhausen's suggestion that miners and others compelled to work on Sundays and feast days should be allowed to hear Mass in the evenings, even if the Holy See gave the necessary permission, he stressed that obligatory work on Sundays and feast days would still remain a violation of religious liberty. From this he went on to destroy the Commander's arguments about the causes of the lack of food in Belgium. The facts quite disproved the General's contention that in peace-time Belgium produced enough food only for half her population and had to import the rest. Even during the occupation Belgium had produced sufficient food to provide the necessaries of life for the entire population, though admittedly the amounts would be small, yet they would nevertheless remove the present state of famine. The same could be argued of industrial products. Was it really necessary to ask where the bulk of Belgium produce and products were going? Since Belgium was thus already making such a high contribution to European economy, was it really necessary to impose forced-labour on the people?

His Eminence then went on to answer Falkenhausen's reproach that the Church in Belgium did not support the anti-Bolshevik struggle. The silence of the Church was quite explicable, he said.

"As Catholic Bishops we wonder what an eventual German victory would mean for the Catholic Church or Christianity in Europe, and, of course, in Belgium. When we hear the thirty

Cardinals, Archbishops, Bishops and other prelates of Germany publicly proclaim in their collective Pastoral Letter published at Fulda on 26th June, 1941, 'It is a question of the existence or non-existence of Christianity and of the Church in Germany'; when many documents issuing from German Bishops regularly express their mortal dread for the future of Catholicism and of Christ's Church in their country; it is quite natural for us to share the same fears. . . . On the other hand, as Belgian Bishops, we have the duty and the right to remain faithful to our country, and to wish, with all Belgian people, for the complete restoration of our independence. But, we do wonder what the fate of Belgium would be in the event of a total German victory. So far as we know, Germany, up to now, has made no reassuring declaration whatsoever on this point, as the other belligerent powers have done. There, Excellency, are the reasons which dictate our silence: believe us when we say that we cannot denounce a distant and problematic danger when we see very near us very real dangers which threaten simultaneously the Catholic Church and Christianity, and which do not spring from Russian Bolshevism."

The whole letter was in similar outspoken and mildly, but irritatingly, sarcastic terms. While there was an overtone of superficial politeness, there was no attempt to conciliate Falkenhausen; on the contrary, there was no equivocation in a single syllable. He could not now be ignorant of exactly what the Cardinal and the Bishops thought of the Nazis and their oppressive measures.

While Falkenhausen was composing his reply to the Cardinal's first letter of 8th May, and his Eminence was drafting his reply, in some way which has not yet been fully determined the text of the 8th May letter became accessible to the public. It was copied and re-copied and passed from hand to hand throughout the length and breadth of the country, and was an instrument for reviving courage and a source of spiritual comfort, so badly needed. Naturally, the Germans soon came to hear of what was happening, and on the same day that the second letter was delivered in Brussels, the Cardinal received a brief, threatening note from Reeder, Chief of the Military Administration, who also sent a copy to each of the Bishops.

After expressing surprise that the letter should have been made public, Reeder listed the following threats: the Cardinal was to be held personally responsible for what had happened, and would be fined on the basis of so much for each copy seized by the Germans; and the publication of a decree which would require all ecclesiastical communications destined for the public, and in particular Pastoral Letters, to be submitted to a German censorship.

The Cardinal replied immediately to Reeder avowing in his own behalf and in the name of all the Bishops that neither he nor they were responsible for the dissemination of the letter of 8th May. He continued that if Falkenhausen wished to publish his reply in the Press, the Church authorities had no objection, but if he did so, then he ought to allow the Cardinal's second letter to be published at the same time. If the fine were imposed, since the Archbishop and Bishops had no funds to meet such a fine, in order to pay it a public appeal would have to be made to the Faithful. As for the proposed decree to enforce German censorship on all ecclesiastical pronouncements, so that there should be no misunderstanding at all, the Cardinal must say at once and bluntly that neither he nor his Bishops would accept such a censorship, whatever might happen to them.

Falkenhausen, in making these threats, had, however, placed himself in a very difficult position. If he imposed them, then it must emerge that the occupying Power had come into open conflict with the Church. This was not at all in keeping with high Nazi policy. They knew quite well that in a predominantly Catholic country such as Belgium, where the Catholic Church was the established Church, such a conflict would only serve to exacerbate relations between the people and the German authorities, and relations were even now, to say the very least, extremely difficult, for by this time Belgian Resistance had become organised and active, and the morale of the population, despite the terrible conditions in which they were living and the increasingly restrictive measures imposed by the Germans, was rising daily.

To extricate himself from his difficulty, Falkenhausen caused an approach to be made to a former Belgian military chaplain, Canon Van der Elst, then Vicar of Our Lady of the Rosary at Uccle, asking him to act as mediator between him and the Cardinal, and when the Canon had asked His Eminence for his views on the suggestion, he agreed to act. As a result of the discussions which followed, the Canon communicated the Cardinal's views on the position of the Church under the occupation under four headings. First, since the general principles of Church government preclude the Church from becoming involved in political agitation, the Cardinal had given instructions to his clergy how to conduct religious services in order to uphold these principles. However, in this connection he would ask the authorities to inform him of any priests or Catholic activities which the Germans believed were threats to public order, and, for his part, he would see that his priests carried out the proper duties of their charge. Second, the Cardinal wished to draw the attention of the authorities to the constant attacks on the fundamental principles of Christianity, the rôle of the Church and the activity of the clergy, in the Press and other organs; and he expressed the hope that the authorities would not allow these attacks to develop. Third, if the German authorities felt that they could not limit the liberty of the Press in order to stop the attacks, then they should accord to Catholics the right to defend themselves against these attacks. Fourth, the Cardinal wished the German authorities to believe that any proposal or any complaint that he might feel constrained to make, he made only because he felt it necessary to do so for the safeguarding of the conscience of the Faithful and for the maintenance in Belgium of the religious customs, convictions and institutions which were the bases of "that Christian civilisation which Germany declares she wishes to maintain and defend in this war".

Again we see in this final phrase the biting barb of sarcasm.

A letter from Reeder on 7th July retracted the threats made in his letter of 6th June. No further mention was made of the fine or the proposed censorship, and he expressed the view that "this affair need no longer be pursued".

While all this had been happening, new and increasingly restrictive measures dealing with forced-labour had been introduced. They continued without abatement throughout the summer and into the autumn of 1942. Until now, however, Belgians seized for forced-labour were ostensibly put to work in Belgium; but on 6th October yet another ordinance decreed that Belgium men between the ages of eighteen and fifty, and single women between twenty-one and thirty-five should be sent to forced-labour in Germany.

Realising that this new measure could not fail to move the

Cardinal to further protests, Reeder called Canon Van der Elst to his headquarters, where he had explained to him what was involved, and asked him to pass the explanations to His Eminence. After pointing out that the measure had already been in force in Holland and France for some time, and that it was by nature quite different from the deportations of the First World War, when Belgian men were arrested en masse and without any consideration of their family situation, Reeder asserted that the seizure of men and women for forced-labour in Germany would be carried out only if the number of volunteers was insufficient for Germany's requirements. Those who were sent to forced-labour would work under exactly the same conditions as if they volunteered, and a commission was to be set up for their protection.

But the Cardinal was not deceived; nor were the Belgian people. There were very few volunteers at any time for any work that would help Germany, and the majority of those who were called "volunteers" had been coerced. So the decree was put into effect immediately, and caused a state bordering on panic among large sections of the population.

On 25th October the Cardinal addressed another letter to Falkenhausen, in which he begged for a revision of the latest decree. But appeals to common humanity and treaties and conventions made no impression on the Nazis, though Canon Van der Elst was told by Reeder that the letter had been brought to the attention of Hitler and of Gauleiter Sauckel, Commissioner for Labour. Once again the Cardinal pressed for permission to send priests to minister to the deported workers; there was a great difference between sending spiritual comforters to volunteers and to deportees; but again his appeal was ignored.

Yet the Cardinal's protest was not entirely without effect. In November His Eminence was informed that the Germans would not impress for forced-labour women under the age of twenty-five.

As the second year of the occupation came to an end, the Germans intensified their forced-labour campaign. But the more the pressure that was brought to bear on them, the more obstinately did the Belgian workers resist. Large numbers went into hiding as soon as they received notice of call-up, and this meant supreme danger to themselves and to those who hid them, and tremendous problems of feeding, for they could no longer use their ration-cards.

The situation reached one of its many climaxes in the spring of 1943, and the Cardinal and Bishops felt compelled to make a public protest, which they did in a Pastoral Letter dated 15th March. Once again the language was blunt and uncompromising and completely unambiguous. To write this at a time when the Germans were arresting, deporting and executing many hundreds of Belgians monthly must have demanded considerable courage.

"These measures providing for the levy of human-beings are absolutely unjustifiable; they violate natural rights, international law and Christian morals. They disregard completely the dignity and essential liberty of the human-being, which are destroyed by compulsion, threats and heavy sanctions; the well-being and honour of families grieviously wounded by the violent dispersal of their members; the supreme interest of society which will suffer fatally as a consequence of the anger and blind hatred sown in thousands and thousands of oppressed hearts. The constraint placed upon the body and the will is serious enough; even more serious is the violence offered to conscience. Belgian citizens are compelled to co-operate directly or indirectly in the military operations of the Foreign Power which unjustly forces upon them an extremely hard régime of occupation, while giving them not the least assurance as to the future and which often forces upon workers, and above all upon women workers, conditions which are morally and religiously seriously damaging. Despite their repeated efforts, your Bishops are unable to obtain permission to send to their exiled flocks, chaplains to help them by their priestly ministrations.

"We are told that these measures are necessary to protect civilisation. But rather than defend European civilisation, is it not to annihilate it that these measures, which violate the essential principles of all civilisation, are applied?"

As with former letters and Pastorals, so this brought comfort and courage to the Belgian people. Among the Germans it was received with mixed sentiments. The moderate among them, whose policy was to avoid all violent opposition, were distressed. On the other hand, the extremists saw in it yet another reason for discrediting Falkenhausen, whom they believed to be too weak and complaisant for his post.

At first it looked as though the extremists would make their point. On 23rd March Canon Van der Elst visited the Military Command headquarters at the instance of the Bishop of Tournai, to plead for the life of Abbé Raymond Marchal, who had been condemned to death on charges of assisting the Resistance. The Canon was told that, because of the Letter, all relations between the Church and the German authorities were broken off. As a concrete reprisal, though they were exempt from forced-labour, all first-year philosophy students in the Catholic seminaries were called up. No official notice of this was given to the Cardinal or the Bishops; they learned of it from the newspapers.

The reaction of the Bishops was immediate and uncompromising. They refused to supply nominal lists of the students, as required by the order. At the same time, the Cardinal sent Canon Van der Elst to protest vigorously to the German Ambassador in Brussels. This call-up, the Cardinal declared, was a serious attack on the rights of the Church, for the students were being prepared for ordination. He supported the Bishops in their refusal to supply nominal lists and the students in their declared intention of ignoring the order unless physically forced to obey it.

The Ambassador stressed to the Canon the extreme seriousness of the situation. He quoted a recent declaration of Sauckel's that the discussion, argument or consideration of the principles of forced-labour could not be entertained. Nevertheless, he persuaded Reeder to see the Canon. At this interview Reeder told the Canon how very seriously the German authorities viewed the Pastoral Letter. Since its publication, he said, there had been a considerable increase in acts of active resistance, and the number of those refusing to obey German orders had greatly increased. In industry and commerce both management and workers had developed scruples of conscience which prevented them from doing their duty. A man like the Cardinal, the second personage in the realm after the King, ought to have foreseen what effect such a pronouncement was bound to have in present conditions. The German authorities would be compelled to take really rigorous measures, for which the Cardinal would have to shoulder the full responsibility.

But though Reeder raved, and stated flatly that the order affecting the students could not and would not be rescinded, he undertook to see if anything could be done to delay its execution.

In the event, there was a delay of two or three months. In July the students were again ordered to report to the Germans, and again refused. Thereupon, with the exception of a few who managed to escape, they were rounded up and set to work. In the diocese of Malines the young men were made to work, from morning to night, in the arsenal to which the railway workshops at Malines had been converted, and submitted to terrible conditions of work and living. Those at Roulers and St Nicholas were sent to the Belgian coast, where they were made to work on the construction of concrete fortifications. In the other three dioceses—Liéges, Tournai and Namur—they fared somewhat better.

When nearly all the students in the Catholic seminaries refused to report to the Germans, security police were sent to the Superiors and Directors to demand the nominal lists. The Cardinal at once issued instructions that the lists were not to be supplied, as a result of which several Directors were arrested and imprisoned.

So that there should be no repetition of the call-up of first-year students in future, the Cardinal decided that there should be no public enrolment. Young candidates for the priesthood were, however, admitted privately to the seminaries, and the number of applications, in spite of everything, was as great as in peace-time. These precautions were fully justified, for in the autumn new orders were issued to the Directors of seminaries requiring them to bring the decree regulating the forced-labour of students to the notice of their pupils. At the same time it was pointed out that though theological students were exempt from the general decrees regulating forced-labour, they were nevertheless required to work for at least one year either in Belgium or Germany.

Again the Cardinal and Bishops refused to comply. The Cardinal informed the Germans that, as far as his own diocese of Malines was concerned, the question did not even arise. "In fact, in the seminary of Malines, there is no first-year course for students," he declared, "and not a single student has been enrolled."

In the midsummer Falkenhausen broke his promise to the Cardinal that young women under the age of twenty-five would not be called up for forced-labour. On 28th June a decree was issued for the registration of all girls and women from the age of eighteen upwards. This order caused considerable distress throughout the whole country. Through Canon Van der Elst, the Cardinal made several attemps to get the order changed, but was unsuccessful.

The German officials at the so-called recruiting offices at Anvers, admittedly contrary to practice in any similar office in Belgium, insisted that the young girls called up should submit to a gynæcological examination, mainly, so they said, to discover the presence or absence of venereal infection. In fact, this examination was purely an excuse for the commission of sexual assaults upon the girls, who, besides being raped, were made the victims of horrible perversions. As soon as the news of this reached the Cardinal, he sent Canon Van der Elst to protest to Reeder. (This was the last time that the Canon acted as intermediary, for he had been a sick man for many months, and he died in Brussels on 10th July, 1944, having rendered great service to his country and to his Church in his rôle as liaison between the Cardinal and the Germans.) No official communication ever reached the Cardinal as a result of his protest, but there was no repetition of the assaults.

Incessantly and with increasing harshness, the Germans pursued their forced-labour policy right up to the Liberation of Belgium in September 1944. In so far as the seminaries were concerned, neither the Cardinal nor the German authorities would budge from the position they had taken up. Since 1943 many Directors of seminaries had been imprisoned, and those still held in custody at the beginning of September 1944 were put on a train for Germany.

The Allied advance was by now so rapid, however, that the train had only reached Malines when it was overtaken, and the Directors were freed.

Though the question of forced-labour as it affected the Belgian people in general, and the question of the Belgian fascists using memorial services for political ends, drew from the Cardinal his strongest and most outspoken protests and his most obstinate refusal to surrender to German wishes, no other injustice imposed upon the country was allowed to pass without his making some representation to the Military Command or Administration.

There was, for example, the matter of memorial services and Requiem Masses for Belgians executed by the Germans, and for Allied airmen shot down and killed over Belgian territory. The Germans raised serious objections to such services being held, seeing in them—as indeed they were right in seeing—a manifestation of anti-German feeling on the part of the population.

In January 1942 Reeder wrote to the Cardinal informing him of a decree which Falkenhausen proposed publishing to regulate Requiem Masses and memorial services for executed Belgian patriots. This decree would permit a Low Requiem Mass, without catafalque and Libera, to be held in the deceased's own parish church provided that the Area, Regional or General Headquarters were informed in advance of the time at which the service was to be held and that not more than twenty of the closest relatives of the victim were present. Members of the German armed forces would attend to see that the order was obeyed, and would not be counted in the twenty persons permitted. The decoration of the church in any way was also strictly forbidden. Reeder requested the Cardinal to bring these regulations to the notice of his clergy and instruct them to conform.

In his reply, the Cardinal reminded Reeder that he had issued strict instructions to his clergy forbidding them to use church services for political ends. But this decree went far beyond a simple prohibition of secular demonstration, for it forbade services ordained by Catholic liturgy for those who had died at peace with the Church; it forbade the Faithful to be present to pray for the souls of the departed. Not only was the decree a measure which ran counter to the sentiments and religious customs of the population, it was contrary to the spirit of Canon Law and to the liturgical rules of the Church. He could not give his approval to such a decree and thus could not instruct his clergy to obey it. "No doubt," he concluded, "the German authorities will wish to accept full responsibility for the decree by publishing it themselves." Realising that the Cardinal would never be moved from his position, Falkenhausen directed the Provincial Governors to make the decree known to the clergy. Some Governors refused on the grounds that it was outside their competence to do so; but others complied.

The case of the Allied airmen provides a striking example of how the Cardinal resisted the wishes of Falkenhausen by adhering to the strict letter of Canon Law.

The Vicar of Houthalen-Centre, in the diocese of Liége, celebrated a mass for the repose of the souls of three English airmen shot down over the district and buried in the village cemetery.

As soon as Reeder heard of it, he wrote to the Cardinal to say that while the Germans, like everyone else, agreed that honours should be paid to all soldiers who fell in war, even to enemy soldiers, the saying of Mass for the repose of their souls, especially when, as in this case, the fallen men were not even Catholics, was not acceptable to the occupying authority, since such Masses could only be interpreted as anti-German demonstrations. Had not the Cardinal given implicit instructions to all his clergy that they were not to hold religious services of any sort that had any political flavour or significance? Surely the curé of Houthalen-Centre had, therefore, disobeyed the Cardinal's strict directions? This being so, the German authority hoped that the Cardinal would take such steps as he deemed necessary to prevent a recurrence of similar incidents, which could only terminate in disturbing both the political and religious life of the country. Reeder would be grateful if the Cardinal would let him know what his attitude to this matter was in principle.

The Cardinal's reply was brief.

"In reply to your letter of 21st July, 1941, I have the honour to draw your attention to the fact that the parish of Houthalen-Centre is not in the diocese of Malines, but in that of Liége.

"As Archbishop of Malines, I have not any authority whatsoever in this diocese nor over this vicar. Canon Law does not permit me to issue instructions to or take measures against the parishes and priests of other dioceses. As the instructions to which you refer are effective only for the archdiocese of Malines, there is nothing I can do in regard to Houthalen."

The Cardinal was strictly telling the truth when he said that his directives were valid only for the clergy in his own diocese. He was the head of the ecclesiastical authority in Belgium and, as such, whatever he said and did had a great effect on the actions and reactions, not only of the clergy, but of the whole population. His moral influence was tremendous. But nevertheless, in so far as the discipline of the clergy was concerned, his writ ran only in the archdiocese of Malines, and each of the other six Bishops had equal powers with his, within their own dioceses. In practice, however, whatever the Cardinal decreed for Malines, the Bishops adopted in their own dioceses, so that, in effect, the Cardinal's disciplinary measures affected the clergy of the whole country. Had the Cardinal chosen to issue a directive to the clergy of the archdiocese of Malines forbidding them to celebrate Mass for the repose of the souls of Allied airmen, should any be shot down over the territory of the diocese, there is little doubt but that the six Bishops would have issued similar directives to their clergy.

It must not be thought that the Germans did not retaliate in any way simply because they did not touch the person of the Cardinal. As will be seen later, many priests played an important part in the active—and what might be termed secular—Resistance of the country, helping to organise escape-routes and hiding-places and occasionally acting as chaplains to *maquis* groups. Numbers of these priests were arrested and sent to concentration camps or shot.

But besides these there were no fewer than 425 parochial and diocesan clergy and 151 members of religious Orders arrested and given terms of imprisonment ranging from one or two months to a year or more. Seventeen of them were shot or executed in other ways. And their crimes? Obeying the instructions of their Cardinal and their Bishops. It was in this way that the Germans tried to punish the Cardinal himself.

It is not possible to say exactly how many petitions the Cardinal made to the German authority on behalf of both these priests and laymen arrested, imprisoned or condemned to death. Very occasionally he achieved some success, but more often than not no reply was made to his entreaties. But if he could not obtain any physical relief for them, he was very often able to gain permission for the priests to have the spiritual consolation of celebrating daily Mass in their cells.

Women Religious were no less immune from the attentions of the Germans than were their brothers. This was particularly true of the English and other Allied members of various communities. On 3rd April, 1941, for example, Gestapo agents arrived at houses in Brussels and Uccle and arrested the English members of the Soeurs des Petits, early in the morning as they were getting up, and took them off to an unknown destination. The Superior General of the Order went at once to Malines and told the Cardinal what had happened, and His Eminence immediately sent his private secretary, Canon Leclef, to Brussels to find out the whereabouts of the Sisters. He discovered them at Gestapo headquarters in the Avenue Louise, and demanded an interview with the Gestapo Commandant, who told him that the Sisters had been arrested as a reprisal for the arrest of German women in England. From there the Canon hurried to the headquarters of the Military Administration, where he saw Oberkriegsverwaltungsrat Thedieck, who was unaware of the arrests, and suggested that the Cardinal should write to Reeder. This the Cardinal did at once.

Reeder did not reply for a fortnight, and in the meantime two more English Sisters were arrested at Anvers. One of them was seriously ill, and had a medical certificate to prove it. Once again Canon Leclef went to Brussels, where he found that the Military Administration officers knew no more about these arrests than they had known of the former ones.

In his reply, dated 19th April, Reeder confirmed the reason for the arrests of the Sisters, and went on: "Because of the brutal treatment inflicted on the German women interned by the British authorities, it is not possible to foresee an abatement of the measures taken against the Sisters, unless the British Government modifies its treatment of German women."

A year later no fewer than twenty-three English Sisters were held in a camp at Beverloo, along with more than a hundred British and American internees. They had been taken from seventeen convents situated up and down the country. The conditions in which they were kept were distressing. All twenty-three were housed in a room twenty-one feet by twenty-one, which was their workroom, refectory and dormitory. Bunks were arranged round the walls, and in the middle of the room was a table with boxes for seats. Each had a cup and a small and a large bowl. They shared the public washrooms with the other internees. In the morning they were given a slice of German black bread with a little fat or margarine; at midday three potatoes boiled in their skins and a ladle of red cabbage; in the evenings nothing to eat, only a cup of black water passing for coffee. This fare was the same every day, and was scarcely enough to ward off death from starvation. They heard Mass once a week and on Sundays. They were provided with cold water only, and their greatest practial problem was washing their clothes. After some weeks the Swiss Consulate and the Belgian Red Cross were able to supply them with extra food.

The Cardinal, on hearing of their plight, reacted vigorously and unceasingly on their behalf, and late in June 1942 the Military Administration agreed to the release of the Sisters provided the

Church would place them all together in a convent approved by the German authority and would give an assurance that the Sisters would never leave the district in which the convent was situated without German permission. The Cardinal immediately called to him the Provincial Superior of the Franciscan Missionaries of Mary, who said that she would receive the Sisters in her own House in the Avenue de Tervueren at Woluwe-Brussels, which was acceptable to the Germans.

Canon Leclef was sent to Beverloo to fetch the Sisters and take them to Woluwe, and he has described the incident thus: "The Sisters could not believe their ears when I told them that I had come to take them to Brussels. But they needed only the time to get together their luggage, and then loaded with bags, packets and even pails, they accompanied me to the station at Bourg-Léopold. Here we found places in compartments reserved for the Wehrmacht and leaving at 12.30 p.m. we arrived at Brussels seven hours later. The Sisters were unable to contain their joy. For them it seemed as though the occupation were over and Belgium already liberated, and on the journey they sang *God Save the King* and *Tipperary* again and again. We arrived at Woluwe at 8.30 p.m. and there they received the warmest of welcomes."

There were, however, yet other English Sisters who were still living in their convents. These the Military Administration now requested to be housed at Woluwe with the others. This request raised two serious difficulties: the convent at Woluwe was not large enough to accommodate them, and their leaving their own convents would seriously undermine the working of those convents. The Cardinal attempted to persuade the Germans to allow them to remain where they were, but without success. But a compromise was reached whereby a number were received at Woluwe and the balance distributed between two other Houses.

Nor was the Cardinal engaged solely in efforts to relieve the fate of his co-religionists, whether clergy or laymen. As early as October 1940 the Germans began their persecution of the Jews. To begin with, the measures they took were not physical, though they were devised to cause distress and suffering. Radios were confiscated, businesses closed, restrictions put on areas of residence, bank accounts blocked, Jews in official posts dismissed, doctors, lawyers and chemists forbidden to practise. Then in 1942 the mass deportations began.

From the moment that their troubles started, numerous Jews wrote to the Cardinal imploring his help and protection. These were, of course, apostate Jews, mainly of Balkans origin, but nevertheless Belgian subjects, who professed the Catholic Faith. The Germans, however, did not take religion into their considerations; born a Jew, always a Jew, they said.

In case after case the Cardinal intervened by one means or another. Sometimes he was successful; at other times, not. Chiefly he approached those Belgian authorities who, by virtue of their office, could legitimately appeal to the Germans on behalf of the Jews. But besides interventions of this kind, His Eminence lent his moral support to other measures of aid. He signed an appeal for funds to help indigent Jews, and particularly Jewish children; and with his direct approval the Brothers of St Vincent de Paul lent to the Jewish Association a large unfurnished property in Brussels to be used as a home for aged Jews.

The Cardinal's efforts on their behalf was known to all Jews in Belgium, and though he was unable to prevent their deportation or imprisonment, they were very appreciative of what he was able to do for them. Hundreds of letters of thanks arrived every day at the archiepiscopal palace for several weeks after the Liberation.

There was one aspect of the occupation in which the Cardinal did not feel himself able to support the activities of his compatriots. This was that violent form of Resistance which included sabotage and the killing of Germans. As the occupation advanced and sabotage increased, so did German reprisals in the form of the seizure and shooting of hostages.

At the beginning the Cardinal made several attempts to persuade the Germans to modify their restrictions against the population, which, he said, prompted, by their harshness, the acts of sabotage. He pleaded against the seizure of hostages, pointing out that the imprisonment and execution of innocent people only served to increase the anger and intransigence of Belgian Resistance. Though he was not often successful—and certainly not at all in persuading the Germans to revise their tactics—there were occasions when his interventions saved the lives of hostages marked down for execution.

But there had to come a time when, in conscience and after long reflection, the Cardinal had to censure those acts which led to the seizure and shooting of hostages. On Sunday, 17th January, 1943, he caused an appeal to his countrymen to be read from all pulpits in the country. After drawing attention to the unhappy state of the people, he went on: "In these conditions, we appeal to the reason, good sense and patriotic sentiments of all our fellow citizens. We do not know the authors of these outrages nor the ends that they pursue; but whatever may be their intentions and the motives which inspire them, we see developing under our eyes the unhappy consequences in which their action, in fact, involves our unfortunate people. On account of these consequences, we do not believe that acts of violence are justified, and we reprove and publicly condemn all attempts on human life. In raising our voice, we have only the well-being of the Fatherland and the preservation of our people in mind. *Salus populi suprema lex.* The preservation of the people must be the supreme law; it is the fundamental postulate of all soundly conceived patriotism. In the name of this concept, we ask that an end is put to all bloody actions, and that calm and patience are reborn in the indestructible hope of a just peace."

Throughout the occupation the Cardinal was in constant collision with the Germans on matters affecting education and the call-up of students for forced-labour, particularly in connection with the Catholic University of Louvain; and besides all these matters of high import there were others in which His Eminence reacted no less vigorously.

Early in 1941 the Germans announced their intention to demolish the towers of churches situated near airfields. The Cardinal made immediate protests to Falkenhausen, but without any success, and many fine and ancient towers were destroyed. He did achieve success, however, in the matter of the church bells.

The Belgians are very proud of and have a great sentimental attachment for their church bells, which are, indeed, fine examples of bell-casting, both ancient and modern. This being so, when the Germans, in July 1941, addressed an urgent request to provincial Governors, commissioners of districts and burgomasters to furnish the number of bells in their region or town, whether they were made of bronze, steel or aluminium, their weight and their age, they were involving themselves in a matter very close to the heart of the vast majority of the population.

The Germans realised this, for the officials were asked to supply the information in the strictest confidence, and to carry out their census in such a way that the public did not get wind of what was going on. This was naturally quite impossible, and almost at once it came to the Cardinal's ear.

Without a moment's delay, he and the Bishops wrote to Falkenhausen. In the First World War, they said, the Germans had proposed confiscating the church bells, and for the very reasons that Cardinal Mercier and the Bishops then protested, so now they made their protest. Church bells were not ordinary objects which an army of occupation might have a right to seize; they were by nature exclusively religious, serving to praise God and to call the Faithful to worship. They were, besides, sacred vessels, dedicated to divine religion by the anointing of holy oil and by prayer. They could not be taken from the churches without the consent of the ecclesiastical authorities, and they, in this present time, would never consent to a seizure which had for its object the conversion of the bells into engines of war. In addition, such a seizure would be regarded as an act of sacrilege by the whole population. Besides, the seizure of church bells was contrary to the Hague Convention, which Germany had signed. They were confident that the German authorities would not take the decision to seize the bells.

Two days after receiving this letter Falkenhausen sent Ober-kriegsverwaltungsrat Thedieck to tell the Cardinal that the decision to carry out a census of the bells had been made in Berlin. But, he said, although the census had been ordered, it was not foreseen that there would be any seizure. For several months nothing more was heard of the matter; but on 30th October Dr Thedieck accompanied by a colleague came to Malines with a communication from Falkenhausen. This said that Hitler had ordered the seizure of all church bells both in the Reich and in all the occupied territories. The military authorities in Brussels deeply regretted being unable to disregard this order, but they had been able to obtain permission to exempt the bells of carillons, one bell in each parish church and bells of an artistic or historic nature. The work of removing the bells would be carried out by Germans, and no Belgian would be called upon to assist. The General hoped that the Cardinal would not oppose the seizure nor provoke demonstrations.

The Cardinal replied that all he could do was to take note of what Falkenhausen had written. He had hoped that the Holy See would have been able to intervene to save the bells. He did not think that the clergy would actively obstruct the seizure, but, on the other hand, they could not be held responsible if there should be popular demonstrations here and there.

The two officials, having expressed their own regrets at being the bearers of such bad news, left the Cardinal, handing him as they did so a copy of the ordinance which was to be published the following day. The same evening, however, Dr Thedieck telephoned Malines asking the Cardinal to receive Dr Reusch, his colleague on the morning's visit, and requesting that His Eminence would not yet make public what he had been told earlier in the day.

When Dr Reusch arrived he announced that at five o'clock that afternoon an order had arrived from the Führer's G.H.Q. not to carry out the decision to seize the bells for the time being. Reusch expressed the hope that the revoking of the order would be permanent.

Indeed, it seemed that it might be so, since, for more than a year nothing further was heard of the matter. Then suddenly, on 12th February, 1943, the Cardinal was informed, through Canon Van der Elst, that all bells were to be seized at once.

Realising that a new protest would be unavailing because of the speed at which the order was executed, the Cardinal caused a resounding public protest, in his own name and in the name of the Bishops, to be read in all the churches. This was the celebrated protest to which reference has been made earlier, touching on forced-labour and deportations, and including also the seizure of the bells; the protest, in fact, which brought about the final rupture in relations between the Church and the Germans.

But the protest having been made, the Cardinal and Bishops gave instructions that all incidents were to be avoided. Nevertheless, in many parishes there were demonstrations.

The seizure of the bells was carried out with great speed. By 30th July, 1944, no fewer than 4,568 bells, weighing 3,794,225 kilograms or approximately 3,700 tons, had been dismantled. Fortunately, the lack of transport and the swiftness of the Allied advance prevented all of these from being sent to Germany, and after the Liberation 373 bells were found still in Belgium.

Despite the brevity of this account of Cardinal van Roey's

stewardship during the extremely harsh years of the Nazi occupation of his country, there emerges the picture of a man of fearless courage who, though helpless to prevent many of the excesses forced upon his countrymen, nevertheless was able to do so much to ameliorate their suffering. But it was in the moral leadership which he gave that the true value of his example, and of the example of his loyal and equally courageous Bishops, lay. In saying this, it is not the intention to detract from the leadership which was displayed by a number of Belgian laymen, notably Burgomaster van Meulebroeck of Brussels; but it cannot be denied that it was the uncompromising stand against the Nazi evil and against the encroachment of human liberties taken by the Church leaders which, probably more than anything else, stiffened the backbone of the unhappy, bewildered and apprehensive people at the moment that they most needed encouragement. Here was a true Prince of the Church, who behaved as a true Prince should when opposed by a rabble.

CHAPTER III

Occupied France

PERHAPS THE uncomplicated framework of the occupation in Holland and Belgium made it easier for the Church in those two countries to determine their stand and their tactics in their countries' struggle against Nazism. The peculiar circumstances which arose in France from the fact that the country was physically divided into two parts, one known as the occupied and the other as the "free", undoubtedly created a situation which needed much careful thought when it came to the point of demonstrating exactly where the Church stood.

It is not the intention here to embark upon a discussion of the rights and wrongs of the actions of the ancient Maréchal. The division of France and the Government of Vichy must be accepted as *faits accomplis*; and within this framework must the actions and activities of the French hierarchy be placed, and the reader left to form his own conclusions, which, according to his acceptance or rejection of the Maréchal, are bound to be coloured white or grey. With this in mind, therefore, we shall record here only facts without comment.

It had long been the custom of the Cardinals, Archbishops and Bishops of France to meet in full assembly at the beginning of each year. This is not to say that the meeting of the hierarchy was the only one held in the year. When events or circumstances of gravity and urgency arose, ad hoc meetings would be called. As this account progresses it will be seen that the hierarchy found it necessary to meet two or three, or even more, times a year.

However, the Assembly for 1940 made clear, in a letter to the Pope, that the Church in France would continue faithful to herself, alive to the needs of the times, conscious of the scope of her mission. Practically, attention was to be concentrated on the work of Catholic Action, since through this great organisation the people could be most easily reached and guided.

But the events of June were to change completely the situation of the country, the lives of all Frenchmen and—the circumstances in which the Church would henceforth conduct her mission. What was now to be the Church's rôle?

As a result of the division of France into two zones, the hierarchy was itself split into two. The Archbishops and Bishops of the occupied zone continued to meet in Paris, while those of the "free" zone met at Lyons under the leadership of Cardinal Gerlier, Archbishop of Lyons.

On 15th January, 1941, the Cardinals and Archbishops of the occupied zone met in Paris, and there decided upon their future policy, which they described in a letter to the Pope in these words: "Being firmly decided to concentrate our efforts on the religious plane, we intend to avoid all political or partisan activities and devote ourselves entirely to the spiritual well-being of souls and the relief of the unfortunate. In the social and civic fields, we profess complete loyalty to the established power of the French Government, and we ask our Faithful to adopt this principle. We wish to draw ever closer to our people who suffer and are in great distress, to share their sufferings, to encourage them with precepts of enlightened piety: we would like to instil in them the desire to pray, to teach them the redeeming value of sacrifice, to exhort them to have patience, strength of spirit, to practice help and Christian charity. We shall endeavour to inculcate in all the conviction that if the redress which is so much desired depends on God, it depends also upon our personal efforts, that it will be real and lasting only in proportion as to how each one of us works for it."

Copies of this letter were sent to all the clergy, who were required to regard it as the directive for their future mission.

A fortnight later, the Archbishops of the "free" zone met under the presidency of Cardinal Gerlier. They, too, addressed a letter to His Holiness in which they associated themselves with all contained in the Paris letter.

In these days, perhaps, the dominant feeling in France was that the present situation would never be resolved in such a way that the country would be restored to her former situation. It was certainly the principle adopted by the Vichy Government, who set about introducing a plan for "the reconstruction of France".

On 24th July another meeting of the hierarchy of the occupied zone, plus Cardinal Gerlier, was held in Paris. This meeting issued the following declaration, which was also subscribed by the hierarchy of the "free" zone.

"We wish that sincere and complete loyalty, without enslavement, will be accorded to the established Power. We regard the Head of State (Pétain) with deep respect and we ask that all Frenchmen, without delay, will unite round him. Unity is always the source of strength.

"We encourage our Faithful to place themselves at his side in the work of readjustment that he has undertaken in the three spheres of Family, Work and Country, so that a strong, united and closely knit France may come into being. In this great work we ask them to join their efforts with those of their fellow-citizens.

"In this connection, we renew that assurance we have already given many times, that in so far as the Church is concerned it will remain, today more than ever, on the religious plane alone, outside all party politics, despite all appeals that may be addressed to us by any side whatsoever."

At the time, and for long after, this declaration was the subject of widespread discussion and controversy. Opponents of it accused the hierarchy of preaching acceptance of the legality of the Vichy Government and submission to all its orders. A number of the Bishops refuted this, the Archbishop of Rennes, Monsignor Roques, being one of the principle disputants.

"The presence of a diplomatic representative at Vichy," he maintained, "signifies only de facto recognition of Marshal Pétain's Government. For if the Church preaches submission to the established Powers, if it treats with them, recognises them in a practical way, points out the necessity of submitting to them and of accepting them for what they are, she does not believe that by so doing she invests them with a legality which they lack. . . . The French Bishops have never, as so many reproach them with doing, preached submission to *all* the orders of Marshal Pétain's Government. They know that there exists a considerable distinction between *constituent powers* and *legislation*, the quality of the laws depending more on the men than on the form of power."

Having made their appeal for loyalty to the established power, the Bishops, in their declaration of 24th July, went on to outline their views on other subjects. With regard to the Faith, they warned every man to be on his guard against all erroneous ideologies and certain "deviations of spirit" which, always blameworthy, constituted in the present times a veritable peril. As for the Christian schools, the Bishops were determined to continue all efforts to maintain and develop them, and to use to even greater effect the school-hours in public schools set aside for religious instruction. Catholic Action the Bishops regarded as the apple of their eye. In respect of the human being, his dignity and essential liberties, the Church would strive always to help and succour him in every aspect of his existence.

The general attitude which the Church intended to adopt was explained by the Archbishop of Cambria, Monsignor Chollet. "Persuaded of the necessity for there to be a firm distinction between the temporal and the spiritual, the French Bishops intend to exclude all that might lead to confusion between the two Powers. They desire neither a clerical government nor a political episcopacy. They claim no privilege whatsoever but simply the rights of religious conscience and the liberty of the Church."

Catholic Action figured prominently in all the Bishops' considerations from the beginning. On 28th August, 1940, the chief of the German Military Administration in France had forbidden the activities of all unions, societies and other associations. The Bishops had immediately declared: "To touch Catholic Action is to touch the Church. The Bishops would always oppose this violation of one of the essential liberties of the Church, its apostolic life. To attack Catholic Action would be to let loose religious persecution in France."

The Germans, however, were unmoved by this pronouncement, and at the meeting of the hierarchical Assembly on 24th July, 1941, Cardinal Suhard, who had been appointed Archbishop of Paris in May 1940, protested once more. "The episcopacy and Catholics of France cannot accept without protest and opposition the amputation of one of the essential organs (of the Church). It will lead to persecution by one side and opposition by the other. . . . The German authorities can count on the firm attitude of the Bishops and on their public protests if the Church is not immediately given satisfaction." Though Catholic Action might be officially banned, its work was continued by the zeal of its members, not only in France itself, but also among French prisoners, deportees and forced labourers wherever they were situated.

As the Archbishop of Lille said in the church of the Sacred

Heart at Roubaix on 15th October, 1944: "We have been accused of being confined within our religious work instead of taking part in the great national movement of the Resistance. I say quite categorically that we do not accept this reproach. . . . (Nazism) tried, by every means, to stifle Catholic Action, by drowning it in a single youth organisation, or by closing its general secretariates and arresting its directors. To all these attempts we replied by opposing them with a resistance, equally as active as passive, of which we have the right to be proud. . . . We have even succeeded in endowing our Catholic Action with a fullness it had never before attained. . . ."

Next after Catholic Action, the fate of the Jews in France caused the Church to raise its voice loudest. The Germans had instituted restrictive measures against the Jews in the occupied zone since soon after their arrival, all of which were merely a prelude to a campaign launched in 1942, and directed to achieving the "final solution".

In the "free" zone, doubtless as a result of German pressure, similar restrictive measures were introduced, and on such a scale that by 15th December, 1941, no fewer than sixteen laws and a dozen decrees affecting the Jews had been promulgated. But as early as December 1940, 20,000 Jews had been rounded up and placed in a camp at Gürs, in the Basses-Pyrénées, an act which had provoked the Archbishop of Lyons to deliver a strong protest to the Vichy Minister of the Interior. On 17th June, 1941, the Theological Faculty at Lyons issued a denunciation of the injustices done to the Jews under a law published on 2nd June. But it was the beginning of mass arrests and deportations in the occupied zone, in July 1942, which roused the Bishops most fiercely.

"Profoundly moved," they wrote to the Head of State, "by the news brought to us of the mass arrests of Jews during the past week, and the harsh treatment inflicted on them, notably in the Vélodrome d'Hiver, we cannot stifle the outcry of our conscience. In the name of humanity and of Christian principles, we raise our voices in protest in favour of the indefeasible rights of the human being. Our protest is also an anguished call for pity for the immense sufferings inflicted on all and particularly on so many mothers and children. We ask, Monsieur le Maréchal, that it may please you to bear this in mind so that the exigencies of justice and the rights of charity may be respected."

This protest was followed in the succeeding months by Pastoral Letters issued by some of the Bishops and read from all the pulpits of their dioceses. Among them were the Archbishop of Toulouse, the Bishop of Montauban, the Bishop of Marseilles and the Archbishop of Lyons. But all such protests were of no avail.

On 4th October, 1941, a law was promulgated which, in fact, constituted a Work Charter. Some of the provisions of the Charter were the setting up of social committees, a tripartite organisation of industry, a wages policy and one, and only one, Trade Union.

For many years the Church had been exercised by the inequality and exploitation of the workers in relation to capital in the industrial organisation of France, and from time to time attempts had been made to formulate a plan for the reorganisation of industry founded on justice and charity and animated by a spirit of collaboration between capital and labour. The Work Charter covered many of the points which the Church deemed to be necessary in any reorganisation along these lines, and on 23rd December, 1941, the hierarchy issued a statement welcoming the Charter in principle, but making certain reservations. The provision to which the Church took the strongest exception was that ordaining a single Trade Union with obligatory membership. If this provision were made effective it would mean the suppression of the Catholic unions. The Bishops therefore concluded their declaration with the plea that the Vichy Government would think again before introducing this provision, so that "the autonomy of the professional associations, the existence of Christian unions, and the vitalising of the professional organisations by the professions themselves, might be safe-guarded".

In April 1942 the Bishop of Lille personally intervened at Vichy to stress the opposition of the Church to the single Trade Union. Referring to this intervention more than a year later, he said: "The fidelity of the Church to the principle of liberty of free association is not in question. The Church will always defend that principle. . . . This single union will not be a true union. It will be a kind of reservoir union which will not possess any constructive qualities. We have conceived a union which would be like a well constructed wheel which would be capable of being geared with others to form the corporation. . . . The ideas and the intentions of the Charter are excellent, but it is necessary that instead of producing a soulless machine, they should give birth to a human, living society."

The majority of French workers were aligned with the Church on this point, and were deeply concerned by the single union idea. But this was not the only trouble with which the workers were faced at this time. As in other occupied countries, so in France, the appeal for voluntary workers for Germany had fallen on deaf ears, and in September 1942 Laval replaced the voluntary system with a compulsory one, with conscription as its basis. At the beginning of 1943 the Germans began to organise mass deportations of Frenchmen for forced-labour.

The Church at once made its position with regard to this policy clear. In February two provincial assemblies of Bishops publicly denounced it, and the Archbishop of Lyons caused a letter to be read in all the churches of his diocese in which he called it "an attack on the natural rights of the family and the prerogatives of the human being".

The stand taken by the Church was this time effective. The Vichy Government, in order to end the direct seizure of Frenchmen by the Germans, introduced a plan for a two-year period of forced-labour. But this time the action of the Church had a deeper significance than merely its success in making the Government retract a little. This was the first time in the history of the French Church that she directly opposed a law decreeing mobilisation. By doing so, she illustrated clearly that she would not allow herself to be involved in a policy of collaboration with the occupying Power which had inspired this legislation; and showed with equal clarity that the moral law took precedence over the positive law.

For the first time since 1940 the full Assembly of the French hierarchy was permitted to meet in Paris in March 1943. Forced-labour held a prominent place on the agenda, and after a full discussion the decision was recorded that "this law of the French State is not binding in conscience, and that no one can be compelled to obey it".

These interventions naturally roused the anger of the Germans, who launched a violent Press campaign of vilification against the Church. But equally they served to guide and inspire the Faithful, and nothing that the enemy could do or say could undo the effect which the unequivocal stand by the Bishops had on general morale.

By this time the Bishops were finding that, though they could keep within the limits they had imposed upon themselves and the Church at the beginning of the occupation, a duty devolved on them, as moral leaders, to take a more and more uncompromising stand against the excesses to which the people were being increasingly subjected; even though in doing so they might sometimes come perilously near to being involved in politics.

The call-up of women and young girls, the massacres of Ascq, Oradour-sur-Glane, Saint-Genis-Laval, Montpezat and Aucambille, and other German activities drew more and more outright condemnation from the hierarchy. And presently the Germans were goaded into retaliation. The Bishop of Clermont-Ferrand was arrested and sent to Dachau, and three other Bishops—Monsignor Moussaron, Monsignor Théas and Monsignor Rastouil—were imprisoned. The Archbishop of Toulouse would have suffered a similar fate but for the frail state of his health. Had France not been liberated when she was, there is no doubt that other prelates would also have been seized.

As we have said at the beginning of this account of the Church in France, the stand taken by the French Church during the occupation caused much controversy among Frenchmen, to neither side of which do we believe it to be right or necessary for us to adhere. We would merely add the words of Pius XII to Cardinal Suhard, Archbishop of Paris, which might with equal justice have been addressed to any of the Cardinals, Archbishops and Bishops of France.

"In the war years," His Holiness wrote, "and during the occupation of your archiepiscopal city by the enemy armies, you did all in your power to relieve the ills of your people. You foresaw the dangers which threatened them, you helped them in their difficulties, you softened the sufferings of all kinds to which they were submitted. Soldiers and prisoners were helped by your spiritual aid; and as for the workers who were compelled to work, in order to live, outside their country, you comforted them by all the means with which your piety and charity inspired you."

CHAPTER IV

Austria

THE HISTORY of the Austrian Republic was unhappy from its inception on 12th November, 1918, until the Allied occupation was terminated in 1955. Economic instability for which no one seemed to be able to find a cure, led to political instability, and in the vicious circle created by the two the seed was sown which was to flower into the Anschluss with Nazi Germany in 1938. The absorption of Austria by Nazi Germany, though generally accepted as being just a part of Hitler's plan for the conquest of Europe, was, in fact, the culmination of a movement within Austria itself which had for many years undulated beneath the surface, and sometimes on the surface, of the Austrian scene. No matter how it manifested itself, whether in the Pan-German movement or the Austrian Nazi movement, it was always there. Only the dictatorship of Engelbert Dollfuss had prevented it from acquiring demonstrable momentum during the early and middle years of the 'thirties; but when it gained the support of the German Nazis, sooner or later it was bound to assert itself. So when the Austrian Republic became Ostmark, a province of the Greater German Reich, in the spring of 1938, though men might protest, and feel afraid, they should not have been surprised.

The events leading up to the Anschluss can be briefly related. After the murder of Dollfuss by Austrian Nazis in July 1934, Kurt von Schuschnigg took over the Chancellorship and continued Dollfuss's policy of eliminating the parliamentary system. Though the Germans appointed Franz von Papen as their Ambassador to Vienna, relations between Austria and Germany remained strained until July 1936, when an agreement was arranged to settle differences in a friendly way, and Hitler recognised the full sovereignty of Austria. It might have been expected that the Austrian Nazis might now have curbed their activities, but, in fact, as part of a well-devised plan, they became more actively troublesome than ever before. Von Papen persuaded Schuschnigg to visit Hitler at Berchtesgaden, and there, on 12th February, 1938, the Austrian Chancellor was faced with an ultimatum—unless he took Austrian Nazis into his Cabinet, his country would be invaded. Schuschnigg bowed before the Hitlerian storm, and gave two important port-folios to Nazis, one of whom was Seyss-Inquart, whom we have already seen as Reichskommissar for occupied Holland. All Nazi organisations were also granted a free hand.

It did not take long for Schuschnigg to see that these steps were merely the preliminaries to a process of nazification from within, and that this would mean the end of Austria's independence. In a vain attempt to prevent this he ordered a plebiscite on the question of the country's independence to be held on 13th March. But on 11th March Hitler issued a second ultimatum—if the plebiscite were not abandoned, he would invade Austria. Again Schuschnigg surrendered, called off the plebiscite and resigned. Seyss-Inquart followed him as Chancellor, his first acts being the arrest of his predecessor and an appeal to Hitler to send troops to preserve order in Austria. On 12th March German soldiers and tanks crossed the frontier, and on the following day Hitler arrived in the capital where, among others, he saw Cardinal Innitzer, Archbishop of Vienna and Primate of Austria.

At the interview, Hitler was at his most deceptively charming, and, it would appear, completely disarmed the Cardinal. He promised that the Church should retain its inalienable rights, declaring: "The Church will not regret her loyalty to the State. . . . We want to show how the Church can be compatible with the National-Socialist State, and Austria shall be the example for the whole Reich." The Cardinal and Bishops, relieved by these fair promises, decided that co-operation would be the means of preserving the influence of the Church in Austria, and, to the horror of much of the Catholic world and to the deep wounding of Pope Pius XI, words of commendation of the Nazis were heard proceeding from the archiepiscopal and episcopal thrones of Austria.

But who is to judge? Hitler had promised to return to Vienna after elections had been held, to enter into negotiations with the Church for the drawing up of a new agreement. To us now, who have the full story of Hitler's treachery and long string of broken promises neatly tabulated in history, the acceptance of a Hitler promise seems to betray an overwhelming naïvety in so great a

77

Prelate. But Hitler had not yet embarked on his programme of territorial aggrandisement. Munich and the rape of Czechoslovakia, the seizure of Danzig and of Memel, the unholy pact with Bolshevist Russia were still many months away. As the Cardinal was to remark later: "I could not assume that the man would lie." Yet, the example of the surrender of the German Church was there to see; and Rauschnig had published his conversations with Hitler—in *Hitler Speaks*—in which the Führer had made plain for all the world to see what his plans for the Churches were. But who is to judge?

It was not long before the Church in Austria was to discover exactly what the Nazis' intentions towards her were. Nazification was put in hand immediately and carried out with a speed which gave practically no opportunity to gather any protesting strength, or devise and execute any obstructive tactics. In the overwhelming embrace of the New Order, the Church was inextricably involved, and in no other country occupied by Nazi Germany was the attack launched so early or so openly.

Within a few weeks of the Anschluss, Catholic organisations were banned. Catholic schools were closed; religious foundations were seized. Catholic Action headquarters were searched, the files removed and the organisation eventually suppressed. As will be seen as this narrative unfolds, the tactics used by the Nazis to render the Church ineffectual were strikingly similar to those employed in those countries which, since 1945, have fallen under Communist domination. It was not the slow, abrasive technique which Hitler had deemed necessary to undermine and destroy the Church by slow, almost imperceptible degrees, but a frontal attack. In permitting those whom he had made responsible for the campaign to depart from his plan, Hitler made a great mistake. For the violence of the attack brought the Church to with a shock by which the reality facing it was made all too clear, but which, at the same time, made it possible for it to make preparations to resist.

The methods which the Church in Austria chose for their struggle for existence are of great interest. Rather than set up an active resistance to authority, it set about strengthening itself from within.

As early as 26th April, 1938, the *Wiener Diözesenblatt* issued some *Instructions to Ministers of the Church*, which illustrate the fundamental principles on which the struggle was conducted throughout the seven years of Nazi domination. First stressing the need for the continuance of the ministry in the face of the greatest difficulties, the Instructions impressed upon the clergy the need for even greater faith, and pointed out that if they were to have any influence at all by their example, the priests must strive to become more deeply religious than ever before. They must continue to announce to the people the precepts of the Church, and work unceasingly to win souls for Christ. In the practical field they were warned against mingling politics with their preaching; rather they must intensify their personal contact with their flock, since it was through such contact that the Church, which relied for its existence on the relationship between God and men, could acquire strength. Thus, there must be a positive application of Christian teaching. Opportunity for confession must be made easier; young people must be encouraged to take part in Marian devotions; routine visits of the sick must be conscientiously performed; a permanent campaign must be put in hand for the recruitment of communicants; Bible-study groups must be organised and emphasis be laid upon the continuation of youth groups; more time must be found for private prayers and devotions; and finally, all priests must submit themselves to complete obedience to and place utter trust in their Bishops, who carried the responsibility before God.

The developments of the next few months, however, showed that as organised at present, the Church could not hope to preserve itself on these lines, and in August a new scheme of organisation for the ministry was announced. This provided for the setting-up of three departments, whose respective functions were to be to provide for the further education of priests for the ministry, the organisation of the Church and the preservation of its rights, and thirdly, to control the financial aspects of the two foregoing departments. With this new organisation it was hoped that the Church would acquire strength to cope with the New Order.

Immense importance was attached to assisting the individual priest to acquire the knowledge, skill and strength which would help him personally in his ministry in these changed times, when the normal difficulties confronting priests had been added to and intensified. While recognising that no priest should feel himself to be controlled by an organisation, and that his ministry was a personal affair, it was felt essential that everything must be done to protect him from the danger of failing in his priestly duties.

To this end a Pastoral Conference was called in the latter half of 1938 which had for its subject: "Precepts for life and behaviour of the clergy—a self-justification in times of oppression." This conference was so successful that it was made an annual event, and at subsequent conferences such subjects as "What qualities do the present times demand of priests?" (1940) and "Ministry among Ministers" (1943) were considered. The Gestapo soon recognised the threat of these conferences and banned them, but this did not deter the Church from continuing to hold them and the clergy from attending them, in spite of the tremendous transport difficulties and the penalties facing them if they should be apprehended.

In addition to these conferences, courses for priests were arranged in religious Houses. Attendance at these courses also called for courage, for when priests from all parts of the country converged on one place, the Gestapo soon got wind of it, and were not slow to confiscate the Houses and evict the Religious. When this happened, at great risk to themselves, monasteries and convents co-operated. Especially worthy of mention in this connection were the Ursuline Sisters of Wien-Wahring, who risked constant danger from the Gestapo by allowing their House to be used for courses.

There had been set up some time before the Anschluss what was called the Seelsorge Institut. It is not easy to find an exact equivalent for this; *Seelsorge* means "the cure of souls", and the Institut was designed to help the priests in their ministry with advice if asked for, and by the dissemination of helpful literature. The influence of the Institut was greatly increased under the new conditions. It added to the help it was already giving by arranging one-day refresher courses, as an aid to bolster the enthusiasm of the priests in these discouraging days. Cardinal Innitzer took great interest in these courses, and expressed the wish that one a year, at any rate, should be held in every deanery. They were subject, of course, to the same difficulties that confronted the conferences, represented chiefly by the undesirable interest of the Gestapo, but also by the problem of accommodation, food for the priests and the selection of a suitable leader. But they were well worth all the trouble, for they were well attended and the priests received great help from them.

Aged and sick priests, no longer able to work, were constantly in the Primate's thoughts. At Christmas and Easter he would write personally to them, encouraging them and telling them how they could still be useful to God by bearing their pain and loneliness with fortitude and trust. Many letters expressing gratitude for the Cardinal's encouragement came back to the Archiepiscopal palace.

In every way, everything possible was done not only to protect the clergy from the evil times and from their own spiritual dangers, but also to strengthen them during their tribulations. By deepening the interest of the clergy in basic theological problems it was hoped, too, to help them resist the temptations placed in their way; such temptations, for example, as that dangled before the priests in difficult parishes by the Nazis, who offered to all those clergy who wished to change their profession good and lucrative work in secular life. For the accomplishment of this, the theological holiday courses which were initiated in 1937 at Altenburg were continued throughout the war years.

For those priests unable to attend such courses, the Seelsorge Institut, which had now been raised to Seelsorge Amt, organised the meetings of specialist groups within each deanery for the discussion of theological problems. So-called work conferences, at which it was not a question of "settling problems" but of evoking interest in them, were also held in Vienna. As a result of this, Vienna became known as the only place in the Reich where lively theological discussion was taking place.

The courses differed from the conferences, in that they were not intended for the solving of new problems, but for the offering of solid knowledge and to fill the gaps in a priest's education. They were so popular that it was often necessary to hold two parallel courses simultaneously, since the numbers who applied for admission to them were too great to be accommodated at one centre. In the autumn of 1942 it was decided to hold two courses yearly: that in the spring to deal with practical theology, while the autumn course would be devoted to systematic theology, dogma and ethics.

But if it was hoped to strengthen what may be termed the theoretical side of the priest's ministry by such means as these, encouragement in his pastoral work was not neglected. Before the Anschluss there had been yearly ministry conferences at Christmas, at which practical problems were discussed and views exchanged. Such a conference was planned for Christmas 1938, but was cancelled when warnings were issued by the authorities. The 1939 conference was also abandoned for similar reasons. But the necessity for them was now greater than ever, and a "legal" way of overcoming the ban had to be found.

It will be worthwhile to digress for a brief moment to consider the attitude of the Seelsorge Amt towards the legality or illegality of their undertakings. The basic principle on which the Amt functioned was: "We will do nothing illegal, but will somehow manage everything legally, even if not in quite the same way that Authority intended." What the individual might do was his own affair, but everything attempted by the Amt, even youth work, had to have the appearance of legality, or it was not to be attempted at all.

This attitude of the Amt caused much shaking of heads at the time, and may do still in some quarters. But it did not betray opportunist or collaborationist tendencies; it was wise and necessary realism. It was absolutely impossible, in the terrible conditions of the times, to do anything illegal which was not immediately discovered by the Gestapo, and dealt with by the infliction of the severest penalties. The post, telegraph and telephone, inns, theatres and private houses and churches were all watched. Little children were encouraged to denounce their parents, and many of them did. All banned political activities attempted during the early years of the occupation ended in the concentration camp or immediate death. The Seelsorge Amt was a public institution. Any mistake it might have made would have been tracked down, and the whole Church might have suffered in consequence.

To give only one example. An enthusiastic young priest engaged in youth work decided in 1941 that he must attempt something more venturesome than the activities in which he was then engaged. So he arranged a Sebastian celebration in the crypt of a certain Jesuit church: a moving ceremony with torchlight and singing which inspired all present. Next day the Gestapo struck. All crypts and other underground rooms in all Viennese churches were closed, thus depriving no fewer than eighty parishes, whose presbyteries had already been confiscated for some time, of invaluable premises for their activities. As for the young priest, he was exiled from Austria, and all youth-workers were placed under even stricter surveillance.

The time was to come when training courses and one-day refresher courses fell under the Nazi ban. But when this happened discussions about the theoretical aspect of the ministry and religious reflection were still permitted. By the exercise of a certain amount of skill it was possible to fit nearly all activities under one or other of these two headings. Thus, the Christmas ministry conferences became "Religious-theoretical-reflection conferences". So that the attention of the Gestapo should not be unduly directed to them, the number of those attending these conferences was kept low. Priests were chosen to attend who would be capable of going back to their districts and disseminating the proceedings of the meetings.

Special conferences were also arranged for deans. The deans, who were the direct representatives of the Bishops, now achieved even greater importance, since the Bishops were not permitted to travel about their dioceses as freely as hitherto. After such a conference the dean would call a meeting of the priests of his deanery, and there pass on all that had happened at the decanal conference.

But it was still necessary to have direct access to the priest if he was to be encouraged, and unless a priest were enthusiastic it could not be expected that his parishioners would be so. So "practical weeks" for priests were arranged. Priests were encouraged to give an account of the year's work, and to submit a work-plan for the coming year. In this way the priest could be helped to view his work objectively and a high degree of efficiency could be ensured.

The duty of the Church was described by Christ as being threefold: "Go ye, therefore, and *teach* all nations, *baptising* them in the name of the Father, and of the Son, and of the Holy Ghost; teaching them to *observe all things* whatsoever I have commanded you." (Matthew xxviii. 19–20). Teach, baptise and observe God's commandments.

One of the most efficacious of all media for teaching—the Press—had been denied to the Church by the suppression of all Catholic newspapers and journals, and even parish notes, and by the closure of Catholic printing-houses, which meant the disappearance of religious books, especially such books for children, and of the Catechism. At the same time, propaganda for the new Philosophy of Life swamped all ages and all classes. In the totally Nazi-controlled Press, in schools, from university to kindergarten, in school books, in ordinary books and magazines, on the radio, in the theatres and cinemas, in military instruction, at firm meetings, in courses for trade apprentices, in courses for teachers and officials, even among the arts, this propaganda infiltrated. The theories of biological materialism, of racialism, and all the other pagan teachings of National Socialism penetrated to even the smallest villages. Besides the spate of words which swamped the people with currents of uncertainty, bribes were offered and threats made to persuade men and women to leave the Church. The bribes were in the form of profitable jobs, the threats chiefly involved dismissal and an embargo on obtaining other employment. Those who went to church were "observed"; in all congregations there were Nazi "spies" who took the names of those present. Meetings of the Nazi youth organisations were arranged to clash with the times of church services. The priest whose sermon contained any ambiguity which might be interpreted as an attack on National Socialism was fined and imprisoned, exiled or sent to a concentration camp. Indeed, no priest whose true desire was to remain loyal to his Bishop could mount the pulpit of a Sunday in the sure knowledge that on the Monday he would not be seized by the Gestapo. The nervous strain on the lonely parish priest induced by all these conditions was extreme, and it was essential that he should be given every aid to maintain belief in the Living Word.

So as to protect his flock from pagan materialism, the priest could no longer preach a sermon that was in the slightest degree superficial. This was no time for bringing out the old manuscripts; and he himself, above all, must take his sermons seriously. The dangers in which this involved him were great. He might legally "preach religiously", but in so doing he might lose touch with the vital reality of the times. It was necessary, therefore, to teach him how to "preach religiously" and at the same time point a lesson which would help the Faithful to deal with reality.

In the autumn of 1941, therefore, a preaching course was held and the pastoral conference of the same year was also devoted to the same object. Under the resulting plan, besides sermons, there were to be Bible-readings followed by brief commentaries, at all services; and daily services were to be introduced at which short talks were to be given on subjects provided by the Seelsorge Amt.

The chief evil of the time was the religious doubt which had been sown in the minds of many of the Faithful. Up to the Anschluss religious instruction had been compulsory in all schools, and communion had been compulsory three or four times a year. The religious instructors had, for the most part, been drawn from the powerful movement of the brothers Pichler, whose catechisms and religious books were famed throughout the world. But now even the educated classes were assailed by doubts. With the banning of religious instruction in schools, a great responsibility devolved upon the parents, who were to be encouraged to become the first religious teachers of their children; and the weekly lessons in Christian doctrine, which the Codex required all priests to give, but which, with the passing of time, had been replaced by the sermon, were reintroduced, and were soon proving valuable and fruitful.

Cardinal Innitzer, in this connection, announced his intention of composing six letters—their subjects: Religion and Confession, the Personal God, Sin, Christ, Salvation, Faith—by which the priests were to be guided in their doctrinal talks. He also gave instructions that when giving the talks the priest should stand before the people, not in the pulpit, and that his tone and phraseology should be simple and homely. Unfortunately, when three of the Cardinal's letters had been distributed, the Gestapo intervened. The publication of single pamphlets was permitted, but the series of letters were considered as periodical publications, which were banned. But in spite of this, the teaching of Christian doctrine continued throughout the War years.

All these measures served to strengthen the Church within, to steady the clergy, to sustain their faith and to create an outflowing power to counter-act the flaunting paganism which infiltrated every aspect of life. In this they succeeded, but they could not have done so had the priesthood looked to itself alone. Equally important was the drawing together of the Faithful by helping them to resist temptation and resolve doubts, and to this end all that could be done to provide opportunities for religious observance was done.

In Belgium, as we have seen, when the Germans turned Sundays and holy days into work-days, so that the Faithful were prevented from hearing Mass, Cardinal van Roey, purely as a measure of opposition, flatly rejected the suggestion of Falkenhausen that Mass should be said in the evenings, giving as his reason the fact that the Holy See had always refused to sanction evening Mass, as indeed it had. In the case of Austria, however, Rome recognised the grave difficulties under which the Church was labouring—for example, religious doubt had become more widespread here than in any other occupied country, causing a falling off in church membership amounting to tens of thousands—and granted a dispensation for the Holy Eucharist to be celebrated in the evenings, when the pressure from outside made it impossible for even devout Catholics to come at the usual time. The period of abstention was fixed at four hours before the time scheduled for the service, and where even this was impossible, it was waived altogether. The success of this measure can be gauged by the fact that the number of communicants increased by over a million in one year. Other measures included the saying of Mass at 5 a.m., 5.30 a.m. and 6 a.m., instead of the usual later hour, and evening devotions were moved from 4 p.m. and 5 p.m. to 7 p.m., 7.30 p.m. and 8 p.m., and met with similar success.

The value of the development of the sacramental life was also stressed. Normally, the meaning of the sacrament of baptism was impressed only upon the newly confirmed. Now it was periodically brought to the attention of the entire parish congregation, and bells were rung for baptism instead of only for funerals. At the beginning of the régime people still considered it socially correct to have their children baptized even when they themselves were adrift from the Church. To combat this attitude the priests were instructed to refuse the sacrament unless the parents would give a solemn promise that the child would receive a Christian education. This caused a good deal of unpleasantness between clergy and people, until the latter gradually became aware of the full significance of this sacrament.

The sacrament of confirmation acquired a new significance, too, and it now became the tendency to encourage the children to present themselves earlier than hitherto. The reason for this was that when the child reached the age of ten the State practically separated him from his parents, and if he was to take a Christian stand in the various Nazi youth organisations which he was compelled to join, he had to be prepared to resist the paganism in which these organisations gloried.

The Cardinal also stressed the necessity for the sacrament of repentance to be readily available to all. In his own Vienna he laid down that at least one priest should be in the confessional throughout the day.

The deportation of Austrian Jews began in January 1939, and was completed by the spring of 1941. The Church had carried out intensive proselytizing work among the Jews and had met with some success, particularly in Vienna. When the persecution of the Jews began, Cardinal Innitzer organised relief work to aid them. Since there was considerable danger attached to doing this, the Cardinal made the archiepiscopal palace the headquarters of this work. The relief which the Church was able to provide in this way was much appreciated by the Jews.

The Church also engaged in other fields of relief, especially in the ministry of the sick. The sick, the weak and the aged were regarded by the Nazis as merely unproductive eaters and a drag on the State, and they were quite prepared to permit the Church to look after the unwanted, on two conditions: that the people were willing to accept the help of the Church, and that the Church provided itself with the necessary funds and materials. The ministry of the sick was hedged about with many restrictions, nevertheless. For example, priests might visit hospitals only within prescribed hours; nurses were forbidden to encourage the sick to take part in religious exercises; the request to be visited by a priest had to be made in writing; the dying who were no longer able to speak might receive the solace of religion only if a crucifix, medallion or rosary were found on them. All these things made the situation difficult, but it was by no means hopeless, and much good was accomplished.

The sick at home were visited by the parish priests, and home-nurses were organised to attend them. The nurses had to be recruited from ordinary lay-women, who were given special courses in nursing. It was particularly heartening that considerable numbers of young women volunteered for this work.

The poor were no longer permitted to be ministered to by the Church. The relief of the poor was one responsibility which the State did accept, and which, since it had great political opportunities, it carried out well. All Church charities for the poor were suppressed, but in many parishes secret aid was still dispensed in really necessitous cases where the victim would not comply with Nazi regulations, and so was barred from State relief.

Laymen had to be recruited more and more to help the Church in its practical work. There was, for example, a serious lack of priests. Seminaries had been closed by the Nazis and their buildings confiscated. The death-rate among priests rose steeply, and many were arrested.

To begin with, the Church drew on men and women already in its service, but soon it had to go further afield. Perhaps the most striking development in this field was the number of women workers recruited. Courses in theoretical and practical training for both men and women were organised, and those who were successful in examinations held at the end of their course took over responsible ministerial work. If out of evil comes forth good, the evil of Nazism certainly proved a blessing to the Church in this respect, for it brought back to full communion with the Church many who had tended to withdraw from Church activities other than purely religious observance.

But there can be no doubt that the greatest challenge to the church came from the threat to youth. To an ideology like Nazism and to people with aspirations like the Nazis, the youth of the country naturally presented the most impressionable material from which the future State and nation might be moulded. As has already been mentioned, Church schools, hostels, children's homes and kindergartens were taken over by the State. Catholic youth organisations disbanded and their members compelled to join Nazi youth organisations. Children were deprived of religious instruction as much as possible, and the paganism of Nazism was pumped into their receptive minds.

Fortunately, such religious instruction as was still permitted was left in the hands of the Church, but this instruction was not enough to be a one hundred per cent effective counter to Nazism. The ministry among the youth was therefore concentrated in the parish. This presented all kinds of difficulties, from practical, physical ones, like suitable places in which classes could be held, to theoretical ones, like the way in which the work could be so camouflaged that it escaped Gestapo prohibition. It also threw a new and tremendous burden on the already over-worked parish priest. But all obstructions were met and coped with, and the results justified all the work and effort.

The workings of the Gestapo mind have always puzzled at least one writer, who is convinced that despite the cruel ruthlessness of their attack on human life and liberty, there was a quality of intellectual naïveté in them which is difficult to reconcile. In the case of youth and the Church, it would seem that while they objected to "organisations", they had nothing against the gathering of young people in parishes for the purposes of pastoral care.

This being so—and as a test of their sincerity on this point—on 7th October, 1938, the Church organised a youth festival in Vienna cathedral, in the presence of the Bishop. Though many Hitler Youth were present at the service, there was no disturbance. After the service the young people gathered outside the Bishop's residence and chanted for some time: "We thank our Bishop! We thank our Bishop!" This was only the second great meeting of Catholics since the Anschluss, and constituted the first act of collective resistance by any Austrians. The police were called and a number of arrests were made, and several youths were sent to concentration camps. The Nazis were furious, and one evening, a little later, Hitler Youth mobs stormed the Bishop's residence. They broke the windows and climbed in, and destroyed pictures, looted whatever took their fancy and threw furniture into the street. The Cardinal himself was got to safety only at the last moment. When their fury against the Bishop was spent, they made their way to the Priests' House opposite, where they knew a youth-worker lived. There they seized a young priest and threw him from a window. The next day the Nazi-controlled newspapers attributed the attacks to the Communists.

Though this showed the Church what the opposition was likely to be, the struggle for youth went forward undaunted. Courses for parish priests and lay-workers were arranged, and a programme for youth activities drawn up. Youth services and classes were arranged, Church festivals celebrated and processions and pilgrimages organised until they were forbidden.

The most encouraging factor in this work was the way in which the youth responded, and soon the Gestapo began to be apprehensive. Pressure was applied both to the youth and their parents, and the youth-workers themselves were often arrested, fined and imprisoned, five from the central office in Vienna being exiled.

The success of these efforts to win over the youth may be gauged from the fact that by 1944 no fewer than 4,000 young Viennese were attending courses and taking part in church services. By this time the conscription age in the Greater Reich had been lowered to sixteen, which meant that it was the child and young adolescent who were mainly concerned. Even so, the older adolescent—that is, those in the senior classes of the secondary schools and the university students whose military service was deferred—were not neglected. Among seniors in secondary schools special courses were arranged to cover the ground which the religious instructor would have normally covered, and in the universities the ministry was carried out by means of Catholic student corporations. Though these corporations came under suspicion from the Gestapo and the Nazi student body, they were not attacked, and survived the War.

The family, naturally, was not neglected as a powerful agent in helping the Church, for it was from the Christian family that the Church derived the greater part of its strength. Now that parish life was threatened it was all the more important that everything should be done that could be done to preserve the unity of the family, indeed to safeguard the very existence of family life, attacked as it was on all sides by the State, which sought to gain its ends by setting brother against brother, son against father.

Before the Anschluss much had been done to foster family relations by the Seelsorge Institut. The Seelsorge Amt set up a family ministry section which arranged weekly consultations for imparting advice on marriage and the family. In many parishes special classes were devised for the mothers of young children, and letters were sent to parents asking for their co-operation in preparing their children for first communion. Young couples were approached to persuade them to be married by the Church, for the State propaganda on behalf of registry-office marriages had become one of the chief threats to the Christian way of life. Premarriage courses were held for these young people, and in 1943 refresher courses were begun. Family communion was also encouraged, and meetings for young families were made a monthly feature of parish life. It is interesting to note that all this work had far greater success among the younger families—the very people whom the Nazis were most eager to detach from the Church—than among the older families.

Perhaps the outstanding difficulty encountered by the Church was in its efforts to reach the men. Even before the War there had been no strong men's organisation, and now the task of getting close to the men was made all the more hard by their being drafted away from their own parishes either into the armed services or into war-work of one kind or another. Many attempts to attract the men to the Church failed, for the majority were embittered and had become hostile to the Church. Those who did play an active part in Church life were those who would have practised Christianity in any circumstances, that is to say, those who recognised and felt the need for religion in their lives.

Truly, the difficulties which faced the Church in Austria were immense. The pressure of the Nazis on laymen and clergy alike is almost impossible to apprehend without the aid of actual experience. It was not the physical threats and the brutality of the attacks, when they were carried out, which were the main protagonists the Church had to face, but the insidious blandishments, bribes, rewards and psychological force which the Nazis called to their aid. Nor was this all: the history of the Republic had been such that men's minds had become receptive to the delvings of materialistic influences. The constant economic uncertainty in which they lived made a promise of certainty attractive, no matter from what source the promise came, nor the methods which would be required to substantiate it. Doubt and uncertainty were the keynote of the pre-Anschluss years, and it cannot be denied that the Church did not face up to the exigencies which they thrust upon it.

This being so, the methods which the Church adopted to oppose the Hitlerian neo-paganism were those which had the potentiality of being the most effective. Any other kind of opposition, whether it was the Dutch kind of out-and-out encouragement to resist or Cardinal van Roey's kind of creating difficulties by strict interpretation of the letter of Canon Law, must undoubtedly have led to immediate, violent and complete suppression of the Church. What, then, would have happened to Austria without the Church?

To attempt to answer this might lead us into unprofitable speculation. But to discover how far the Church was justified in organising its resistance as it did, it is necessary only to look at the Church in Austria today. There you will find a strong, united Church which has a personal contact with the Faithful difficult to find elsewhere, and from which it derives its main strength. Perhaps no other Church in Europe so clearly exemplifies the declaration of Pius XI: "I would glady have lost more ground than I have in the Vatican City to be able to show more clearly that the Church needs no worldly authority, no bracchium saeculare, no territorium. She can and should be effective supported solely by her mission in the Holy Ghost." For the Church in Austria, when deprived of all her worldly authority, became the Good Shepherd.

CHAPTER V
Italy

THE BEST way of getting from Austria to Italy is by way of the Brenner Pass, and it was at the Italian end of this pass that Mussolini stationed his armies when Chancellor Dollfuss was murdered in 1934. If Hitler had marched into Austria then, there is little doubt that an armed clash between the two fascist Powers would have followed. Mussolini's rapid action deterred Hitler, and it was something for which the Führer never really forgave the Duce.

When we consider the pitiful figure cut by the saw-dust Caesar in the later years of the war, it is difficult to remember that there was a time when Mussolini was the dominant fascist leader. Those qualified to know have always insisted that the Duce surpassed the Führer in intelligence and culture. For him fascism was a means by which Italy could be saved from the political and economic morass into which post First World War Governments had dragged her. It never became for him the obsessive credo which National Socialism became for Hitler. The neo-paganism of Nazism made him smile; for racialism he really had no time—though, purely from opportunist motives, he was to adopt a very modified form of it at Hitler's request in 1938; and though no churchman himself, he saw in the Church, as Hitler saw, a strong and powerful institution which he felt, unlike Hitler, it would be wiser to conciliate than to exterminate.

The "Roman Question", or *dissidio*, is a complicated matter which only the learned can unravel with many words. The quarrel between the Holy See and the Italian State, which had had its origins in the Church's opposition to the Risorgimento, the movement for the unification of Italy in the middle of the last century, reached its climax in 1870, when Rome was made the capital of a unified Italy and the Pope was deprived of his states and temporal power. From that date until 1929 the Question remained a burning issue between Church and State.

Two events occurred in 1922 which were to provide the answer to the Roman Question. On 22nd January, Pope Benedict XV died unexpectedly and was succeeded by Cardinal Ratti as Pius XI. In October the Fascists seized power in Italy, and Mussolini took over the reins of government.

Now, before Mussolini realised his ambition he had maintained an attitude of cautious friendliness towards the Church, and though the majority of the Party might possess anti-clerical sentiments which some, like Farinacci, expressed in uncompromising terms, it was evident to the Vatican that the new head of Government was an outstanding leader, determined to mould the future policy of his régime according to his own ideas and with very little regard for the views of his followers. This "reading" of him appeared to be strengthened when, in his first parliamentary speech as Prime Minister, he declared: "All religious faiths will be respected, with special regard for that which is the dominant faith, Catholicism." In addition to this, the Holy See, though issuing a circular to all members of the clergy strongly urging them to hold themselves officially aloof from the party struggle, knew that there was nothing in the programme of the Party to prevent good Catholics from supporting it, even to the extent of becoming members.

For many spectators of the events of the first years of the fascist era in Italy, much happened to cause bewilderment and surprise. It was too early yet for Mussolini's inconsistencies—and probably no political leader of modern times has been more importantly inconsistent—to be appreciated. In his early days as an agitator he had been a "blasphemer"; then, as we have already said, he had adopted a cautious friendliness towards the Church; now he began to show it definite and open respect which he marked by several actions.

The first of these was an official visit on the Feast of the Epiphany 1923 by the fascist Commissioner for the City of Rome to the Cardinal-Vicar to offer the greetings of the citizens to their Bishop, the Pope. Not long afterwards the Government presented to the Vatican Library a magnificent collection of books and manuscripts dealing with the history of the Vatican, which the Government had bought in 1918. Without looking boorish, the Vatican had to make some gesture in response, so the Capella Paolina in the Quirinal—the palace in Rome which had been taken from the Pope in 1870 and had since been the official royal residence—was freed from the interdict which had been placed upon it as a result of the seizure of the palace.

In many other ways, too, Mussolini illustrated his attitude towards the Church. Mass was always included in public functions attended by royalty and members of the Government. The crucifix, which had been banned in schools and public institutions by an upsurge of secularism in 1870, was brought back. When the Holy Year of 1925 was announced, the Government eagerly collaborated with the Church authorities to make it a success. Religious instruction was reintroduced into primary schools; chaplains were appointed to army, navy and fascist militia; certain Church feasts—S.S. Peter and Paul, Corpus Christi and the Annunciation—were declared public holidays; the stipends of the clergy paid from public funds were increased. These were but a few of the signs of goodwill which Mussolini made to the Church.

It would be wrong, however, to imagine that Mussolini demonstrated this goodwill without requiring a quid pro quo. The return he demanded can be simply stated thus: The Church must conform to the dictates of Fascism, the Faithful must be good Fascists as well as good Catholics. But despite the simplicity of this statement, the practice of it was complicated, for Fascism contained many pitfalls for the unwary Christian and traps for the Church. For example, if the Church accepted the dictates of Fascism, sooner or later it must become identified with Fascism, and even while he had been accepting Mussolini's favours, the Pope had found it necessary to denounce some elements of the new doctrine as heretical. It was essential, therefore, if Fascism and the Church were not to come into a collision that would very likely be fatal for one or other of them, for a *modus vivendi* to be found; and any *modus vivendi* must necessarily include a settlement of the Roman Question.

The first approaches of the régime and the Vatican were made in great secrecy. Beginning early in 1926, they extended over three years. Many difficulties were exposed, for the Pope was as shrewd a bargainer as the Duce. By the first weeks of January 1929 it looked as if negotiations had entered the final phase and at this crucial moment the Government delegate, Councillor Barone, died. Barone had conducted the negotiations single-handed, reporting results only to the Duce. Any delegate now appointed to replace him would, therefore, have to be made familiar with the course of the negotiations, and this would mean a further delay which neither the Vatican nor the Duce considered desirable. To overcome the difficulty, Mussolini decided to conduct the remaining discussions on the Government's behalf himself.

By this time Mussolini's desire for a settlement had become intense, and he threw himself into the negotiations with an energy which drew unstinted admiration from the Papal delegate, the Marchese Pacelli. At least twenty drafts of the Treaty and Concordat were presented; so Mussolini could justly claim later that "every article, every word, one might even say every comma, has been the object of frank, unimpassioned and exhaustive discussion".

The news of the Concordat was first publicly announced by the Pope shortly before midday on 11th February, 1929, at an audience to the Lenten preachers. After dealing at some length with possible subjects for their sermons—indecent fashions, the fetish now being made of sport, among them—His Holiness went on: "This very day, this very hour, and perhaps at this very moment, over in Our palace of the Lateran—talking to parish priests We had almost said in Our parochial house—a Treaty and Concordat are being signed by Our plenipotentiary, his Eminence the Cardinal-Secretary of State, and the Chevalier Mussolini as plenipotentiary of his Majesty the King of Italy."

The signing ceremony was brief and simple. Within half an hour the news was all over the city; within two hours the whole country knew. The public reaction was widespread, heartfelt delight; foreign reaction congratulatory to both sides. The Roman Question was settled after more than a quarter of a century of disagreements and enmity.

If anyone imagined that the Lateran Agreements, as the Treaty and Concordat came to be known, would settle *all* questions between Church and State, they were to be disappointed. Between 1929 and 1943 the Church and Mussolini clashed several times over such issues as the Catholic youth organisations, Catholic teachers' organisations, the national minorities and racialism. In the outcome of any struggle, however, it was the Church that had to compromise. The writer would not have it thought that he approved of Italian Fascism or would be its apologist; nevertheless the fact remains that the Church in Italy under the Fascist régime experienced no persecution such as that which the German Nazis inflicted upon it whenever it came within its orbit.

What, then, can be the claim of the Church in Italy to be inluded in this narrative?

Simply this, that between September 1943 and April 1945 the *Germans* and some rabid Italian Fascists inflicted upon the Italian people atrocities which in number and horror are scarcely surpassed by their abominations in any other occupied country.

On 25th July, 1943, after a meeting of the Fascist Grand Council, at which a majority of malcontent members had voted Mussolini out of the supreme command of the Italian armed forces, the King arrested the Duce, and called upon Marshal Badoglio to form a Government. As a result of this, German forces began pouring into the country, and though the Badoglio Government was frightened out of its wits by what was happening, it delayed asking for Allied assistance against the Nazis until 12th August.

From the Allied point of view the fall of Mussolini had come too early for them to take immediate advantage of it. However, an armistice was arranged and signed on the same day, 3rd September, that the Allies landed on the Italian mainland. An arrangement was made to keep the armistice secret until 15th September, the reason being that the Germans would be bound to attack as soon as it became known, and their first objective would be Rome. Attempts were being made to collect all available Italian troops round Rome, and this could have been achieved by the date agreed upon. However, for some reason which has not yet been made absolutely plain, the announcement of the armistice was made on 8th September, with the result that these preparations were far from complete.

When the Italian Government, less than twenty-four hours before, learned of the Allied intention to announce the armistice, they fell into a state of panic, and, accompanied by the King and the High Command, they left Rome for Brindisi, behind the Allied lines. The move was made with such haste that no one was appointed to take command of the capital.

The fall of Mussolini had caused a serious disintegration of the armed forces. Officers and men, divided in opinion and loyalties, and left to their own devices, went their own particular way. But the disintegration was not complete. North of Rome, the Arriete

Armoured Division commanded by General Cadorna on the Bracciano–Monte Rossi line, held back the German 3rd Panzer Division, which had been ordered to repulse the Allied landings at Salerno. Elsewhere there were other stands of less importance, but a German threat to bomb Rome forced an armistice on 10th September. The Germans occupied Rome on the pretext that the Italians were holding armed forces there, and pushed south until they occupied all Italy to a line south of Naples.

Meanwhile Mussolini had been liberated by the daring German Otto Skorzeny and S.S. troops, and after a brief meeting with Hitler, had returned to Italy and set up a Fascist Republic at Salo on Lake Garda. Throughout the rest of the conflict the Fascists who adhered to him were to vie with the Germans in inflicting atrocities on their own people.

In the south the Allied armies met stiff resistance from the Germans, and made only slow headway. The story of this fight up the armoured spine of Italy is now too well known to need repetition here. But during this slow and costly progress, which was to take eighteen months before it overcame the Germans, the Italians organised a Resistance which was destined to restore to the nation its lost reputation and its honour.

The conditions in which Italian Resistance was born were far different from the conditions which gave the impulse to resistance elsewhere. Certainly there was confusion; but there was no stupor! The armistice with the Allies and the overthrow of Mussolini produced not a numbness, but a totally different emotion, which at the outset was translated into an almost general relief, and an indescribable joy that the war, which the great majority had never wanted, was over. Soon, however, the true facts were to change the relief and joy into a stubborn will to resist the new Nazi enemy.

When the Allies landed at Reggio on 3rd September, the Germans, who since the fall of Mussolini in July had had time to re-group their forces, already had twenty well-equipped divisions in Italy. The twelve divisions of the Italian army in Italy were rendered ineffective, not only by inferior equipment, but by a lack of fuel, which made them practically immobile. As has already been remarked, the course of events had also led to a very large degree of disintegration. Those commanders who, like General Cadorna, held their forces intact, might have prevented a general disintegration by their very example, had they been supported by authority and directions from the Government and High Command. As it was, those soldiers who had not laid down their arms and departed to their homes were seized by the Germans, and though many were able to escape, no fewer than 600,000 were interned in Germany.

But as soon as the air had cleared a little, officers and men became aware of a reawakening of the old spirit of resistance to oppression, of the urge of the ideals of patriotism and liberty and of the courage of their ancient ancestors. Many of those who had escaped the Germans had done so only by going up into the mountains to hide. They were now joined by others prompted to do so either to avoid recruitment for forced-labour by the Nazis or the desire to resist actively. Everywhere parties and groups organised themselves and within a very short time had begun to harry the Germans. Their value was recognised by the Italian High Command and by the Allies, and high-ranking officers were sent to aid them; British and American officers trained in guerilla warfare were parachuted in to them, and every effort was made to turn them into an effective organisation.

Under the Fascist régime there had been a certain clandestine political activity, notably among the Communists. Since the overthrow of Mussolini these small groups had become more active, until the turn of events persuaded them that they must still operate underground. Among their clandestine activities, they, too, organised guerilla bands in the mountains and shock groups mainly for sabotage in the cities.

At first the guerillas, or Partisans as they preferred to be called, formed themselves into small independent bands, which were autonomous and fed and supported by the local populations. Among these bands were many British officers and men who had escaped from prisoner-of-war camps in the confusion which reigned at the armistice, and other prisoners of all nationalities.

Within a short time these forces of Resistance numbered between 20,000 and 30,000. Such an army could not be left without some general direction, so in each region National Liberation Committees were set up, composed of representatives of the six main political parties. The military also set up its own commands, and for a time the two organisations worked without co-ordination.

99

A turning point was reached, however, in the early summer of 1944, when all groups were co-ordinated into a single organisation. The Military Committee of Milan was transformed into the General Command of the Corps of Volunteers for Liberty. General Cadorna was appointed General Commander of the Liberation Army (CVL), and a Central Committee of Liberation (CLNAI) was set up to direct the struggle against the enemy and to take over the administration when the Allies liberated northern Italy.

The new Fascist army which Mussolini had formed with the founding of his Fascist Republic was composed entirely of fanatics. The Germans were also roused to a pitch of fury and ferocity, and, through fear, used terror in their attempts at quelling the opposition of the Liberation Army. Hostages were shot, ten for every one German or Fascist killed, women were violated, often in the presence of their families, and again and again whole villages were burned.

The simple peasant population were the greatest victims of this indescribable brutality. The peasants might have been forgiven had they submitted to the Germans and refused to help the Partisans. Instead, their anger roused, they rebuilt their houses, often three or four times, and did all they could to help the Partisans by warnings, and by going hungry themselves so that the soldiers might have the strength to fight on.

The life of the Partisans in the mountains was a hard one. It was difficult to obtain sufficient food, and the lack of clothing made the already abnormally fierce winters of 1943/44 and 1944/45 a trial which was hard to sustain in the caves and hideouts among the mountain peaks. Yet by mid-June 1944 the numbers had risen to 80,000, by August to 100,000 north of the Apennines, while to the south there were another 20,000. When early Liberation became a certainty in the spring of 1945, the numbers reached a quarter of a million. The moment had come for final action, and the Partisans came down from their mountains.

If any idea of the overall contribution of Italian Resistance can be achieved from its losses, it was certainly no mean contribution. In a little more than one year 150,000 Italians gave their lives— Partisans, regular soldiers, civilians (massacred) and military and political deportees in concentration camps in Germany.

And what was the Church doing during these times?

The Vatican, in duty bound, beyond refusing to recognise Mussolini's Fascist Republic of Salo, maintained a façade of neutrality. Behind the façade, however, much was done to relieve the sufferings of the more unfortunate. Many prominent anti-Fascists were granted asylum within the Vatican City; numbers of Jews owe their lives to the protection of the Holy See; money was made available for soup kitchens which were organised under Vatican auspices for the starving people of Rome.

But it was outside the Vatican that the Church really played its significant rôle in these horrible days. To cite the number of religious communities all over the country who risked all, even the lives of their members, to hide and succour escaped British and other prisoners-of-war, and Italians on the run from the Germans, would take a book double the size of this one. There was one convent in Rome, for example, which had undertaken to look after some of the many children whose parents were in difficulties, and which for several weeks hid two British soldiers until arrangements could be made for them to join Partisan groups. Time and again German soldiers searched the convent, but were never successful in proving their suspicions.

Unhappily not all of the hierarchy were prepared to become the champions of the people fighting for their liberty. When Partisans killed the well-known neo-Fascist, Fagiani, the Bishop of Reggio Emilio felt constrained to send the following telegram to the officer commanding the 79th Legion of the Republican National Guard: "Profoundly grieved by brutal crime resulting in Fagiani's death. Accept our condolences and prayers. We earnestly hope that the divine laws will triumph over the powers of darkness which prompt such bloody deeds of violence." Then there were the Pastoral Letters, almost identical in content and phrasing, issued in the spring of 1944 by the Bishops of Lombardy, Piedmont and the Veneto. Without drawing any distinction between the two sides, with no consideration as to whether there was oppressor and oppressed, the Letters deplored all the excesses on both sides. Morally the Bishops may have been right not to draw any distinction on the ground that the rightness of a man's cause does not permit him to defend that cause by every means whatsoever; but there was no doubt that the Letters did real disservice to the Resistance by adding bewilderment to all the other trials to which the Faithful were being subjected.

There were, on the other hand, other prelates who were prepared to risk all for the Faith and the cause of right. In March 1945 a public gallows was erected in the Piazza Capitello in the city of Belluno, and on the evening of the 17th four captured Partisans were placed upon the gallows. Priests approached and requested permission to administer the Last Sacraments to the condemned men, but were refused. One ran and told the Bishop of Feltre and Belluno, Monsignor Bottignon, a Capuchin, who immediately hurried to the piazza, shouldered his way through the cordon, laid his cloak at the foot of the gallows, mounted the steps and administered the Last Sacraments to the men and gave them the kiss of fellowship and peace. The Bishop was naturally accused of inciting and encouraging the Partisans by his action, but the news of it spread throughout all northern Italy and brought great comfort to all who heard it. There was also Cardinal Schuster, Archbishop of Milan, who never let there be any doubt as to where his sympathies lay, and who acted, towards the end, as intermediary between the CVL and Mussolini. And there was Monsignor Giovanni Sismondo, Bishop of Pontremoli.

Monsignor Sismondo, like many another Bishop, hoped at first that the Church would be able to exert an influence as a Christian and neutral force, but when it became clear that the Germans had no intention of regarding it in this light, and subjected priests to persecution that often had no rhyme or reason, he became what was called a "collaborator" with the Partisans. This meant that he watched the Germans and reported their movements to the Partisans. When two of his priests were murdered he issued an angry denunciation of the Germans, which, of course, directed their attention towards him. But, though they kept him under constant watch, they did not dare to attack the Bishop, who was also Count of Pontremoli and a Prince of the Vatican State.

But it was among the simple parish priests that the greater glory accrued to the Church. In Italy, as in every other occupied country, it was the simple parish priest who came into direct physical conflict with the enemy. It was natural that this should be so, for it was to their priest that the villagers looked for guidance, and the priest could not fail them, no matter how he might become involved.

In innumerable cases the priest acted as liaison between the Partisans and their families. More often than not he acted as "collaborator", keeping watch over the Germans in the village or the neighbouring countryside, reporting their movements and plans to the Partisans. No Partisan was ever turned away from a presbytery; no prisoner-of-war on the run sought refuge from the parish priest in vain. Often when the Germans realised the rôle the parish priest was playing, he escaped to the mountains, too, and bore arms and ministered to the spiritual needs of the Partisans.

Among the outstanding warriors of the Resistance are many priests. In Rome there was Don Pietro Morosini, who was arrested and tried on charges of having collected arms for the Partisans. When he was condemned he declared to his judges: "Had you acquitted me I should have continued to do all in my power to help the patriots of Italy." And there was a day when St Peter's Square was crammed with a vast crowd waiting to receive the papal blessing. There were many Nazis and Fascists in the crowd, and Don Paolo Pecoraro; and the priest raised himself above the people, and at the top of his voice exhorted them to drive the Germans from Italian soil.

In Piedmont, Don Agnesi turned his presbytery into a re-cruiting centre for the Fourth Garibaldi Brigade. In Genoa, Don Gaggero became head of the local Committee of National Liberation. In Reggiano, Don Pasquino Borghi organised the first Resistance group and was subsequently caught and executed.

The list is endless!

If the contribution of Italian Resistance was one of immeasurable value to the Allies, the part played by the priests of the Church from prelates to *paroccos* was no mean one. The opposition of the Church to the Nazis in Italy was not made up of protests and legalised arguments—valuable though these were elsewhere—but direct, brutal, physical contact; and the light of the Church in Italy shines brighter for it.

CHAPTER VI

Dachau

IN THE foregoing pages mention has been made time and again of the activities of the simple priests of all the occupied countries. Whatever might be the hierarchy's method of opposing the Crooked Cross, the parish priest, besides carrying out the instructions of his spiritual superiors, could, according to his own conscience, engage in forms of opposition more akin to active Resistance; and there were few whose consciences kept them aloof from this kind of activity. In many cases the priest became involved on his own initiative, but the great majority found themselves caught up in it willy-nilly. There can be little wonder at this, for any parish priest who has the right to the title is the father of his flock, their confidant and comforter. So, when his people were caught up in the active struggle and found themselves in need of help, where should they turn but to their priest? and if his flock could risk their lives to harry the enemy, was there anything to prevent the priest from doing likewise? Is a priest's life more precious than a layman's? Does a priest possess a different kind of conscience from a layman?

There would be small point in trying to discover the motives which involved the priest in active Resistance. Let the fact be accepted that there were priests taking part in every aspect of Resistance—with the exception of sabotage or any activity involving the taking of life—in every occupied country. In Holland they hid the "divers" or found hiding-places for Jews, distributed clandestine newspapers, acted as couriers or as scouts. In Belgium one of the chief "intelligence" networks was for a time headed by a priest, and others were engaged in organising escape-routes. In France, too, this was one of the favourite Resistance occupations of priests; and many others acted as liaison between local Resistance headquarters and *maquis* groups, while others joined the *maquis* as chaplains, sharing the privations and risks of those courageous men. In Italy we have already seen how they participated.

But for almost every priest who resisted there was one who was arrested and imprisoned or sent to concentration camps. Sometimes it was because they were trapped in Resistance activities, but more often than not it was because they preached "inciting" sermons or broke the Nazi laws in other ways. Often they had committed no crimes at all, and were arrested simply because they were priests, though charges were trumped up against them.

How many priests were thrown into concentration camps and prisons it has not been possible to discover, but it can be said with certainty that the numbers ran into many thousands. And of these thousands many hundreds achieved martyrdom by cruel death. For in the concentration camps themselves they continued to resist.

To make a detailed record of the simple clergy who resisted would take a library of books, and though the history of each priest would make an exciting story and demonstrate many examples of personal courage and resource, the greater part would be repetition. We believe that those who escaped arrest and death would prefer that, instead of recounting their exploits, we should close this brief account of the Church's struggle against the Crooked Cross with a tribute to those who knew the horrors of the concentration camp and still resisted, and who, resisting to the end, gave their lives for His Name's sake.

Whatever is said here of Dachau is equally true of any other concentration camp—Mauthausen, Buchenwald, Belsen, Gusen, Ravensbruck, Sachsenhausen, Auschwitz, Natzweiler, Gross-Rosen . . . there is no end, it seems, to the list of them.

The world of the concentration camp was in most cases a world without God, and without human dignity in every case. Priests arriving at Dachau were automatically drafted into the punishment squad, merely because they were priests. Most of the prisoners consigned to this squad, which was given the hardest tasks and denied all privileges, were kept in it for twelve months, but Jews for as long as they lived. The treatment was monstrous. The priests were mixed with other prisoners and wore the same drab, threadbare uniform. In addition to constant hunger, exhaustion and illness, there was always the brutality of the S.S. guards and, perhaps worse than that, the brutality of the Capos, the "trusty" prisoners set in authority over the rest and chosen from hardened criminals.

In Dachau—though this was not the case in a few of the other camps—no display of religion was permitted, let alone the carrying of the ministry to the lay prisoners. But many confessions were heard, not only among the priests themselves, for laymen would come secretly to the priests. Every secret corner of the camp served as a confessional, though the safest way was in the open. During the midday break and in other rest periods it was customary for the prisoners to walk along the camp roads. Priest and penitent walked side by side, and to the distant spectator appeared to be two men in earnest conversation, which was not an unusual sight. The priest held his dedicated right hand tucked in the lapel of his jacket, from which position it could be raised in absolution without attracting attention.

The German Bishops, aware of the conditions under which the priests lived, approached the Nazi Government to try to persuade them to alleviate their sufferings a little, and the Government miraculously agreed. This was at the beginning of 1941, by which time there were no fewer than 2,600 priests of twenty-two nationalities representing 136 dioceses in Dachau alone. The Bishops made four requests to the Nazis, three of which were granted: that the priests should live all together in special barracks, that they should be provided with a chapel and be allowed breviaries, and that they should be given only light work, so that they might have strength and time for intellectual work and the performance of priestly duties. The request that was refused was that priests who died might be buried according to the rites of the Church.

So the priests were concentrated in Block 26 and work was begun on building a chapel in the block. It was finished on 21st January, and the first Mass was celebrated the following day. What this meant to the priests can be imagined. No laymen were permitted by the S.S. to attend the chapel, but many were smuggled in by the priests. To some, Communion was a great need, and so the priests would carry the Sacraments to work. A handshake and a consecrated wafer lay in the prisoner's hand, and he would go off to find a quiet place where he could receive Christ's Body from his own hand. The Sacrament was smuggled, too, into the sick-bay, and it was possible to administer the Last Communion to many on the point of death. Those who were being moved to camps where there were no priests were nearly always able to communicate before their departure.

Among the Dachau priests, whose numbers were eventually to exceed 4,000, there were more than 1,600 Polish priests, 846 of whom were to die in the camp. From 1941 to 1944 these Poles were barred from the chapel, but this did not prevent their saying Mass. A watch would be set, and the celebrant would stand hidden by a stove, the edge of a table his altar, a rough home-made stole over his prison uniform, his paten a small piece of metal, his chalice a water-glass. In the quarries and in the plantation, too, they secretly celebrated Communion, and though many Polish laymen attended, they were never once betrayed.

The winter of 1941/42 was one of the most terrible periods in the camp. No fewer than 500 prisoners died of starvation alone. But in the middle of the year, purely to get more work out of the prisoners, conditions were improved. The punishment squad was abolished and the prisoners were allowed to receive parcels.

With the arrival of the parcels, the priests were able to trade groceries and tobacco for the services of craftsmen to make fittings for the chapel, though both food and tobacco were as gold to every priest. Most of the materials for these fittings were smuggled in from outside. In the plantation, which was partially outside the camp boundaries, there was a stall which sold seed and flowers grown in the camp to the inhabitants of the town of Dachau. It was in the charge of a priest-prisoner, Dr Ferdinand Schönwälder, who for more than two years risked his life daily, by bringing into the camp over 400 pounds weight of medical supplies, more than 2,000 illegal letters and large quantities of food, which came chiefly from the Jesuits of Pullach, the Sisters of Freysing and pious Dachau laymen. The materials for the chapel entered the camp by the same route.

There was always a risk of losing the chapel, for Berlin could be capricious. No order came, but at the beginning of September 1944 there was a dangerous crisis. By this time the conditions in the camp caused by overcrowding were terrible, and the priests were asked by the camp authorities voluntarily to surrender the chapel, this being the only way in which Berlin's orders could be circumvented by the S.S.

Father Schelling, the leader of the priests, who had been appointed Dean of Dachau concentration camp by Cardinal Faulhaber of Munich, refused to comply with the request in the name of all the priests. He presented his reasons in writing, which were read in chapel before being despatched; and his reasoning was so irrefutable that the S.S. did not mention the matter again.

There is no doubt that the chapel not only brought great spiritual comfort to the priests, but also strengthened their power to resist the evil in their midst; and this they did constantly, many of them even unto death. By the cookhouse door stood two large barrels of water, and one day an S.S. man seized a priest and a Jew and ordered them to insult God. When they refused, he held them head down in the water until both were dead. A priest working with barbed wire was asked by his guard: "What about a crowning of the thorns?" and was compelled to make a crown of barbed wire, which the S.S. man forced upon his head. Tens of priests were so brutally punished that they died; others died at the hands of doctors who conducted experiments on them; some were crucified head downwards, so that the cause of death might not be determined.

Yet nothing daunted these priests—neither hunger, nor punishments, nor lice, nor typhus, nor threats, nor death itself.

In the camp there were two Bishops, one a Pole, who died there and who is to be Beatified, and the other Monsignor Piguet, Bishop of Clermont-Ferrand. It came to the Monsignor's knowledge that there was in Dachau a young German deacon, Karl Leisner, from Cleve in Westphalia, who had been arrested before he could receive priest's orders. He had been in the camp for five years, and had a lung infection which was killing him. Monsignor Piguet had letters to the Bishops of Munster and Munich smuggled out of camp, asking their permission to ordain Leisner priest before he died, which was readily granted. Robes for the Bishop, a "gold" ring and pectoral cross were manufactured in the camp, and holy oil and the order of service were smuggled in from Munich.

On 17th December, 1944, the Bishop of Clermont-Ferrand ordained Karl Leisner priest in the presence of 1,000 fellow priests. Nine days later the newly ordained priest said his first—and last—Mass. He was now very ill, but he survived until the liberation of the camp by the Americans, and died shortly afterwards, reunited with his family.

"I strove," said Dean Schelling, "to raise the prestige of the priests in the camp by three means: by their moral–religious example, by their charity and by their industry at work for the benefit of their fellow-prisoners."

How the priests responded and gave more than was asked of them has written a golden page in the history of the persecuted Church. They died and suffered that we might have life, and might have it more abundantly; and we betray them when we let the new materialism make us forget Him Who gathered them unto Him in everlasting glory.

PART TWO

The Church's Struggle Against Communist Persecution

CHAPTER VII

The New Threat

THE UNCONDITIONAL surrender of Hitlerite Germany brought to western Europe a future heavy with hope. Much had happened during the years of fighting which had roused a determination in the minds and hearts of men not to allow the bad things of the past to exert an influence on their lives any more. The drawing together of all sorts of men into a cohesive whole in the face of the common threat had given birth to a new understanding of "the other man's point of view". Barriers of class had, for the most part, been demolished, and the right of all to a full share in the cultural and industrial wealth of the nations had been recognised. Exploitation of men in any field whatsoever was never to happen again. All were to have equal rights and opportunities to all educational resources, and a fair return for labour of hands and minds.

That this has been only partially achieved is the tragedy of our times. What had not been taken into account was Man's spiritual weakness once the threat to his body had been removed, and in the glow of resolution to build a new world it had been over-looked that this spiritual weakness creates a vacuum which materialist instincts are only too eager to fill. The materialism of western Europe and American today is scarcely surpassed by the dialectic materialism of Russia and her Communist satellites and fellow-travellers. Looked at from one angle, the materialism of the Communists is more honest than the materialism of the West, for while the Communists preach materialism as the supreme tenet of their creed, we in the West attempt all the time to disguise our materialism under all kinds of camouflage. The only thing in which the West is superior to the Communists is the liberty of thought, conscience and action we are still permitted to exercise; though this, too, might be argued as being to our detriment, for our thoughts and consciences direct our actions away from spiritual things, and leave us free to pursue our materialist desires.

In every country in western Europe and in America those who practise religion are a tiny fraction compared with those who do not say their prayers or go to church.

This is not the place to consider whether the Churches are to blame for this state of affairs, as the majority of us protest. Undoubtedly some of the blame may be apportioned to them. When men were afraid for their bodies during the War, and turned to God for protection and consolation, the Churches were given a great opportunity. Perhaps they were so happy when the altar-rails were full at the administration of the Sacraments, or when the high vaults vibrated to the sound of many prayers, that they were content to live only in the present. "Take no thought for the morrow." Perhaps it is true to say that the mid-twentieth-century Churches have made no effort to keep abreast of men's needs, and by thus being unable to help men with their new problems have dangerously weakened themselves. But however the argument may go about and about, the blame is not all on one side, and despite what has happened, the Church, whether Catholic or Protestant, had a right to share in the great hopes for the future.

The Catholic Church had struggled valiantly against the paganism of Nazism and Fascism. Though it had suffered, it had emerged with the secular powers, triumphant, if bruised, and could look forward to an era of recuperation and a great future. That a period of even more violent and vicious persecution should be its lot could not have borne contemplation.

The layman must wonder whether it was foreseen by the politicians who dealt the cards of the future at Yalta and Potsdam. Or are the minds of politicians engraved only with one groove which plays only a secular tune?

It is easy to be wise after the event, but have we not the right to expect our leaders to be wise for the future?

Until 1939 the Western Powers had done all they could to isolate Russia from the rest of Europe. Admittedly, Russia's own policy was partly responsible, but from the beginning of the Communist régime there it was the aim of all the democracies, and of the two dictatorships, to weaken Communist influence by containing Russia within her frontiers and preventing her from becoming a member of the European political and economic set-up.

When Russia became an ally of the West, and began to display her strength, did it not occur to the Western leaders that she could never again be forced back to the old position? The Russian leaders did not fail to see the opportunity presented to them by their victories of redressing the balance of power in Europe. Did none of our leaders foresee that the Russian occupation of the eastern zone of Germany, of Bulgaria, Rumania and Hungary, and the necessary arrangements for the movement of Soviet troops to and from the Soviet Union to East Germany across Poland would have an influence on the political structure of those countries? Did they really believe that the Russians would not so arrange things that these territories, which constitute, with Russia herself, more than half of Europe, would enter the Communist camp? Did they ask the Russians to define exactly what they meant by free elections? Did they really expect the Russians not to use every machiavellian trick to gain the end which was of such value to them?

But even if our leaders had been so forward-seeing, the fact remains that there was little they could have done to change the course of events short of going to war with Russia as soon as the war with Germany was at an end. There was one stage of the War when there might have been a possibility of preventing part of what has happened. The British Government in 1943 were strongly in favour of attacking Hitler in the Balkans, but the American military men were so opposed to the plan that it never got to be more than a suggestion. And even supposing that the Western Allies had liberated the Balkans, Yugoslavia would still have gone Communist, and the communisation of Bulgaria, Rumania and Hungary would only have been delayed until Allied occupation troops had left. Poland, East Germany and Czecho-Slovakia would still have gone as they have.

Did the Church see the dangers lying ahead? Without definite evidence to the contrary, it must be surmised that they did. Then why did they not make preparations to withstand the imminent onslaught? The only answer to this question can be that without organising the Faithful on a military basis, there was nothing practical that could be done.

Like a lamb to the slaughter the Church was led by events to physical and spiritual persecution of a violence not experienced by her for nearly 2,000 years. Yet there are few who are aware of the extent of the Church's sufferings. We are angry and sad when we hear of the arrest of a Primate, but for the most part we have been content to relegate the little knowledge we have to the deeper recesses of our minds, where it cannot trouble our comfortable materialism. But we have a duty towards the persecuted of any Church. The knowledge that prayers are being offered for them can bring comfort to those most harshly persecuted, for those prayers mean that we are remembering those in trouble; and the knowledge of the trouble they are in must exert, eventually, a great moral power before which the forces of evil must retreat sooner or later.

In the following pages we provide the knowledge, and if there is any truth in the axiom: Knowledge is power, then perhaps, helpless though we are in other ways, we may still—if only we will—come to the aid of our unhappy, persecuted brothers in Christ.

CHAPTER VIII

The Baltic States

On the Baltic seaboard of Russia, to the south of the Finnish Gulf, there were, in 1939, three small independent sovereign powers—Estonia, Latvia and Lithuania. In 1939 they had enjoyed independence for just on twenty years, for before 1919 they had formed provinces under the Russian Imperial Crown, and as such they had been subjected to the laws of Tsarist Russia to the same degree that the remainder of that vast country had been.

The Constitutions of the three new countries recognised and guaranteed freedom of conscience and religion. The peoples of the three countries possessed markedly different national characteristics, which were reflected in their ways of life and in their religion, though both of these were conditioned somewhat by the influence of the various great Powers who had had relations of one kind or another with them before they were finally annexed to Russia by Peter the Great in 1719. Thus, Estonia and Latvia derived much from seventeenth-century Sweden, while Lithuania was greatly influenced by Poland. In Estonia and Latvia the predominant religion was Lutheran. When independence was declared in Estonia there was no Catholic Church, while in Latvia about one-quarter of the two million inhabitants were Catholic. Lithuania, however, was predominantly Catholic, 80 per cent of the three million population belonging to the Latin Rite.

When Hitler invaded Poland, the Russians demanded from the three Baltic States facilities for setting up military bases within their territories. The three small countries had no alternative but to comply. Within a few months the Russians had taken over, a kind of *coup d'état* had been organised and the legally elected Governments had been replaced by Communist Governments, each of which petitioned the Kremlin to be granted the honour of becoming members of the Union of Soviet Socialist Republics. This the Kremlin was graciously pleased to permit.

In Estonia the 2,000 Catholics had been ministered to by eleven priests and twenty Religious, both men and women, under the Apostolic Administrator, Monsignor Edward Proffittlich. Their Church was only about fifteen years old, and this, with their small numbers, presented no great problem to the new rulers. First of all, priests of German nationality, of whom there were six, were compelled to leave the country, and not long afterwards the Administrator and one of the remaining priests were deported. All Church property was confiscated and endless difficulties put in the way of the four priests who remained and of the Faithful. Extra taxes were imposed and a levy was exacted for the performance of all religious ceremonies. The funds and property of relief organisations were appropriated and all Catholic literature burned.

In 1941 the Germans occupied the country, and remained there for nearly three years. During this time there was a period of comparative peace for the Church, but when the Russians drove out the Germans, the persecution was renewed, and in 1945 only two priests were active. Since then no news has come out of the country, which is held incommunicado, because of the Russian intermediate-range ballistic missile bases on the islands off the Estonian west coast.

The Church in Latvia, though a minority Church, had always been well looked after by the State, which had made grants of land to it and provided a subsidy. It was, indeed, a very flourishing Church, with a Press producing four periodicals and numerous magazines, and owning two high schools and a senior and a junior seminary. There was a faculty of Catholic Theology in the University of Riga. Catholic associations were numerous.

The first step in the persecution of the Latvian Catholic Church by the new régime was the breaking off of diplomatic relations with the Vatican. The Latvian representative was recalled from the Holy See and deported to Siberia, while the Apostolic Nuncio was expelled. Though the new Constitution recognised liberty of religious worship, the Church was excluded from public life. All Church property and funds were confiscated by the State. Even the sacred vessels and vestments were included in "property", and the State hired them back to the Church at extortionate rentals. A levy was also made on every religious ceremony, and all ceremonies outside the church were forbidden, which meant that Catholics could not be buried by the Church.

Deprived of all means of income, it was almost impossible for the Church to meet the taxes, rentals and levies imposed upon it. An attempt was made to reduce costs by combining two or three parishes, under the ministration of only one priest. When this happened the churches thus left vacant were taken over by the State and put to secular uses.

Religious books were confiscated and destroyed, the Catholic Press suppressed, the celebration of Holy Days was forbidden and, as religious instruction was banned, the Catholic schools and the Faculty of Theology in Riga University had to close. At the same time an anti-religious campaign was conducted among the young, to imbue in them the principles of Marxist materialism. All Catholic associations were suppressed, the religious Orders expelled and monasteries and convents confiscated. Bishops and clergy were compelled to leave their houses, which had been nationalised.

But besides these so-to-speak collective measures, direct action was taken against those individual priests who showed themselves difficult to subdue. The only way in which their influence could be broken was by liquidation, and since this could not be done secretly without arousing suspicion, some semblance of legality was aimed at, and priests were arrested on the most fantastic charges. The parish priest of Indra, for example, was accused of setting fire to his presbytery after it had been nationalised. Another was arrested, charged with taking payment for cemetery plots; another was accused of deceiving the people by having performed a marriage ceremony in church. Before the victims were brought to court they were handed over to the Secret Police, and as a result of their attentions made full confessions.

When Germany marched against Russia, the Communists launched a bitter attack on the clergy and Faithful, an attack of such brutality that it is not possible to give an idea of the number of priests who were murdered without being arrested, or who were arrested, tortured and either deported or executed. It has been estimated, however, that in the eighteen months of Soviet occupation in 1940–41 no fewer than 34,000 Latvian Lutherans and Catholics were massacred, among whom were 6,000 Catholic intellectual élite.

The Germans, during their occupation, followed the example of the Russians with regard to the confiscation and nationalisation of Church property and to processions outside churches. But the celebration of religious ceremonies and religious instruction in schools were permitted, except that no mention of the Old Testament could be made, though the reason for this peculiar ban is not known.

Russian troops returned to Latvia in October 1944, and the persecution of the Church was renewed with a violent wave of arrests, deportations and executions, among the first victims being the Auxiliary to the Archbishop of Riga. Within a short time more than fifty of the 187 Catholic priests in Latvia were eliminated.

Today Catholic rites and ceremonies may still be performed in Latvia, but under extremely difficult conditions. For example, Mass may only be celebrated if the priest has paid the levy fixed for the celebration of Mass and if his parishioners have paid the rents and taxes imposed.

The Church functions as best it can in the face of all these difficulties and of a violent anti-religious campaign. It would seem that the régime is now content to rely on time finally solving the religious question for them.

The democratic Government of Lithuania was compelled to resign on 15th June, 1940, the day on which the Soviet Army entered the country to reinforce the garrisons already there. A Provisional Government consisting mainly of Communists was formed, and general elections were fixed for 15th July. Under Soviet tutelage, the Provisional Government also decreed the separation of Church and State, the Concordat of 1927 was renounced and the Apostolic Nuncio was given two months in which to leave the country.

During the night of 12th/13th July more than 2,000 Lithuanian intellectuals were arrested, so that they should be unable to influence the popular vote. At the elections a single list of candidates, selected by the Communists—who, before the arrival of the Russians, did not exceed 2,000 in the whole of the country—was put up, with the result that the new Parliament was entirely composed of Communists and fellow-travellers. Early in August, at the request of the Government, Lithuania was admitted to the U.S.S.R. as the fourteenth Soviet Republic.

But even before this happened the attack on the Church had begun. Though the land had been nationalised under the democratic Republic, a new nationalisation law reduced the amount of land held by former owners to seventy-five acres, though Catholic parishes were allowed to retain only a tithe—seven and a half acres. On 6th August all private enterprises employing more than twenty people—later the figure was reduced to five people—were nationalised. This measure deprived the Church of its printing presses and bookshops. All religious books were seized and destroyed, as were all objects of piety. Later in the year all dwelling-houses over a certain size were nationalised, the owners becoming the tenants of the State. Where the tenants were clergy, rents were fixed at three roubles a square metre, whereas workers were charged only one rouble a square metre.

By these measures the Church was deprived of all its property and sources of income, and had to rely on donations from the Faithful. But these were soon drastically curtailed when a devaluation of the *litas* and the confiscation by the State of all shares and bonds and of all bank deposits and savings in excess of 1,000 roubles reduced the whole nation to extreme poverty.

Within a week of the Provisional Government being set up all religious instruction had been banned from schools, and the faculties of Theology and Philosophy in Kaunas University were closed. Then followed rapidly the nationalisation of all private schools, and the reorganisation of the school and university curricula in accordance with Marxist–Leninist materialist doctrines. The buildings of Catholic seminaries were commandeered by the Red Army and the Party.

The loss of the Church schools and the ban on the teaching of religion in schools was a grave blow, and after some consideration the Bishops decided to counteract the latter by organising small classes in churches. This was not permitted to continue for long, and in the spring of 1941 all clergy were warned that if they continued to give religious instruction to children of school age in churches or private houses they would be liable to the severest penalties. The arrival of the Germans in the middle of 1941, however, rendered the ban ineffective.

It was the aim of the régime not only to insulate the young from all religious influences, but also to rid the grown-ups of their religious "superstitions". The profession of any religion was declared incompatible with Party membership, State officials and members of the armed services were forbidden to attend church and all military and prison chaplains were dismissed. Public processions were forbidden, and Holy Days were declared full working days, with severe penalties for those workers who absented themselves to attend church. All Catholic associations were suppressed.

Simultaneously with these repressive measures, an intensive anti-religious campaign was organised. Its programme was two-fold: it aimed at showing the benefits of atheistic materialism, and at unmasking the futility and emptiness of religious superstitions. Secret police agents spied on all the clergy, some even going to the lengths of presenting themselves at the Confessional in the hope of trapping the priest into an anti-Communist pronouncement. Equally active measures were taken to hold up the clergy to ridicule and to destroy their prestige. Bishops' palaces, the houses of the religious Orders and the buildings of charitable organisations were commandeered by the Red Army. The Religious were dispersed. Vestments were used as door-mats.

Efforts were also made to coerce the clergy into becoming agents of the secret police. Priests who were arrested were offered their liberty if they would undertake to become police agents, with the alternative of imprisonment or deportation to Siberia for refusal. No fewer than twenty-seven priests who were arrested for this purpose were imprisoned or deported.

The arrival of the German forces in the summer of 1941 relieved the sad situation of the Catholic Church somewhat, and prevented, for the time being, the accomplishment of a vicious plan ordered by Serov, the Commissar of Security Police (NKVD). All anti-Soviet men and women of the Baltic States were to be arrested and deported to Russia. Lithuania alone was required to supply 700,000. The plan had already been initiated when the Germans' attack on Russia halted it, but not before 60,000 Estonians, 34,000 Latvians and 30,000 Lithuanians had been deported. On the return of the Russians in 1944 the plan was restarted, and reliable information states that at least half a million Lithuanians were moved to Russia before the deportations finally ceased. As these wretched people included almost all the priests and a vast number of devout Catholics, the strength of the Church was very effectively undermined.

After the return of the Soviets the persecution of the clergy was reinstituted with the greatest severity and vigour. They intensified their attack on the Pope, and attempted to separate the hierarchy from the clergy by falsifying documents and letters. Attempts were made to cause a split among the clergy with a view to setting up a National Catholic Church. As elsewhere, so in Lithuania, there have been a small number of renegade priests who have become willing tools of the Communists. These "independent" priests were often put in to replace a priest who had been imprisoned or deported, but it was not long before the Faithful discovered him to be a Communist agent and rejected him. But though new and most determined efforts to found a National Catholic Church were made again in 1952, it would appear that there has been little progress in achieving this.

It is not widely known that after the end of the War in Europe quite a strong guerilla organisation carried on harassing operations from the great forests of Lithuania against the Communists. The activities of the Partisans reached such proportions in 1946 that the Minister of the Interior felt compelled to call upon the Catholic Bishops and the heads of other religious bodies to aid the authorities. He requested the Bishops to condemn the resistance movement and to advise the Partisans to give up the struggle.

When the Bishops refused to to do this, extreme measures were taken against them. On 3rd January, 1947, the Bishop of Telsiai was condemned to death by a secret tribunal in a Vilna prison. Whether the sentence was carried out or not is not known. He had been arrested in the autumn of 1946, together with his Auxiliary, who was deported to Siberia, and in 1955 was known to be undergoing forced-labour at Abyz, in Russia. Not long after this the Bishop of Kaisedoris was arrested, and when last heard of, in 1955, was confined in a home for old people in Moldavia. The Apostolic Administrator of the Archdiocese of Vilna was confined to prison for some years before he died, still in confinement, on 8th November, 1953.

Since the Bishop of Kaunas and his Auxiliary, and the Auxiliary Bishop of Vilkaviskis went into exile on the return of the Russians in 1944, out of Lithuania's eleven Bishops only one was left at liberty after all these arrests. He was the aged Bishop of Panevezys, who was nearly eighty. The authorities later, however, gave their approval for the consecration of two new Bishops, but so far as is known there have been no more new consecrations.

But more than anything else, it is the burden of taxes which has been responsible for the gradual elimination of the Church in Lithuania. The taxes are so extortionate that sooner or later all resources are exhausted, and there is nothing to be done but close the church. In this way the Lithuanian Communists believe that the Catholic Church will be forced out of existence, and it seems that nothing can be done to prevent it.

But while they are waiting for this to happen, they seek to impede the work and ministry of the Church by every possible means. Very little now exists but the "exercise of worship" carried out in such buildings as the State permits. Yet even this, so long as it lasts, feeds hope.

CHAPTER IX

Yugoslavia

WHEN TITO and his followers, having fixed themselves in the saddle of Government, drafted a Constitution for the new People's Federal Republic of Yugoslavia, a first reading of Article 25 must have momentarily lit some hope in the hearts of the Faithful. The Constitution recognised, the Article stated, liberty of conscience and liberty of worship.

But the Yugoslav Communists were guided by Marxist principles as thoroughly as any other Communist régime elsewhere, and they had not overlooked that tenet of Marxism–Leninism which states that the liquidation of the Church should not be carried out if that liquidation threatened to hold up the sovietisation of the country and its economic development. Though the elections which had put Tito in power appeared to prove that 99·89 per cent of the population supported him, in actual fact this was a gross exaggeration, and the Yugoslav Communists knew it. They realised that they had before them a giant task in their efforts to consolidate the new régime, and that until consolidation was complete some attempt must be made, while keeping the Church within circumscribed bounds, to do nothing which would make the Church the centre of national unrest.

As late as June 1952, Krstulovic, President of the Croatian People's Assembly, declared: "The revolution has enabled us to break the old middle-class frame-work, to destroy the main foundations of this middle-class and to bring everything under our control. But we cannot destroy the Church as an institution.

This is not because our country or our Government are too weak to do so, but because there still exists in the conscience of many citizens, and particularly peasants, remnants of faith to which they tenaciously hold. We know that, as an institution, the Church will soon have disappeared. In our struggle against it we must carry the fight into the political and cultural arenas, enlightening the conscience of the people at the same time that we raise their standard of living, so that they may come to understand better that the world did not develop under the guidance of the Holy Spirit, but according to the Laws of Nature. To this end, we must mobilise public opinion in the towns and villages against the destructive work of the priests."

Besides recognising liberty of conscience and liberty of worship, the Yugoslav Constitution provided for the separation of Church and State, banned the abuse of the Church and of religion for political ends, declared political organisations with religious backgrounds to be illegal and permitted religious communities whose teachings were not opposed to the Constitution to carry out their religious functions and to perform their religious rites. For the Constitution of a Communist State this appears reasonable enough; but what was unwritten was as important as what was written—perhaps even more so—and even what was written needs consideration in order to arrive at a true interpretation.

In all Communist States religion is a private matter for the individual alone. That is what liberty of conscience means. The Constitution provides for it. But the members of the Party have a duty imposed upon them by the superiority of their knowledge to persuade those whose consciences involve religious beliefs how greatly in error they are to let themselves be deceived by superstition, which is what religion is. The enlightened Party members must, therefore, use every weapon—propaganda, persuasion and, in obstinate cases whose example may lead others astray, the ultimate weapon of liquidation—to eliminate religion. This, which is not written into the Yugoslav Constitution, was clearly stated in *Nedeljne informativne novine,* in its issue of 4th May, 1952: "But liberty of religion does not merely signify liberty to practice such and such a religion: it also allows the liberty of the ideological struggle against religious mysticism and religious prejudices." It is not necessary to itemise the ways and means which are open to the Enlightened to perform this duty, since they become self-evident when the nature of the Communist State is considered.

Even while permitting liberty of worship, the State could legitimately withhold the right of the Church to perform any function other than the celebration of services. Since a great deal of the work of the Church is performed outside the churches—in schools, for example, in youth organisations, in works of charity —its influence could be greatly curtailed by denying to it all forms of expression except as defined by the letter of those three words "liberty of worship", which is quite a different thing from liberty of religion.

It was not long before the architects of the new régime were making clear exactly what their attitude towards the Church was. In Yugoslavia, as in other occupied countries, the early months of the Liberation were marked by the arrest, trial and punishment of collaborators and war criminals. In the Yugoslav purge of these undesirable elements many priests were arrested. Charged before military tribunals with crimes no more specifically described than "enemy of the people", "reactionary" and "traitor", the verdict was a foregone conclusion, the sentence for the great majority, death. Until they were brought into the court-room scarcely any knew with what they were charged; often the accused were not allowed to defend themselves or to have any legal aid.

Nor was it the simple parish priest who suffered this fate. Between April and August 1945 the Bishops of Krk and Krizevsi were arrested, the latter being condemned to death; the Bishop of Dubrovnik disappeared, and what was believed to be his body, identified from scraps of clothing, was later found at the bottom of a well with a heap of other bodies; while the Bishop of Ljubljana was tried *in absentia*, and condemned to eighteen years' confinement, ten years loss of civic rights and the confiscation of all his property. Two other prelates—the Bishops of Sarajevo and the Bishop of Banja Luka—escaped to Austria, where the latter died shortly afterwards.

So terrible was this persecution that the Bishops felt themselves compelled to denounce it in a Pastoral Letter dated 20th September, 1945. "The sad and terrible fate of many of our priests fills our hearts with grief and uneasiness. Even while the war was being waged many had fallen, not only on the battlefield, but before the rifles of the civil and military authorities. Since the ending of hostilities the execution of Catholic priests has continued. Our information is that 243 have been killed, 169 are in prisons or concentration camps, while 89 are missing, making a total of 501, in addition to whom, 19 seminarists,

3 brothers and 4 nuns have been killed. Such a thing has been unheard of in Balkan countries for centuries. But our crowning sorrow is that these victims, as well as hundreds and thousands of others, were refused the solace of their religion in their last moments, which in any civilised country is accorded even to the worst criminals."

This physical persecution of prelates and priests was not the only manifestation of the Government's attack on the Church in the early months of the régime. One of the first things that the Communists did on achieving power was to reorganise the educational system. All schools from now on belonged to the State, and though private schools might be permitted to function, they would still be regulated by the State.

The Communists, like the Nazis and Fascists, recognised the importance of youth as the adults of the future. The main task of the schools, therefore, was to educate the children to grow up into good Communists, steeped in materialist principles, "the study of which", as Milovan Djilas put it, "permits teachers to inculcate in their pupils a sound outlook on the world, which removes them from the influence of the clergy and the diverse ideological theories of the middle classes." At the Fourth Party Congress, Tito had occasion to criticise the results of socialist education among university students. "It is necessary", he said, "to take measures for the formation of the children in secondary schools so that these young people may become, in the more or less distant future, the true socialist intelligentsia. The faster we set to work, the sooner we shall withdraw our intelligentsia from the influence of various foreign ideas, and the sooner shall we have a sure support to accomplish successfully the building of the new society."

Yugoslavia is a federation of republics, each separate one of which has its own way of administering federal laws. In Croatia, where there was a large Catholic majority, at the beginning priests were permitted to give religious instruction in schools outside ordinary school hours, if the parents of the children made a request in writing for this to be done. In Bosnia-Herzegovina, Slovenia and Montenegro, however, no religious teaching was allowed in schools, and even religious instruction given in churches was forbidden on the grounds that such teaching converted the churches into private schools, which had no authorisation. In yet other parts of the country a more liberal policy was introduced; at least, it was ostensibly a more liberal policy. The teaching of religion was permitted throughout all primary schools and in the lower classes of the secondary schools. In the lower classes of the primary schools parents were required to make written application if they desired their children to be given religious teaching. One day, and one day only, was set aside at the beginning of the school year for handing in these requests. In making the announcement the master, more often than not, added the comment that when the applications were handed in, it would be seen who were the reactionary parents who wished their children to hear the nonsense of the priests. There was a special form in which the application had to be made, and if there was the slightest error in the wording, the application was declared void, and no second one could be submitted.

The children of the upper classes of the primary schools and in the secondary schools had to make the decision for themselves. Many inducements and obstacles were placed in their way to dissuade them from choosing to attend religious classes. Walks and games were organised for those pupils not attending religious classes; while in many schools the time for instruction was set so late in the day that the children who might have attended would have been unable to reach home before nightfall.

Only one hour a week during a maximum period of three months in the school year may be devoted to religious teaching. The priests who take the classes must have permission from the authorities, and to obtain it, they must send one copy of their application to the local Committee, one to the District Committee and a third to the Provincial Committee.

All schools and colleges owned and run by the Church have been closed, and their buildings taken over for Government or Party use. As for seminaries for the preparation of young men for the priesthood, more than half have been closed and their buildings confiscated. Those that have been permitted to remain in being often have to share their buildings with Party organisations, and all work under tremendous difficulties, since all their funds have been confiscated by the State, and very few gifts in money or kind are allowed to be sent into the country from abroad.

No boy under fifteen years of age may be admitted to a seminary. This means that he must attend a State school for eight years, where he will be subjected to the teaching of atheism. The number of would-be priests entering the seminaries is, therefore, very small compared with former times, and there is no doubt that the Communists are using this as a direct instrument to curtail the life of the Church.

Another measure early introduced by the new régime was a wide agrarian reform, under which all land was nationalised. The Catholic Church in Yugoslavia had partly supported itself by the income from estates which had been in its possession for very many years. Now no religious community could own more than twenty-five acres, and in many cases the prescriptions regulating expropriation were exceeded.

At the same time that the income of the Church was thus seriously diminished, all State subsidies were withdrawn. This double blow reduced the Church to a state bordering on destitution. The Bishops, however, accepted the condition of poverty, and looked for the assistance of the Faithful to support the clergy, the seminaries and the few other religious institutions that remained.

Before the Bishops issued their Pastoral Letter of 20th September, 1945, Monsignor Stepinac, Archbishop of Zagreb, had made courageous protests against the violence of the régime towards the Church, and particularly against the arrests, imprisonment and execution of priests and prominent Catholic laymen. At the beginning the Communists attempted to win over the Archbishop, but when this failed, a Press campaign of vilification was started. He was accused of being a war criminal and was arrested and held in prison for fifteen days. In November 1945 an attempt was made to assassinate him. None of these attacks caused him to swerve from his resistance to Communist violence, and on 27th August, 1946, he made yet another protest. This letter determined the régime to get rid of him.

In September he was arrested, and on the last day of the month was brought to trial on charges of a political nature. Most of those who might have given evidence on his behalf were arrested before the trial opened, and though the prosecution called a long array of witnesses, the defence could produce only one or two. Step by step, with clear argument, the Archbishop refuted every charge, and none of the "proofs" brought forward by the prosecution would have satisfied any court which observed respect for the law. This did not prevent the tribunal, however, from sentencing him to sixteen years' hard labour, with a further five years' loss of civic rights.

The trial of the Archbishop was but one of a series. During the next four years many priests were arrested and imprisoned. In 1948 the Bishop of Mostar was arrested on a charge of collaborating during the War with Pavelits' Croatian fascist militia called the Ustashis. The charge was so ill-founded that the prosecution had to rely on patently false witnesses, and the Bishop had no difficulty in proving their testimony a series of lies. "The only reason why I stand before you," the Bishop declared to his judges, "is because as a Bishop I have defended the rights of the Church and of religion. And that is a right recognised by the Constitution." He was sentenced to eleven years' imprisonment. For refusing to give evidence against his Bishop, the Bishop's secretary was sent to prison for eight years.

So it went on. But false imprisonment was only one of the weapons used to try to coerce the clergy. Bishops were attacked by gangs on their way to administer the Sacraments. Other hooligans threw rotten eggs at priests celebrating Mass. Gross insults were showered on priests in the streets, and obscene slogans were daubed on walls.

Whenever Bishops carried out pastoral visits in their dioceses they were required on their return to submit to questioning by State officials. These interrogations often lasted for days at a time.

But it was not only the clergy who were the objects of State-organised or State-encouraged threats. Everything was done to discourage or prevent the Catholic layman from performing his religious duties. Agents mingled with congregations and noted the names of those worshipping. Workers were forbidden to be absent from their work on Church festivals, which were no longer recognised by the State. Ration cards, which were in force in Yugoslavia for several years after the War, were withheld from Catholics who disobeyed these instructions, and many of them were deprived of employment. The sick in hospitals, prisoners, and particularly those condemned to death were not permitted to receive the Sacraments.

By State and Party organs the Church was held up to ridicule. The Vatican was called "the representative of Italian imperialism", "the home of reaction", "the age-old enemy of the people".

The State radio broadcast a parody of the Lord's Prayer and blasphemous so-called Litanies of the Blessed Virgin. In fact, everything was done to discredit the Church, particularly in the eyes of the young.

The Church had no medium of retaliation, for even before the régime was established Tito's Partisans systematically destroyed Catholic bookshops and printing-houses in each town as they liberated it. After the Communists had achieved power, one of the first ordinances to be published laid down that all publications must be authorised by the Government. This authorisation was withheld from all Catholic newspapers, with three exceptions, the *Verski List* of Maribor, the *Gore Srca* of Zagreb and the *Oznanilo* of Ljubljana, and even these three had eventually to close down, chiefly because the State withheld adequate supplies of paper. All Catholic printing-presses not destroyed were taken over by the State, a step which prevented any religious books, even the Bible, from being printed.

In 1948 Tito broke with Stalin and the Cominform, and for a time there appeared to be an easing of the conflict between Church and State. Certainly there was still some persecution, but not on the previous scale, and the Government seemed to be exercising care not to give the Church new grounds for complaint. This is not to say that the State did not continue, without abatement, its efforts to undermine and sweep away the influence of the Church and to replace it with dialectic materialism.

But there was a relaxation of the anti-religious propaganda campaign—a campaign which would require a whole book to give the reader an adequate appreciation of its violence of language and its volume. A limited number of copies of the Bible and the Catechism were allowed to be printed. The nomination of six new Bishops was permitted in 1950 and 1951. Priests who had been barred from their parishes were allowed to return to them. Repairs to churches were authorised in a small number of cases. The nine seminaries still existing were permitted to seek a limited amount of money from abroad. The Faculty of Theology in Zagreb University was once more able to confer degrees. In some places nuns were given permission to live again in communities, and some community houses were even returned to them for this purpose. (The women's Orders had been particularly harshly treated. All schools, colleges, homes and other institutions and a number of convents were confiscated. The nuns were forbidden to wear their habits. Large numbers were set to work on menial tasks, like clearing the streets, particularly on Sundays.) Religious instruction in schools was not so openly opposed as it had formerly been. Some priests were included in the amnesty granted to 11,000 prisoners on 1st June, 1951. Finally, Marshal Tito attempted to solve the case of Archbishop Stepinac.

Shortly after the trial of the Archbishop, Tito had said at a meeting in Zagreb: "We are accused of having arrested Stepinac to get rid of him. When Monsignor Joseph Hurley, the Apostolic Nuncio, called on me, I said to him: 'Take him away to avoid his being sent to prison; if not we shall arrest him.' And we waited several months before doing so." Now he offered to set the Archbishop free if he would go into voluntary exile. The Archbishop refused; nevertheless, he was released from prison and confined, in conditional liberty under police supervision, to his native village of Krasic.

At the same time that this moratorium of persecution was operating, however, other methods were being brought into use to undermine the influence of the Church and bring it to ultimate dissolution. Perhaps the most important of these was the setting up by the Government of Ecclesiastical Associations, as they were called.

Ever since the beginning of the régime the Government had attempted to cause a split between the lower clergy and the hierarchy. Despite their attacks on religion, it served the Government's purpose to appear to have the priests on their side.

Now, some years before the War a certain Father Joseph Lampret had been arrested on a charge of being a Communist. When released, he had left his diocese of Maribor and had fled to Dalmatia, where Tito's Partisans had found him during the War. Lampret was not the only priest to be attracted by Communism, and in 1949 a number of them, calling themselves People's Priests, had asked Tito to receive them. He had done so, and had suggested that now that the Government had broke with the Cominform, did they not think they might break with Rome?

The priests agreed, and as a beginning a bureau for religious questions with the resounding title of the Religious Commission accredited to the Presidency of the Council of Ministers of the

People's Republic of Slovenia, was set up. Its function was to act as liaison between the Government and the hierarchy. Lampret was installed as President of this Commission.

Lampret now formed the Secretariate for the Pioneering Projects of Priest-members of the Liberation Front. The Liberation Front was a Communist organisation, and the priests, recognising that they were forbidden to join Communist or even political organisations, for the most part refused to join it. Despite an extensive propaganda campaign, Lampret's efforts to attract priests into the Communist camp failed miserably, but not entirely. The few who did join him met in conference at Ljubljana in the summer of 1949, and there founded the Association of Saints Cyril and Methodius of the Catholic Priests of Slovenia.

The Government saw in the Association an instrument perfectly suited to their purposes, and did all they could to promote it. Imprisoned priests were offered their freedom if they would join, and many succumbed. Many others fell for the favours held out to them. They were, for example, promised greater freedom in the performance of their ministry; and were offered membership of the Social Insurance Scheme, under which they were made eligible, on the same basis as workmen and officials, for such benefits as free medical attention, insurance against illness and a retirement pension.

The Bishops were naturally opposed to the Association. On the other hand, when the number of priests joining the Association reached serious proportions they declared themselves ready to approve the statutes of the Association if amended along certain lines, and then obtained the approval of the Holy See. The Association agreed to amend the statutes, but would not agree to the approbation of the Holy See being sought. This closed the door, and there was nothing left but the excommunication of the members of the Association. But, despite excommunication, other similar Associations sprang into being in other parts of the country.

Suddenly, towards the end of 1952, the Government seized on the excommunication of the People's Priests and the activities of the Bishops vis-à-vis the Associations as pretexts for breaking off diplomatic relations with the Vatican, on the grounds that the excommunications constituted interference in the internal affairs of a sovereign State. In October 1945 the Holy See had appointed Monsignor Joseph Hurley, an Irishman, as Apostolic Nuncio to

Belgrade, but the Yugoslav Government showed him nothing but hostility from the moment that he began his mission, and obstructed him in every possible way.

As a matter of fact, it was the news which reached Belgrade on 29th November that really brought matters to a head. This was that Pope Pius XII intended to create Archbishop Stepinac, still in conditional liberty in his native village, a Cardinal. Both Government and every instrument of propaganda at once declared that by this act the Holy See was offering intolerable provocation to the Yugoslav State, and on 17th December the Apostolic Nunciature was closed.

The termination of diplomatic relations between the Vatican and Yugoslavia was the signal for new propaganda campaigns designed to improve the position of the People's Priests. The burden of the propaganda was that now all possibility of "foreign intervention" in the internal affairs of the State had been removed, the way was clear for an early improvement in relations between Church and State. Indeed, towards this end Tito called to him a number of Bishops to discuss with him the possibility for arranging a *modus vivendi*. The Bishops, however— as they were reminded by the Holy See—could not legitimately enter into any agreement of this kind, which was solely within the jurisdiction of the Holy See. So the move came to nothing.

A new wave of persecution was now directed against the Church. Today, six years later, it has still not receded. The main instrument in this attack is what might be defined as an economic blockade.

We have already seen the effect of the agrarian reform on the economic life of the Church, and how, as a result of it and of the withdrawal of State subsidies, the Church was reduced to such poverty that it had to rely on such financial aid as the Faithful could provide. In many parts of Yugoslavia it had become the custom for groups of men and women to act as collectors. Now all collections outside church were forbidden, and the collectors were often arrested and fined or imprisoned. Similarly, the age-old custom of house-blessing, which was performed by the priests every year, was accompanied by offerings to the Church. This was now interpreted as begging, which was forbidden by law. Money collected for bells, for the saying of Masses for the repose of the souls of the departed, and funds for church repairs, were confiscated. Even ordinary collections in church were forbidden, except in those churches where a People's Priest was in charge. But most stringent of all were the taxes imposed upon the clergy.

Up to 1952 the incomes of the clergy had been taxed at 4 per cent. Now Inland Revenue officials began to check every item in every return. To do so they visited Bishops' residences, presbyteries and convents, demanding to inspect the books. They verified every sum, and took the gross amount as the basis for their levy, making no allowances for expenses or repairs, and so on, which had previously been allowed. Not only did they do this for the year 1952, but reassessed taxes, on this basis, for the years 1947 to 1951.

To give an example of the workings of the collectors, a community was regarded as a physical person. If the community consisted of fifty nuns, it was more than likely that only ten of them would be able to work, and the money made by those who could work would be devoted to the needs of all. But the collectors took the sum of the money earned by the ten nuns as though it were the income of one person, and tax was levied at that rate. And not only levied at that rate, but multiplied by the number of years for which the arrears were demanded. The sum, more often than not, equalled a tax of 50 per cent on the income of 1952.

If a priest could not pay immediately, anything movable was seized—furniture, radio sets, sewing machines and very often clothing. The Apostolic Administrator at Matibor, Bishop Drzecnik, was assessed for more than a half a million dinars, and the current account of the bishopric was blocked until the sum was paid. The Administrator appealed to the Ministry of Finance without success, and the current funds of the Bishop were so greatly reduced that it was practically impossible to continue work.

The tax collectors proved extremely diligent in their work, but they were not the only ones to turn the screw in this way. Unless a priest had a special permit—and such permits were not often given—he could not accept any gift freely made to him by his congregation. In June 1952, in a parish in Slovenia, there was a young priest about to say his first Mass. This is a great occasion in the life of a priest and is generally marked by a small celebration. The family of this young priest was very poor, so the neighbours got together and brought food and wine and small presents. The police heard what was happening, and on the previous evening they confiscated everything that the neighbours had contributed. If a priest accepted any gift without holding a permit, both he and the donors were liable to arrest and a fine or imprisonment.

Needless to say, the priests who were members of the Association were not treated in this way. They received very favourable consideration from the Tax Commissioners, and were allowed to receive gifts without permission. Many faithful priests were approached and told that if they joined the Association their taxes would be considerably reduced or entirely remitted; and, unhappily, some numbers of them succumbed.

So curtailed did the activities of the Church become under all these restrictions that those Articles of the Constitution regulating the affairs of the Church became a mockery. Between the 23rd and 26th September, 1952, the Bishops met at Zagreb under the leadership of the Archbishop of Belgrade, since the Primate was prevented from attending by his confinement. During these four days they drew up a Memorandum to send to Tito, in which they set out the exact position of the Church after nearly seven years of Communist rule. No religious liberty existed in Yugoslavia, they stated, despite Article 25 of the Constitution, which spoke of safeguarding liberty of conscience and the free exercise of religion; and they set down examples of what had happened and what was happening. It was an extremely outspoken and courageous document, but a few days after it had been sent to Tito it was returned to the Archbishop of Belgrade without comment. The Bishops, however, were determined that Tito should see it, and when seven of them were summoned to a meeting with him in December of that year, they presented it to him in person. But it had no effect at all on Government policy. If anything, it added fuel to the already fierce fire of opposition.

In 1953 anti-Church propaganda was intensified, the people being incited particularly against the Bishops. The Auxiliary Bishop of Zagreb was attacked for a Pastoral Letter in which he had explained how Christians should regard the Person of Jesus Christ, which was interpreted as an attack on Communism. The Bishops of Split, Zadar and Sibenik were accused, in connection with the census of 1953, of wishing "to exploit the census to create confusion and a psychosis of religious persecution". The census form required every citizen to state whether he was an atheist or a member of a religious denomination, and the Bishops had advised the Faithful to state that they belonged to the Catholic Church.

For some years past members of the hierarchy had been subject to violent physical attacks, one of the most serious being that on the Apostolic Administrator of Ljubljana, who was seized at a railway station by a crowd who attempted to burn him alive, while police merely looked on. But in 1953, after the Central Committee of the Communist Party of Yugoslavia had met at Brioni and urged their followers to intensify the struggle against the Bishops, these physical attacks multiplied. Between the 1st July and 31st August three assaults were made on the Auxiliary Bishop of Senj, and one each on the Bishop and Auxiliary Bishop of Split, on the Auxiliary Bishop of Zagreb, on the Apostolic Administrator and on the Vicar-General of Sibenik, on the Apostolic Administrator of Backa and the Apostolic Administrator of Banja Luka; and these were only a few among many. The assailants were never identified and, therefore, never punished.

Arrests and imprisonments on trumpery charges are still the order of the day. There is no slackening in the customary severity of the sentences. For example, arrested in August 1956 on the vague charge of making "propaganda against the State and the existing social order of the country, of spreading fascist ideas and of misusing religion for political ends", the Rector of the Theological Seminary of Split, and Professor Father Ostrojic and two students were sentenced to five and a half years, four and a half years, two and a half years and one and a half years of hard labour, respectively.

True, there has been a falling away in the numbers of the Faithful; true, there are now only 4,000 priests, where before there were 6,000; true, the youth of the country have been detached from their parents and from the Church; but the fact remains that, despite all the severity with which priests and Faithful are attacked, despite all the difficulties that are placed in the way of the priests administering religion and of the people following religion, the Catholic Church in Yugoslavia is still alive. The State has still a long way to go before it succeeds entirely—as *Borba*, the leading newspaper of Yugoslavia, stated on 1st March, 1952—"in withdrawing our workmen from the influence of religion and mysticism".

CHAPTER X

Bulgaria

Out of a population of six million, the Catholics in Bulgaria numbered only 57,000, of whom 6,000 belonged to the Byzantine Rite. The Catholic Church, however, was extremely active, and characterised by an intense unity, which gave to it a strength equal at least to numerically stronger Churches elsewhere. Nevertheless, it will be appreciated that the problem it presented to the Communists was not a formidable one, when once the whole machinery of the State was directed towards its destruction. For this reason, it seems, the new régime in Sofia was content to leave the Church in relative peace for the first two or three years of the post-war era.

The accession of the Communists to power in Bulgaria was achieved in much the same way as in Rumania and Hungary. When King Boris died, in 1943, in mysterious circumstances after a visit to Hitler, he was succeeded by his son Simeon. As Simeon was a boy of only six, a Council of Regents governed for him. When the Germans retreated from Bulgaria in 1944 the Soviet Union demanded that Bulgaria should declare war on Germany. The Bulgarian Government not making a satisfactory reply to what amounted to an ultimatum, Russia declared war on Bulgaria, who at once asked for an armistice.

Russian troops entered Sofia on 9th September, 1944. The following month the democratic Government was dismissed under pressure, and a pan-Slav Fatherland Front administration was formed of the Communists and parties of the Left, with the full support of the U.S.S.R. Bulgaria then declared war on Germany.

In March 1945 a Congress of the Fatherland Front adopted a Communist resolution calling for free parliamentary elections to be held as soon as possible. The elections were announced for August, but Great Britain and America let it be known that the proposed conditions under which the elections were to be held would make it impossible for them to recognise as democratic any Government so elected. So the elections were postponed, and during September measures designed to make the election policy more liberal and to give the Opposition more freedom were announced. Eight days after the abolition of martial law (10th November, 1945) the elections were held. As the Opposition boycotted them, the Fatherland Front were returned. As a result of a referendum held in September 1946, Bulgaria was declared a republic by an overwhelming majority.

The Communists now set about consolidating their position, chiefly by removing their political opponents. Nichola Petkov, leader of the Agrarian Party, for example, was executed in November 1947, and within a year all opposition had been liquidated and the Communists were in undisputed control.

The fact that there was an opposition had not prevented the Communists from introducing a new Constitution which provided for the institution of a communistic State. It contained the usual clauses guaranteeing freedom of conscience and religion, separating the Church from the State, forbidding political organisations with a religious basis and bringing all the schools under State control—all to be the subject of special laws.

The law dealing with the nationalisation of the schools was promulgated in August 1948. Under it the first direct blow was aimed at the Catholic Church. This is not to say, however, that there had been no hostility shown towards the Church before this date. Several individual priests, for example, had been imprisoned on trumped-up charges, while others had been deprived of their ration cards. Then all foreign priests and nuns had been required to leave the country. The Government had requested the only Catholic weekly newspaper to include a Government article in each issue, and arrested one of the paper's collaborators; in view of which the Church decided to suspend publication, so as to remove what might prove to be an instrument turned against it. Chiefly, however, it was through an intense and vicious propaganda campaign, conducted in the Press and over the radio, and directed against the Pope, that the Government sought to harass the Church.

Then, as has been said, in August 1948 the direct campaign was opened with the confiscation of all Catholic schools under the law ordering the closing of all foreign schools, religious and lay. By this law the Church lost nine schools at which more than 5,000 boys and girls had been taught. All staff of foreign nationality were expelled from the country, and later nearly all the

Bulgarian teachers were arrested. All school buildings were taken over by the Government and Party.

In December the Apostolic Delegate in Sofia announced his intention to visit Rome, but before he left he asked for formal guarantees that he would be permitted to return. These were given. But he had scarcely left the country when a Press and radio campaign was opened demanding his expulsion. Consequently when he applied to the Legation in Rome for a visa to return to Bulgaria, it was refused. Thus all contact between the Church and the Holy See was cut off.

In February 1949 the law on Religious Denominations was published. Under it the Church was separated from the State; only Bulgarian citizens might be appointed to ecclesiastical offices; all religious ceremonies were forbidden without the consent of the Ministry for External Affairs; the education and organisation of children and youths were specifically reserved to the State; the Church might not conduct orphanages, hospitals or other similar institutions; the Church was debarred from having relations with institutions or persons abroad; the Houses of all foreign Orders, congregations or missions were to be closed; anyone organising a political association on a religious basis or using the Church and religion for anti-State propaganda would be liable to severe penalties; and the Church was required to draw up statutes which were to be approved by the Government.

Following upon this, the State embarked upon the progressive liquidation of the Church. The Catholic hospitals were confiscated and twenty Sisters of Charity were expelled. The Sisters of the Blessed Eucharist were turned out of their orphanage and novitiate at Sofia. The Jesuit seminary at Sofia was closed, and later all other seminaries. The Congregation of the Annunciation was dispersed.

Simultaneously, every difficulty that could be devised was placed in the way of the clergy to prevent them from fulfilling their ministry. Sermons were permitted at the celebration of Mass, but since police spies were always to be found in the congregations, whatever the priest said had to be so vague as to be almost useless. Under extreme coercion, Catholic laymen were being compelled to spy upon and denounce their priests. Every week large numbers of priests and laymen were held for exhaustive interrogation, and priests were imprisoned in increasing numbers.

In 1952 a series of trials was staged. The first involved the Superior of the Capuchins in Sofia, who was charged with defamation of the Government, disparagement of Soviet Russia and spying for the Vatican and the capitalist Powers. The Superior had been in prison for nearly two years before being brought to trial, and when he was eventually condemned on 14th January, 1952, two years were added to his sentence of ten years, for difficult behaviour in prison.

Yet another Capuchin was next brought to trial. Arrested in May 1950, he was sentenced to the maximum penalty allowed under the Bulgarian penal code—twenty years' imprisonment.

The third trial was organised in the Communist grand manner. The chief accused was the Bishop of Nikopol, who was arrested on 16th July, 1952. On 25th September he was brought to trial in the Palace of Justice accused of espionage, the illegal possession of arms, anti-Communist propaganda and a number of lesser crimes. With him in the dock were twenty-six priests, two nuns and two former editors of the Catholic newspaper. On 3rd October the Bishop and three priests were condemned to death; the two nuns to five and six years; the remaining priests' sentences ranged from eighteen months to twenty years; while the two editors received twelve years each. The sentence on the Bishop had not been carried out when the last news of him was received at the end of 1955.

During the trial of the Bishop, the Vicar Apostolic of Sofia was arrested at the request of the Public Prosecutor on a charge of having had contact with the Bishop. He is still in prison. The third Catholic Bishop, the Exarch Apostolic of the Eastern Rite, was also arrested, set at liberty, re-arrested in December 1956 and again released under police supervision.

The arrest and imprisonment of the majority of priests, the arrest of the three Bishops, the dissolution of the Orders, the confiscation of the schools, orphanages, hospitals and other institutions, all succeeded in reducing the former united and strong Bulgarian Catholics to a terrified, scattered and bewildered remnant. Within the space of a few years, so effective was the persecution of the Communists that the Catholic Church in Bulgaria was completely destroyed. In scarcely any other country have the Communists been so successful in eliminating Catholic opposition.

CHAPTER XI

Albania

ALBANIA IS a mountain country with an area of 11,000 square miles, less than one-tenth of the size of the British Isles. It has a population of 1,100,000, of whom, in 1944, 730,000 were Muslims, 220,000 members of the Orthodox Church and 124,000 Catholics.

On Good Friday, 7th April, 1939, Italian fascist troops invaded the country, drove out the King and annexed it. From Albanian territory Mussolini launched his disastrous and humiliating campaign against Greece in October 1940. When the Germans came to the aid of their Italian ally in the Balkans, they occupied Albania.

Against both Italians and Germans, Albanian Partisans, living in the inaccessible mountain districts, conducted a ceaseless warfare. By far the largest of the Partisan organisation was that organised by the Communists, so it was not surprising that as the Partisan Army, under the leadership of Brigadier E. F. Davies, chief of the British Military Mission which landed in Albania in April 1943, pushed back the Germans, and captured Tirana, the capital, on 18th November, 1944, the Communists should claim and acquire a dominant position.

Indeed, as early as 8th September, 1943, a predominantly Communist Congress had placed at the head of a National Anti-Fascist Committee of Liberation their own leader, Enver Hoxa. In October 1944, as the capture of Tirana became imminent, the Committee transformed itself into a Provisional Government and issued a declaration that guaranteed freedom of the Press, of association and of religion. Soon after the Provisional Government set itself up in Tirana, however, the real intentions of the Communists began to emerge. On 11th January, 1945, the People's Republic of Albania was declared, and from that moment the persecution of the Catholic Church began.

Now, although the Catholics in Albania represented little more than 10 per cent of the population, for many years they had wielded a powerful influence in the cultural life of the country.

They had pioneered schools, hospitals, orphanages, charitable institutions and printing-presses, and were looked upon with affection by both Muslims and Orthodox. All these activities were under the direction of a hierarchy which was composed of two Archbishops and four Bishops, all of Albanian nationality, in northern Albania, while southern Albania constituted a single circumscription under an Apostolic Delegate.

Franciscans, Jesuits and the Society of Don Orione, together with Sisters of the Holy Stigmata and of Charity of Brescia, Servite nuns and Salesian nuns, numbering more than 240 in all, worked for the Faith in northern Albania, while the south was served by six Albanian secular priests and seven Conventuals, of whom four were Basilians and two Lazarists, together with seventy nuns and fifteen Basilian Sisters of the Oriental Rite. Taken all in all, these Religious were roughly 50 per cent Albanian and 50 per cent Italian. It was against these men and women, their Faith and their work, that the destructive forces of Communism were set in motion, operating in such fashion that in the history of this modern persecution of the Church in Europe no greater brutality can be found than in the persecution of the Albanian Catholic Church.

The first measures against the Church were taken within a month of the capture of Tirana by the Partisans. By an arbitrary act, on the grounds of "public necessity", the Communists seized the entire Catholic Press. Within a few days of this happening, Catholic Action groups were attacked, many of their members being arrested, beaten and imprisoned, on the excuse that they were fascist societies. On 15th December an armed search of the Pontifical seminary and the Jesuit House at Scutari was carried out, and several secular priests were arrested. These searches were to be increased in number and intensity in the coming weeks, so much so that on 2nd February, 1945, the Jesuit House at Scutari was searched for the sixteenth time. The building was surrounded by soldiers armed with machine-guns, and while the Religious and students were locked in the refectory, for six hours the searchers ransacked the whole building, staving in ceilings and floors and destroying valuable possessions.

The object of these searches, which were made also at the Franciscan House, the Archbishop's Palace and at the Apostolic Delegation, as well as a Mantilate convent, was to discover alleged caches of arms. The public mind had been prepared for them by an intense propaganda campaign in which caricatures and faked photographs played a prominent rôle. These caricatures and photographs depicted confessionals crammed with rifles and machine-guns, altars covered with arms and statues of Saints filled with dangerous documents and plans.

By the middle of March the prisons of Scutari were already accommodating 1,000 prisoners arrested as a result of the searches, and at the end of the month a People's Court pronounced the first sentences of death. Father Lazarus Shantoja, accused of being Italophile, was tortured, then hanged; Father Andrew Zadeja, considered the greatest Albanian poet of modern times, accused of supporting the National Front Party during the Italian and German occupations, was hanged; Father Anthony Harapj, a former member of the Regency Council, was shot on 7th April; and Father John Shallaku, accused of having helped to form a party opposed to the Communist régime, was shot on 13th April.

During March and April measures were put into effect which, in the space of two months, completely destroyed every facet of Catholic life in southern Albania. The Sisters of the Holy Stigmata at Korcia, were dismissed from their orphanage and kindergarten, and turned out of their House. The Sisters of Charity of Brescia were turned out of their hospital, and, because they were Italians, deported to Italy. The kindergarten of the Servite Sisters at Elbasan was closed and the Sisters chased from the town. At Berat the church was closed and the Houses of the Sisters and missionaries confiscated. All kindergartens, workshops and nuns' Houses everywhere else were taken over, and the six secular priests, who were all Albanians, were expelled from southern Albania, while the seven Conventuals were arrested and repatriated. In no other country was a Church serving such a vast area as southern Albania completely destroyed in so short a time.

Monsignor Nigris, the Apostolic Delegate, protested to Hoxa, by letter and in person, against every outrage committed. Hoxa merely ignored his protests. At the end of March, Monsignor Nigris decided to visit Rome to ask for help for the suffering population and was assured before his departure that he would be allowed to return. Hoxa even asked that the Delegate should convey his personal respects to the Pope and suggest that the Holy See should accredit a representative to the Albanian Government.

On 24th May, Monsignor Nigris returned to Tirana, but immediately he stepped from the aircraft he was placed in a room at the airport, where he was kept for seven hours, and then, without any farewells, put on an aircraft and returned to Rome, expelled as undesirable by the order of the Government.

In May all kindergartens conducted by nuns in northern Albania were closed. In private schools all Catholic teachers were replaced by State teachers. In June all private elementary schools were closed or taken over by the State. For a time the Catholic high schools escaped because there was a shortage of teachers necessary for taking them over, but sections of the Anti-Fascist Albanian Youth Front were forcibly introduced into them, and special State teachers had to be allowed to give political lectures.

With the property of the Church confiscated and the work of the Church—with the exception of the ministry—brought practically to a standstill, the Government at once turned its attention to the elimination of the clergy. This process was begun in January 1946 with the arrest of the Rector of the Pontifical seminary at Scutari and the Vice-Provincial of the Jesuits, on charges of distributing anti-Government propaganda leaflets. With them were charged also a Franciscan brother and six students. Their trial lasted almost a month, and sentences were announced on 22nd February. The Rector, the Vice-Provincial, the Franciscan and two students were condemned to death, three students sent to life imprisonment and the other to ten years' forced labour. The death sentences were carried out at the same time as those passed on ten eminent Catholic laymen from Scutari on 4th March, and the bodies were left lying all day in the rain where they fell.

In January also all Italian Religious were deported at twenty-four hours' notice. No help was given them to reach Durazzo, where they were ordered to report. Having arrived there, they were kept a month and then put on a ship for Italy. Of all the Italian Religious in Albania in 1944, only the Sisters of Charity of Brescia, who worked in the hospitals, now remained, and they only because other staff could not be found to replace them.

With the removal of all the Italians, Government attention was next turned to the clergy of Albanian nationality, who had so far escaped imprisonment. Between March and December 1946 this campaign was conducted in the most ferocious fashion, and as a result thirty-two priests and Religious were imprisoned and fifteen priests and Religious killed.

In April 1947 the Government staged their last official trial of the clergy. The victims were prominent priests, and the trial was conducted in the grand manner. The charges included spying for the Vatican and foreign Powers and sabotage of the Government's reconstruction scheme. When the sentences were announced, Father Stephen Curti received twenty years' imprisonment, Father Meshkalla fifteen years, and Monsignor Bonati and Father Roch Oboti five years each. After this trial the clergy were eliminated without any pretence of legal process on the part of the Government.

With the clergy thus seriously undermined, in February and March 1948 steps were taken to liquidate the Albanian episcopate. The Archbishop of Durazzo, who had become head of the Church on the death of the Archbishop of Scutari in 1946, was imprisoned and after torture sentenced to thirty years' forced labour. He died in prison in August 1952. The next to be arrested was the Bishop of Shappa, who, without trial, was terribly tortured and shot on 3rd February. Next was Monsignor Gijni, who had directed the Apostolic Delegation after the expulsion of Monsignor Nigris. Originally arrested in November 1947, and held in a cell of little more than a square metre in area, so that he could not lie or stand, he was released at the beginning of December. Re-arrested at the beginning of March 1948, he was shot without trial, with eighteen others, on 11th March, 1948.

With the death of Monsignor Gijni, now only the eighty-year-old Bishop of Pulati survived, and he was held under house arrest in his palace in the mountains in the extreme north of Albania. Left without leaders, the surviving clergy elected Vicars-Capitular, who were at once arrested and imprisoned.

By the end of 1948 the Government might fairly have claimed to have achieved their object. With its hierarchy non-existent, with more than half of its priests and Religious dead or in prison or deported, the Church was a poor shadow of its former strength, and one wonders what the Government had to fear. The fact remains, however, that it was not content until it had completely subjected all the remnants, to do which it resorted to an expediency with which we shall become familiar in later pages, though here it had a slight variation from the norm.

In December 1949, following the example of Rumania and Bulgaria, the Government issued a decree requiring all religious denominations to draw up statutes for the approval of the Ministry of Internal Affairs. Where they found the courage and the strength is certain, but it is nevertheless a matter for wonder that the crushed and tortured remnants of the Church held out for nearly two years against this decree. Eventually, in order to have their way, the Government had to resort to extortion and fraud. Two of the supposed signatories of the statutes had already been dead for two years when the Government claimed they had signed, while another ten had been in prison for some time.

Now, these statutes had been drawn up by the Government, and besides purporting to be the statutes of the Catholic Church, they, in fact, created a new Church called the National Catholic Church of Albania. The National Catholic Church of Albania was deprived of all independence: of dependence on the Pope in its organisation, economics and policies; of the right to make appointments without the approval of the Government; and of issuing Pastoral Letters without prior submission to Government censorship. All clergy were required to take an oath of loyalty to the State, and undertake, as one of their chief duties, to "promote among the Faithful, sentiments of loyalty towards the people's authority and the People's Republic of Albania, love of the Fatherland, the cause of peace and of national prosperity". In effect, the National Catholic Church of Albania was permitted to function only as the State wished, and for so long as the State wished, and was required to support the activities of the State, no matter how those activities might clash with the religious and ethical standards of the Church.

It is under these conditions that the Catholic Church in Albania lives and works today. Its true and traditional work has been brought almost to a standstill by the necessity to adhere to the conditions laid down in the statutes. For the last three or four years very little news has come out of Albania concerning the state of the Church. It is known, however, that although the statutes provided for two archbishops and four bishops, there is now only one Titular Bishop in the whole country. If this is an indication of how the statutes are being observed, it is to be feared that the Church in Albania is still suffering the full weight of Communist persecution.

CHAPTER XII
The German People's Republic

FOR A proper understanding of the situation of the Catholic Church in the German People's Republic, it is necessary to consider briefly the territory which it involves and the people, and to have some knowledge of its conception and birth.

As the defeat of Nazi Germany became more and more imminent, so that even the German people themselves could see that the end was not far off, despite the orders of the authorities that the population must stay where it was, so as not to impede the operations of the military, a great movement of the people began. This movement was chiefly from the east towards the west. The Allies had made known in advance that they intended to divide conquered Germany into four zones, each of which would be controlled by one of the Great Four Powers. Fear of Russian reprisals and of Communism sent hundreds of thousands of Germans hurrying from the eastern territories of the Reich to the west, where they knew they would receive humane treatment, despite the fact that they were defeated enemies.

In addition to this, Article 13 of the Potsdam Agreement provided for yet another movement of population on a vast scale. By the Potsdam Agreement the German Territories east of the Oder–Neisse line were transferred to Poland, and Article 13 arranged for millions of Germans living in these territories to be moved, whether they wished it or not, to German territory west of the line. The same Article provided for similar treatment of Germans living in Hungary and Czecho-Slovakia. Altogether, thirteen million Germans were involved, ten million of whom were distributed between the three Western Zones, and the remaining three million settled in the Soviet Zone.

This redistribution was carried out mostly without any pre-arranged plan, and in consequence the whole balance of the religious basis of Germany was upset. Places which previously had predominantly Catholic populations now found themselves predominantly Protestant, and vice versa. As will be appreciated, this tended to throw entirely out of gear the whole organisation of the Churches. It placed upon the Catholic Church an extraordinary burden in times when the burden upon the Church was already severe as a result of the terrible conditions brought about by the almost total disintegration of a great nation. This must be borne always in mind when the position of the Catholic Church in what is now the German People's Republic is considered.

The Western Allies had agreed at Potsdam that though Germany was to be divided into four separate zones, each of which was to be controlled by one of the Powers who should administer it according to its own conception of what was best, nevertheless the administration in all four zones was to be based on democratic principles. Stalin agreed to this, but the Western Allies completely overlooked the fact that the word "democratic" has an entirely different interpretation for them from the interpretation put upon it by the Communists. How this point came to be overlooked is one of the several mysteries attaching to the Potsdam meeting.

It soon became evident that the Soviet Union was intent upon controlling her zone in her own way, and upon principles very different from those the Western Allies proposed to use for their guidance in their zones. This being so, it emerged also that the Soviet Union did not intend to follow the general administrative policy worked out by the great Powers. Indeed, it is doubtful whether they could have done so in view of the difference in interpretation and outlook.

As soon as the Western Allies realised what was happening they united their three zones into one overall unit, which they called the German Federal Republic, with its capital at Bonn. The Russian retorted by transforming their zone into the German Democratic Republic. This happened in 1949.

Under the Military Administration the Russians had permitted the formation of four political parties: the German Communist Party, the German Social-Democratic Party, the Christian Democrat Party and the Liberal Democrat Party. But even before the first elections these were reduced to three by the merger of the Communists and Social-Democrats into the United Socialist Party.

At the 1946 general elections the United Socialists were permitted to present their lists in all the 11,623 districts of the zone, whereas the Christian-Democrats were allowed to present theirs only in 1,182 districts, and the Liberal-Democrats in only 2,082. In spite of this the United Socialists polled only 52·4 per cent of the votes, to the other two parties' combined total of 39·9 per cent. The same picture emerged in the local and regional elections.

A German People's Council was set up for the purpose of drafting a new Constitution. In the elections to this Council the Communists allowed no opposition, and established themselves firmly in power at later elections in May 1949, when they and their fellow-travellers presented a single list of candidates.

On 5th October, 1949, the Russian Military Administration transformed the German People's Council into the People's Parliament, and the creation of the German Democratic Republic was announced. Wilhelm Pieck, President of the United Socialists, was appointed Head of State, while Otto Grotewohl and Walter Ulbricht, both United Socialists, were appointed President and Vice-President of the Council, respectively, in a Provisional Government to which the Russians transferred the legislative and administrative functions of the new Republic.

The Constitution of the Republic, which was sanctioned by Moscow and approved by Parliament in May 1950, guaranteed personal liberty, inviolability of domicile, secrecy of the Post, freedom from censorship, free expression of thought, right of assembly, the recognition of Sundays and Holy Days as days of rest, the right of parents to choose their children's education, freedom of teaching, freedom of religion and conscience. It all looked very well, until one reached the phrase: "within the limits of the law in force for all", which in effect nullified the fundamental meaning of "right", putting in its place any interpretation which the State might wish to put on it.

Gradually the German Democratic Republic was brought more and more in line with all those Soviet satellite States which had a Communist régime. In every sphere it was required to be totally submissive to the wishes of Moscow. After yet more elections in October 1950, the process of Communisation was speeded up, for the results of the voting for a single list had resulted in a spectacular success for the régime, the United Socialists receiving 99·4 per cent of the votes, and in recent years the picture emerging has not been very different from that in the other satellite States.

Now, the fixing of the eastern frontier of the German Democratic Republic on the Oder–Neisse line has given to Poland large territories that formerly belonged to the Reich. This has meant that the organisation of the Catholic Church in the Democratic Republic has been seriously upset, for the greater part of the archdiocese of Breslau, the diocese of Ermland and the prelacy nullius of Schneidemühl are within the Polish frontiers. In the diocese of Berlin the strange situation has arisen of the Bishop living in the western sector of the city while the greater part of his diocese lies within the Russian sector and in the Democratic Republic. The remaining circumscriptions consist of the dioceses of Fulda, Wurtzburg and Osnabrück, the greater part of the archdiocese of Paderborn and a small part of the archdiocese of Breslau. Out of a population of 17,300,000, only 2,100,000 are Catholics.

From the moment that the Soviet Military Administration took over the Zone, Marxist–Leninist philosophies and ideological conceptions began to acquire a dominant position in all aspects of life. This process was naturally continued by the Provisional Government and subsequently by the Government of the Democratic Republic. At first the economic and political disorder which followed the unconditional surrender of the Nazis occupied the attention of the authorities too exclusively for them to dissipate their energies in pursuing anti-religious policies in a practical way, and so led to a kind of truce. This period of truce was equally welcome to the Church, for the Church throughout all Germany had been so disorganised, first by the Nazi persecution and then by the disruption of life in all its aspects during the closing phases of hostilities and the immediate post-war months, that the whole edifice had to be rebuilt almost from the foundations.

But as soon as the political and economic life of the Democratic Republic began to be stabilised, the Government began to take active measures to impede the work and ministry of the Church. Beginning in May 1946, a series of decrees were directed to the limitation and curtailment of the influence of the Church. The first of these decrees dealt with religious instruction, and are now familiar to us. On 31st May all religious teaching had to be omitted from the curriculum of all State schools; if religious instruction was given at all, it had to be outside school hours.

At the same time the teaching of atheistic materialism was made compulsory. In conjunction with these measures aimed at withdrawing the youth of the country from religious influences, official Communist youth organisations—the Free German Youth and Pioneer Youth—were founded with the object of taking the young outside home and family influence. Much was done to make religious observance among the Faithful difficult. Political meetings, for example, were timed to coincide with the celebration of Church services and ceremonies, and as failure to attend political meetings could result in heavy sanctions being placed upon the absentees, it became difficult for the Faithful to attend church at these times. Secular Party festivities were organised on the great feast days of the Church in competition with Church festivities. The Church was excluded from all activity that was not strictly religious. Finally, pressure was brought to bear on the clergy, particularly in regard to their economic situation, in order to coerce them into giving their support to Communist teachings.

When the hierarchy attacked and condemned these measures, they were accused of meddling in politics or of being hostile towards the people. The situation became so serious, however, that on 29th December, 1949, the Catholic Bishop of Berlin, Cardinal von Preysing, sent a letter to the Vice-President of the Council of Ministers deploring all that had happened. In spite of the guarantees given in the Constitution, the Cardinal said, freedom of religion and liberty of conscience did not in reality exist, and the exercise of religion was obstructed in every conceivable way. The Vice-President replied that because the letter raised serious problems, Parliament would be consulted before an answer was given; but when this reply had not been received four months later, and even more restrictive measures had been imposed, his Eminence wrote again, this time to Herr Grotewold, President of the Council. There was no ambiguity in the language of this courageous letter, which was reminiscent of several of the communications made by Cardinal van Roey, the Belgian Primate, to General von Falkenhausen during the War.

"I wish to point out," the Cardinal wrote, "some facts and conditions that constitute a true oppression of the Christian conscience. At the same time I wish to make certain demands in connection with the situation and which, should they not be taken into consideration, would go to prove that one cannot speak of liberty of religion and of conscience in the Republic."

He then went on to attack materialism which he called "the exclusive Weltanschauung professed by the State: it is the exclusive religion of the State, to which, both in theory and in practice all activities of the nation are subject". In schools, universities, youth organisations, in fact, everywhere "only the materialist outlook on life and on the world is tolerated in the education of individuals". This was an inadmissible state of affairs for Christians, and to withdraw them from it he demanded, first, that materialism should cease to be the exclusive State Weltanschauung, second, that instruction given in schools which pupils were compelled to attend should cease to follow anti-Christian principles, and third, that children and adolescents should not be compelled to join the Young Pioneers and Free German Youth.

On 1st July, 1949, an ordinance had been published which required the Church to give notice of meetings well in advance and granted to the police powers to ban or control such meetings as they deemed necessary. This, the Cardinal said, was only one manifestation of the way in which the State was seeking to limit all religious activity to the performance of liturgical rites. Such restrictions struck at the liberty of religion, and since it was the announced aim of materialism to use these means, and others, to liquidate religion, the Cardinal demanded that all attempts to limit religion to acts of worship in consecrated buildings should cease, and that Christians should be given the unrestricted right to pursue those aims which were according to their conscience, especially with regard to work among youth organisations, charitable works and religious instruction.

The Cardinal then attacked the intensity of, and methods being used in, the propaganda campaign to force dialectic materialism upon the people, and the compulsion used to get adults to join organisations and to attend meetings, whose spirit and methods were irreconcilable with Christian conscience. This propaganda and compulsion should cease, and neither the family life nor social position of any man should be endangered by his refusal to join such organisations or attend such meetings.

Materialism, the Cardinal continued, enjoyed a complete monopoly of expression and dissemination. The Church had been deprived of every single periodical, so that it could not present its

arguments against materialism. In addition, the police had intervened to prevent the distribution of Catholic literature coming
into the country from abroad. This also struck at freedom of
religion and conscience, to safeguard which the Cardinal demanded that the Church be allowed to publish periodicals enjoy-
ing the "freedom of the Press", so that it might be able to defend
itself; and that literature published outside the Republic should be
permitted to be distributed "without the police or a one-sided
censorship intervening in a despotic manner".

"Finally, I wish to point out that the rape of Christian consciences is becoming more and more frequent in the German
Democratic Republic. The discontent resulting from this de facto
situation is increasing. The demands presented by me in this
document are not privileges, but are founded on the Potsdam
Agreement and on the Constitution of the German Democratic
Republic. Considering the seriousness of the situation and the
importance of my statement I dare to hope for a speedy and clear
reply."

No speedy reply from the Government was forthcoming,
whereupon the Cardinal issued a pamphlet to the public entitled
*Is there Freedom of Religion and Conscience in the German Demo-
cratic Republic?* This compelled the Government to reply, and on
14th May, 1950, at the Third Congress of the United Socialist
Party, the following resolution was passed:

"The Constitution of the German Democratic Republic
guarantees full liberty of religion. The greater part of the Faithful
is even enrolled in the democratic organisations and parties within
which, together with hundreds of priests, they fight in the
National Front for the peace and unity of Germany. However,
the Heads of the Churches have paved the way for a reactionary
struggle against the peace and democratic order of the German
Democratic Republic by putting forward arguments not of a
nature to serve the best interests of the Church, but rather tending
to upset the existing political order. While claiming for themselves liberty of teaching in the theological faculties, they desire to
forbid the same liberty to dialectical materialism. They take
disciplinary measures against priests who join the National
Front, but have no objections if, from the pulpit, someone utters
reactionary propaganda. They protest because youth as a whole
is turning towards the National Front, and they would like to

refuse it the free exercise of its civic rights guaranteed by the Constitution. This had happened, because, up to the present we have not paid much attention to them, and have given only small encouragement to the activity of progressive priests. Hundreds of priests have taken sides with the people; we must help them."

The reference to priests joining the National Front—though the numbers were exaggerated—gives point to a situation which was unfortunately developing. The Government, as we have seen, tried in every way to make the work and even the personal life of the clergy extremely difficult, having in view a single object which they were attempting, by these means, to achieve with a two-pronged attack. The difficulties with which the priests were confronted were designed to make their work ineffective, if not quite impossible; and the simultaneous offer of privileges to those priests who became members of the National Front, was designed to split the clergy. Economic pressures, physical violence and imprisonment, though not on such a scale as in other satellite countries in similar circumstances, were the means used for coercion, and unfortunately there were a number of priests who retreated into compliant co-operation. These were the progressive priests.

The Cardinal's courageous protest had no effect upon the situation, and between 1950 and 1952 relations between Church and State deteriorated rapidly, and from mid-1952 the position of the Church became more and more serious. The anti-religious propaganda campaign was maintained with great intensity, its object being to drive a wider wedge between the Church and the people. The theme of the propaganda was that the hierarchy was under the influence of the Western Powers and was constantly trying to separate the people from the Government by constant criticism of the latter.

Government and Party leaders added their voices to the propaganda churned out by the Party Press. President Pieck, at the inauguration of the Republic of Young Pioneers, said in his speech: "There is no doubt that they, the Church dignitaries, thus fight against the national interest of the people and push them in the direction of new wars." And Prime Minister Grotewohl, after a meeting of the Berlin Curia had declared that the tension between Church and State was due to the restrictions imposed by the State on the clergy and Faithful, said at a Press conference: "Clergy taking part in the struggle for peace and in the National Front fear the reactions of the Church. Exercise of religion is guaranteed by the Constitution. . . . If an ecclesiastic should be hindered in the free exercise of his civic rights and duties, he will be protected by the Government." Government spokesmen also made it quite clear that the Church could not expect any relaxation of the special laws in force, such as that dealing with the notification of the police of public meetings organised by the Church, and that concerning religious instruction, nor could the Church be granted special facilities for communicating between Berlin and the Eastern Sector. The restrictions on the free communication between Berlin and the Republic particularly hampered the movement of the Bishop of Berlin between his residence in the Western Sector and his diocese in the Eastern Sector and the Republic. It was made practically impossible for him to visit outside the city boundaries, and very often Confirmations had to be abandoned at the last moment because the official decision was delayed as long as possible, and then pronounced to be negative.

In 1953 even more restrictive measures were introduced. The authorities announced that they would no longer collect the taxes from which the subsidies for the Churches were provided, with the result that the Church was made responsible for providing all the money which was required. This was followed by the confiscation of all Church property, the particular owners of which—Orders, Congregations, charitable institutions and associations, for example—had their headquarters outside the Republic. Through this measure the Church lost eleven buildings in Berlin alone, among them being a hospital, an orphanage and a kindergarten. The nuns were expelled from the kindergarten at Bad-Saarow, which was owned by the great Catholic organisation *Caritas* and run by the Sisters of St Hedwig. The State took over the teaching and its administrative management. Catholic youth associations were subjected to all manner of persecution in an attempt to bring about their dissolution. Paper was withheld from those Catholic publications still permitted to publish, so that the circulation had to be drastically reduced, and all kinds of restrictions were placed on distribution. The relief work of Caritas was made exceedingly difficult by restrictions on the distribution of parcels and other assistance. A campaign of revilement was launched against the clergy, who were arrested on such charges as the distribution of forbidden literature, the ill-treatment of children, encouragement to commit acts of sabotage, and more and more were imprisoned for long periods.

Then suddenly the German workers could no longer support the conditions of life to which they had been reduced by the Government, which claimed to do everything for their welfare and protection, and on 17th June, 1953, they revolted against the reign of terror. When calm was restored, the surprised and frightened Government, as a part of the appeasement policy they found themselves bound to adopt, called upon the Church leaders to meet them to discuss a *modus vivendi*. Agreement was reached on 10th July, and resulted in a number of the restrictions being abolished, among them those on religious instruction, care of the sick and prisoners, and the collection and dissemination of information through the Press.

For the remainder of 1953 and throughout 1954 the improvement was maintained, though the Communist leaders lost no opportunity to preach dialectic materialism and to urge German youth to accept it. Then in 1955 the Government suddenly returned to its former policies. Religious instruction in schools was again prohibited, renewed efforts were made to attract the young people to atheism, pressure was exerted on the clergy and Press to make them support Government policies, and a move was begun for the creation of a National Catholic Church separated from Rome.

Now, to assist them in inculcating the youth of the nation with the Communist ideology, the Party had instituted a yearly ceremony which they called *Jugendweihe*, the Dedication of Youth, and which they defined as "a solemn ceremony marking the passage of youths to adult life". Before being so initiated, all young Democratic Germans had to undergo a course of twenty lessons, in which such subjects as the origin of life (Darwinism), and human society and woman's place in it, were studied. This Jugendweihe was condemned by Protestant and Catholic leaders alike.

In November 1954 all the propaganda organs of the Democratic Republic announced that in the spring of 1955 the ceremony of Jugendweihe would again be held, only this time it would be celebrated far more extensively than ever before, in fact, on a nation-wide scale compared with previous efforts, which had been confined to large towns. The Churches protested at once, only to have their protests completely ignored, and in February the preparatory course was begun. All boys of fourteen who were intending to leave the elementary schools at the end of the academic year were required to be Dedicated.

On 6th March, the Bishop of Berlin, Monsignor Weskamm, who had been appointed to the See on the death of Cardinal von Preysing, issued a Pastoral Letter which was read from all the pulpits of his diocese on that day. The Jugendweihe, the Bishop declared, was contrary to all Christian teaching, and those who took part in it would *ipso facto* be denying the Faith. He protested most vigorously against the pressure that was being brought to bear on the pupils who, with their parents, feared that refusal to take part in Jugendweihe would result in their automatic failure in their school-leaving examinations, in which fear they were fully justified, knowing the methods which the Communists used. Parents were afraid that they would lose jobs and livelihood if their children did not attend the Jugendweihe.

The leaders of the Protestant Church, under Dr Dibelius, Bishop of Berlin, took an equally fearless stand, with the result that large numbers of boys fled to the West rather than undergo Jugendweihe, and thus frustrated the Communists' great hopes. Angry, but not discouraged, they announced an even bigger and better Jugendweihe for 1956, and began their preparations earlier, increasing the course of instruction to almost double the number of lessons.

The chief plan of the Communists was now to attack the Church through the youth, and they concentrated on making religious observance extremely difficult. This they did in a number of ways: by organising activities to coincide with the hours of Mass, for example, by opening youth centres only on Sundays, and by planning drives by militant Communist youth among their school-fellows, and so on.

In the German Democratic Republic, as elsewhere, the Communists, while maintaining all manner of pressures on the Church in all aspects of its life, seems, however, to be relying on time as their greatest ally in the struggle. Unfortunately, they may have some justification for hopes of eventual success. The grave difficulties which their restrictions on the Church create in the secular aspects of life, add to the already heavy burden which economic and other restrictions impose upon individuals. Faith must be uncommonly strong to resist all these pressures, and when Faith cannot be inculcated in youth from childhood to the exclusion of all other ideologies, it can be understood if youth takes the easier road of compliance. Sacrifices to make a firm stand lose much of their meaning without the backing of an unquestioning belief in Christianity, and compared with the Communists the Catholic Faithful are a mere handful. The future of the Church in East Germany will not be easy; apart from this, it is impossible to say anything with certitude.

CHAPTER XIII

Hungary

DESPITE ADHERENCE to the Berlin–Rome Axis and the Anti-Comintern Pact, the rulers of Hungary were able to maintain the neutrality of the country for almost the first two years of the War. In June 1941, however, under German pressure, Horthy and his Government declared war on Russia. It was an act the Russians were never to forget.

In August 1944 the Russians entered Hungary. Horthy fled to Germany; the Hungarian Commander-in-Chief went over to the Russians. A Provisional Government was set up in Russian-occupied Hungary, which declared war on the Germans in December. Before Christmas, Budapest was surrounded by the Russians, and by mid-April 1945 the last of the Germans had been driven out of the country.

In the previous month the Provisional Government had introduced sweeping reforms. In 1938, despite previous reforms, land owned by 1,200,000 peasants amounted to 950,000 acres, while thirty-six great landowners together owned more than a million acres. All land now belonged to the State.

On 4th November, 1945, general elections were held under a new law which provided for universal, secret and equal suffrage for men and women. In these elections the Smallholders Party gained 245 seats, the Communists 70, the Socialists 69 and other parties 25. By the wish of the Allies, however, a coalition Government was formed, in which the dominant party held seven portfolios, the Communists three, the Socialists three and the Agrarian Party one.

Though they were the vastly stronger party in the Government, the Smallholders were unable to make the normal use of their power, and the political life of Hungary consisted of a series of manufactured crises, with the Communists manœuvring all the time for more and more power, in which they were aided by the fact that one of their three portfolios was the outstandingly important Ministry of the Interior, and no less by the support of the High Command of the Soviet occupation forces. During the winter of 1946–47, the Ministry of the Interior arrested some 300 army officers and members of the Smallholders Party, alleging that they were conspiring against the State. On 25th February, 1947, Bela Kovacs, Secretary-General of the Smallholders Party, was arrested by the Russians on a charge of acting against the occupation forces and for participating in the alleged conspiracy.

Towards the end of February several of those arrested were brought to trial, and after a hearing lasting seven weeks, three were sentenced to death, and the others to long terms of imprisonment. British and American Notes were presented asking that a tripartite inquiry should be held into the arrest of Kovacs. The request was rejected by the Russians.

Yet another crisis was precipitated in May, by the refusal of Prime Minister Ferencz Nagy, who was on holiday in Switzerland, to return to Hungary. A new Government was therefore formed, one of whose first acts was to introduce a new electoral law, and a second general election was set for 31st August. In February a peace treaty had been drawn up and signed by the Allies and Hungary. It was due to come into force at midnight on 15th/16th September, and since under it the Russian occupation forces would have to leave the country, the motive underlying the manipulations of the Communists was to make certain that before the Russians withdrew a Government should be in control that was willing to respond to the wishes of the Russian puppeteers.

In the 1945 elections the formation of a Catholic Party and several other parties had been forbidden. For the 1947 elections many different opposition parties were authorised. This was a wily Communist tactic as the results of the elections showed. The coalition parties gained 60 per cent of the votes, and the opposition parties 40 per cent. The Communists gained only 22 per cent, but this was the largest percentage won by any single party, and so gave them control.

Now, although the peace treaty had provided for the cessation of Russian occupation, it did, however, permit the Russians to keep fairly large numbers of troops in Hungary in order to facilitate their occupation of Austria. Thus, the Hungarian Communists had for their support, as they set about consolidating their régime, quite a strong sympathetic force. From 31st August, 1947, the Communists in Hungary never looked back; and from this day the persecution of the Catholic Church in Hungary began to be intensified.

The Catholic history of Hungary goes back for a thousand years. The first King of Hungary was Stephen, the son of Duke Geysa, and his Christian Duchess, who had brought up her son in her Faith. From the moment that he knew he was to succeed his father, Stephen was determined that his people should be converted to the new religion. He was recognised as monarch by the Pope, who granted him the title of Apostolic King, which title all the rulers of Hungary—except the Regent—bore until the country was declared a Republic. Stephen was successful in his mission, and forty-five years after his death he was canonised. From his time Hungary has always been a predominantly Catholic country. In 1945, out of a population of ten millions, seven millions were Catholics.

Since the Faith had been introduced by the King, the Church had from the earliest times been very richly endowed. Though the vast patrimony which St Stephen had bestowed upon it had been progressively reduced over the centuries, in 1945 the Church still owned large estates, with the income of which it carried on its great and important social and cultural works. On education alone it spent six million dollars a year in the upkeep of 3,344 schools of all kinds, that is, 45 per cent of all the schools in the country. Its works of charity were tremendous in scope; its Press rivalled the secularly owned Press; its influence on the social life of the country through its many societies, associations and movements, enormous. The Catholic Church, in fact, leavened the whole life of the nation.

We have said that from 31st August, 1947, the persecution of the Catholic Church was intensified. It will be recalled that as soon as Soviet Russia had occupied a part of the country, a Provisional Government had been set up at Debrecen. This Government promised respect for religion and the inviolability of private property, among other guarantees that it gave. While the struggle against the Germans was still raging, the Russians were more than willing to show respect for the Church, and the Hungarian Communists, for their part, showed themselves only too anxious to ingratiate themselves. Very often members of the Party would offer their services to the priests of their parish to help in rebuilding or repairing damaged Church property. For this work they refused all payment, asking only for a written expression of thanks for their generosity; which was at once prominently displayed in the newspapers. Many Party members also applied for membership of Catholic organisations and attempted to have themselves elected to parish councils.

One of the first acts of the Provisional Government, long before the whole country was cleared of Germans, was to introduce a measure of agrarian reform. Though it could be only partial in its scope, Church estates were nevertheless involved in it. But whenever a parish could prove distress on this account, land was allotted to it. As in Belgium and many other Nazi-occupied countries, so also in Hungary, the Germans had confiscated the church bells. Such bells as had escaped the melting-pot and were still in the country were returned to the churches by the Provisional Government.

All this ostensible friendship, however, was merely part of a plan to lull the Church, for the time being, into a sense of false security. It did not last long.

On 4th April, 1945, Russian occupation officials called at the Nunciature and served an expulsion order on the Apostolic Nuncio, who had participated in the siege of Budapest, and by his intervention had saved thousands of Hungarian Jews from extermination by the Nazis. Not long afterwards new and much wider agrarian reforms were introduced, which resulted in the Church being deprived of the greater part of its estates. Following close on this, a decree was published to regulate the supply of news-print and all other paper by a so-called rationing scheme, which reduced the Catholic newspapers and journals to a very small percentage of their monthly circulation of a million and a half copies, while at the same time the Communist newspapers received all and more than they needed. In the summer of 1945 new laws relating to marriage were introduced, requiring all couples to be joined in a civil ceremony, and laws facilitating divorce were brought into force. In July the Communists began to emerge into the open with the organisation of discussions against religion throughout the country and attacks on the Church in the Press. As an example of these attacks, a manifesto, published by the so-called Hungarian Democratic Youth, described St Stephen as "a criminal blinded by incense, who created the thousand-years-old system which has sullied our history in a loathsome way".

While this was going on, preparations were in progress for the general elections, fixed for 4th November. On 1st November the Primate of Hungary, Cardinal Mindszenty, Archbishop of Esztergom, addressed a special Pastoral Letter to the Faithful. After stating that the Church had nothing but goodwill towards the rising democracy in Hungary, he continued: "We must regret that the matrimonial bond has been weakened by the Provisional Government, which in our opinion had not the right so to act and by doing so has contravened the will of the people. . . . With regard to the redistribution of land, it has been presented as a means of destroying a certain class among the citizens, and the agrarian law has been put forward as a penal measure. Is such a motive in conformity with justice and the natural law? We do not criticise the redistribution of land, but the spirit of vengeance which is displayed. Yet more terrible is the number of people who have been sent to prison for paltry reasons or through the abuse of power by provincial tyrants. For attempting to prevent the dissolution of a Catholic association in his village, a priest, who has been suffering from tuberculosis for many years, has been sentenced to forced labour; so has another for preaching on the Feast of St Stephen. The prefects of police have declared that priests who oppose the present régime will be deported to Siberia. . . . We appeal to you to vote only for those candidates who can be relied on to fight so that Hungary may be spared suffering, error and immorality."

The very large majority gained by the Smallholders Party in the elections—245 seats to all the other parties' combined total of 164—gave the initial impression that happier times might be ahead for Hungary. On account of their overall majority, the Smallholders claimed the all-important Ministry of the Interior, formerly held by the Communists in the Provisional Government, for one of its members. However, Marshal Voroshilov, who was president of the Control Commission set up by the Allies, vetoed this decision and insisted that the portfolio should be retained by the Communists, though they had only seventy seats.

The next step in the Communist plan of attack on the Church

was directed at the Catholic schools and Catholic Action organisations. The campaign was skilfully devised and executed. The Communists did not make a frontal attack, but prepared the ground for the eventual take-over by the State with a propaganda attack aimed at denigrating the Catholic schools. The schools, they said, neglected the children of the people and devoted themselves primarily to the children of the wealthy.

Cardinal Mindszenty counter-attacked at once. In a speech at Kalocsa in May 1946 he said: "There is a rumour in circulation that the Catholic schools, especially those directed by priests, concern themselves more with the children of the wealthy to the neglect of the children of the people. Again and again I have heard this charge in Budapest. When I arrived here, I asked for a list of all the children in Catholic institutions in this district, with the profession of the father noted against each child's name. From these lists I have gathered the following data. At the Jesuit College only forty per cent of the pupils belong to the well-to-do, in which I include minor officials; the remaining sixty per cent are the children of small tradesmen and workers. In the professional schools, thirty-five per cent belong to the wealthy classes, and sixty-five per cent to the workers. In the high schools and normal schools, seventeen and a half per cent are from wealthy families, and eighty-two and a half per cent are from workers' families. In the kindergartens 233 children have well-to-do parents, while the parents of 366 are workers. In the girls' normal schools 104 belong to wealthy families and 488 to workers' families. All this proves the contrary of that with which we are reproached."

The Communists also claimed that the State schools possessed much better equipment, while the teaching staffs were much more highly qualified. But in a plebiscite among parents a large majority declared their preference for the Catholic schools, and even Government inspectors had to admit that the claim about equipment was not true.

Losing ground rather than making it by this propaganda, the Communists went over to a new tack. Declaring the Catholic schools to be democratic, and therefore anti-Communist in bias, they began to circulate stories of "plots" against the Red Army being hatched in the Catholic Schools at many places, including Budapest and Esztergom, the diocesan capital of the Primate.

When these claims reached the Cardinal, he immediately sent a memorandum to the Government in which he asked for proofs, but the Government neither acknowledged nor replied to the memorandum.

With regard to the Catholic Action associations, leaders of Catholic Action were accused of hoarding, secretly, fascist newspapers and propaganda leaflets and even dumps of arms and ammunition. An eighteen-year-old youth, whose mother had been raped and killed by Russian soldiers in the early days of the occupation, killed a Russian soldier in revenge. The youth was a member of a Marian society, and at once the Communists declared the killing to be part of a plot. Twenty boys, aged between fifteen and eighteen, members of the local Marian Society, and Father Salesius Kiss, president of the Society, were arrested and Communist students in Budapest demonstrated, demanding the death penalty for Father Kiss and the dissolution of the Catholic associations.

Not long after this incident a Russian officer was killed outside a Budapest bar. A young member of the Catholic Young Peasants' Association was arrested and charged with the murder of the officer, and General Sviridor, commanding the occupation forces, complained to the Hungarian Ministry of Justice of a plot against the Soviet military forces. The Catholic associations were chiefly responsible for the plot, the General asserted, and he demanded their suppression by the Government.

The text of Sviridor's letter was released to the Press, who gave it the widest publicity, with the result that demonstrations were organised and other similar charges were trumped up against the Catholic associations. The pressure of the Communists became such that the Government was forced to issue a decree enabling the Communist-controlled Ministry of the Interior to suppress such of the associations as was deemed necessary from the Communist point of view. Under the decree, roughly 4,000 associations were dissolved, their property confiscated and many of the leaders arrested. Cardinal Mindszenty protested to the President of the Council immediately the decree was published and against the action taken by the Ministry of the Interior. "We must solemnly protest against the grave measures based merely on suspicion which have been taken against our associations and against some of their members," he wrote. "We cannot keep silent on this matter any more than on the propagandist publicity." But his protest was ignored and the militant Catholics were swept away.

The impression which these acts made not only on the Church, but on the great bulk of the nation, was extremely disturbing. The Government realised this, and in an attempt to calm public reaction, a proclamation was addressed to the clergy, to the exclusion of the Bishops, asking them to lend support to the maintenance of peaceful co-existence between the Hungarian people and the Russian occupation forces. "The Government of the Republic declares itself ready," the proclamation stated, "to guarantee the right of the Church in future, and to aid her in fulfilling her religious mission," the implication being—"in return for your support."

The fact that the proclamation was addressed to the lower clergy, and not to the hierarchy, showed that the Government was hoping to cause a split between the Bishops and the clergy. This was soon to become a definite policy, as also were the constant attempts to isolate the Primate from the Bishops by the circulation of rumours that Cardinal Mindszenty's attitude towards the Communists and the Government was not shared by his fellow prelates.

Within a few days of the proclamation being published the Cardinal sent another letter to the President of the Council. In it he refuted the charges made against the Church up to that time— August 1946. His Eminence concluded with these words: "So long as we continue to be the target for charges that lack all real proof, it is impossible for us to accede to the request made in the Government's appeal. But when reparation has been made for the outrages inflicted on the Church and when we have received an assurance that we shall be allowed the free exercise of our religious activity, then we shall be ready to accord our unreserved collaboration."

But throughout the remainder of 1946, and the beginning of 1947, the Communists continued with increasing vigour to bring about a split among the clergy. The attack on the Catholic schools was also intensified.

In this latter the Communists effected a change in their tactics. They were subtle and cunning in their moves. Through a number of the members of the Smallholders Party whom they had managed to bring under their influence, they demanded the abolition of compulsory religious instruction in the State schools. The Cardinal at once protested vigorously to the National Assembly, and large numbers of Catholic parents demonstrated their displeasure, with the result that the Government had to withdraw its motion.

The Communists seized on the failure of their plan to make propaganda against the Smallholders Party, but in doing so they cleverly came out on the side of the Church. Matyas Rakosi, Secretary of the Party, in a speech in the workers' quarter of Budapest on 9th May, 1947, said: "Free teaching of religion is an essential element of democracy, and as such is naturally approved and supported by the Communist Party." Then, after reproaching the Smallholders Party for stirring up trouble by bringing up the abolition of compulsory religious teaching in State schools, he went on: "In our view it is absolutely necessary to fix relations between the Church and the Democracy, and that this should be done as soon as possible, first by holding negotiations and then by making an agreement with the leaders of the Church."

If Rakosi were to be believed, what a topsy-turvy world the Communists were attempting to foist on the people of Hungary!

To console themselves for the failure of their plan, the Government introduced regulations curtailing the freedom of the Press. The permission of the Ministry of Information was required by all existing and all new newspapers, and no printed work might be published without similar permission. Though in theory Pastoral Letters were exempt from these regulations, in practice the regulations were applied, despite a strong protest from the Bishops. Simultaneously with this, the attack on the Catholic associations continued in full vigour, the great charitable institution Caritas (Karitasz) being the principal victim. Caritas, with the help of similar Catholic organisations in western Europe and America, had been able to bring great relief to the suffering population of Hungary in the distressing immediate post-war period.

Now, the background to these early events in 1947 was the arrest and trial of the army officers and members of the Small-holders Party, among them Bela Kovacs, Secretary-General of the S.P., and the refusal of Ferencz Nagy, the Prime Minister, to return to Hungary from holidaying in Switzerland. As a result of the "discovery" of these supposed plots against the Russian occupation forces, a list, known notoriously as List B, was compiled of those elements said to be dangerously "anti-democratic". The Communist Press now accused Caritas of helping people named on List B, asserting that the organisation was therefore behaving illegally. The Government at once intervened, ordering Caritas to hand over 80 per cent of all relief received from foreign sources to the Ministry of Social Welfare. The remaining 20 per cent it could distribute only through Communist-controlled local committees.

The result of this was naturally to halt the flow of foreign relief, and since it was practically impossible for funds or gifts in kind to be collected in Hungary, within a short time Caritas was forced into almost complete inactivity.

The pattern is now emerging. Up to August 1947 there were attacks on the schools, freedom of the Press was so restricted that the Catholic Press was forced out of existence, Catholic associations were dissolved, religious processions and the celebration of religious feast days forbidden, and an attempt made to split the clergy. However, the Communists had not been in full control, and the Church was still alive and active.

As has been said earlier, from the elections of 31st August, 1947, the Communists in Hungary never looked back. With all political opposition effectively removed, they rapidly consolidated their position, and only one obstacle—the Church—now blocked the complete Communisation of the country. The obstacle must be removed, and soon the Cardinal Primate was to be in constant, almost daily, conflict with the Government. But still Rakosi could declare: "We want everyone to know that we will in the future continue to be the defenders and supporters of liberty of conscience and of the true interests of the Church."

One of the first acts of the régime was an attempt to compel Catholics to join the Party. The Cardinal at once protested against this violation of democratic liberty and at the same time spoke strongly against "the spy system of the State Security Police, whose agents interrogate people, including priests, on trumped up charges. By means of threats these agents try to induce the accused to spy on the Bishops and on Catholic associations." But no protest was going to stop the Communists.

The first step, naturally, was directed towards separating the young from the influence of the Church. Caritas was forbidden in future to carry on with its child-welfare work, for which the State would become responsible. Once more the propaganda campaign against the "inferior conditions" in the Catholic schools was revived with greater violence, this time with the outspoken claim that nationalisation of all Catholic schools was the only answer. But though Catholic schools would be taken over by the State, it would be an administrative measure only. Religious instruction would still be obligatory.

The Communists realised, however, that if serious trouble was to be avoided, because of the predominance of Catholics in the population, they must so regulate matters that it appeared that nationalisation of the schools was the decision of the people. So meetings were held and petitions organised among teachers, professors, business employees and workers. Refusal to sign led to the suspension of teachers and professors, and to the dismissal of employees and workers.

A deputation of Bishops, who had been authorised by the Primate to discuss a *modus vivendi* between Church and State with Rakosi, now a vice-premier, had no success, since they demanded the restoration of the Catholic associations, the authorisation for at least one Catholic newspaper to be published and the Catholic schools to remain untouched. Thereupon, Cardinal Mindszenty, in the face of the intensified campaign against the schools, sent a memorandum to the Minister for Public Instruction. Couched in unambiguous terms, the Cardinal indicted the technique of persecution employed by the Communists against the Church.

In support of the Cardinal, many members of the Association of Catholic Parents protested to the Government. Public demonstrations of protest were also organised in many places, some of which unfortunately got out of hand. The police were ordered by the Government to prevent or disperse the demonstrations by any means, and many people were arrested.

So violent did the struggle become that on 4th June the Minister for Public Instruction wrote to the Cardinal asking him to put a stop to the fight against Hungarian "democracy". To this his Eminence replied that the Minister's implication that he was leading the fight was altogether gratuitous, and he went on to denounce those who endangered the peace of the country by bringing up so disquieting a subject and focusing public attention on it by every means.

The Government retorted with measures even more severe, and ordered school buildings to be occupied by the police. At the same time they blamed the hierarchy for the lack of progress in reaching a *modus vivendi* between Church and State. Then on 16th June, brooking no further delay, a bill for the nationalisation of all schools was placed before Parliament, and after a three-day debate became law by a majority of 230 votes to 63. The new law provided for the expropriation by the State of all private schools without compensation. Church control and supervision were restricted to the teaching of religion. So on 22nd June, when the law became operative, the Church in Hungary lost 3,163 schools and 177 colleges, with a total of 600,000 students.

How the public might react worried the Communists somewhat, and to soften the blow, Rakosi announced: "Religious instruction must continue to play its rôle in our schools even after nationalisation, in conformity with the religious sentiments of the Hungarian people." The Minister for Public Instruction in a similar announcement assured the people that compulsory religious instruction was to be taught "by the same teachers using the same texts for the same number of hours. We, therefore, guarantee to the Church the right to give religious instruction".

In yet another attempt to mollify the Church a little, the Government had proposed leaving to the control of the Church ten of the more historic Catholic schools; and that Religious should continue to teach in their former schools after nationalisation. In a joint Pastoral Letter on 16th July, 1948, the Bishops rejected both these proposals, tempting though they were, since "acceptance . . . would have meant the abandonment of all our principles".

Censorship of religious broadcasts was now introduced. The State was not satisfied that the Church should take up a neutral position in its broadcasts, but that it should lend moral support at least to the régime and all that it stood for. Cardinal Mindszenty would not countenance this, and eventually the Cardinal and Bishops decided to withdraw from religious broadcasting.

A campaign of interference with the celebration of public religious ceremonies was also begun. Processions and other religious manifestations were made as difficult as possible to carry out, and measures were often taken to prevent them altogether. The State railways, for example, withdrew reduced fares for people travelling in groups; buses and lorries were forbidden to carry pilgrims to the places of pilgrimage; quarantine regulations, which confined many of the Faithful to their homes, were promulgated.

And all the time that these insidious anti-Church campaigns were being conducted, no relaxation in the intensity of one other campaign was permitted—the campaign to separate the Primate from the clergy and the people. A whispering campaign was inaugurated by which blame was to be attached to the Cardinal for the withdrawal of Religious as teachers in the schools after nationalisation, and for the failure to reach a *modus vivendi* between Church and State. Direct access to the Cardinal was made more and more difficult, and even the medium of the Pastoral Letters was restricted by making them subject to the censorship laws. This also applied to circulars emanating from the Bishops. An attempt was made to bring about a rift between the Primate and the Bishops. Every day some Government official or other would complain to a member of the episcopate of the aggressive policy of the Primate towards the State. Every day, too, the State newspapers carried violent attacks on the Cardinal; fictitious or misquoted statements were attributed to him; and similar tactics employed *vis-à-vis* the Bishops, so that the situation could be entirely confused.

To reduce the confusion, particularly in the minds of the more simple Faithful, and as an expression of their own loyalty, on 3rd November, 1948, the Bishops published a declaration of their full confidence in the Cardinal, expressed amazement and sorrow at the attacks made on him, and protested against these attempts to slander him. But their efforts were unavailing. The campaign was continued with even greater violence, and fifteen days later the Cardinal issued a statement to the people, in which he summarised the attacks being made upon him, and denounced the régime.

Now, at a Party meeting held at the beginning of 1948, Rakosi had made a speech in which he had said that relations between Church and State must be settled one way or the other by the end of the year. "If we cannot establish order by means of a reciprocal agreement," he concluded, "very well, then, we shall obey the will of the people and establish it by the strong arm of the State."

The "agreement" mentioned by Rakosi meant a declaration by the Church of loyalty to the State. Such a declaration had already been demanded of the Protestant Church and had been given when, on 4th May, 1948, Rakosi demanded a similar declaration not from the Cardinal, but from the Archbishop of Eger. The Bishops refused to make such a declaration until the State recognised that the Church possessed certain inalienable rights, and once more there was an impasse.

The Government was by now quite convinced that the Primate was the chief obstacle to solving the problem, and as the year progressed it was decided to remove him as soon as a suitable opportunity presented itself. To foster the opportunity and to accustom the people to the idea, the Communists organised student and worker demonstrations at which the removal of the Cardinal was demanded.

The first moves were made on 19th and 23rd November, when the Cardinal's secretary and two priests attached to the Curia of the Archdiocese, all being close collaborators of his Eminence, were arrested. The Cardinal read these signs correctly and began to make preparations. On 20th December he sent a letter to all the clergy begging them to be constant in the Faith no matter what might happen to them, and on the same day addressed the now famous letter to the Bishops in which he said: "Since I have not taken part in any plot I shall never resign. I shall not speak. If after this you hear that I have confessed this or that, or that I have resigned my office (even though this should be authenticated by my signature), you should realise that such a declaration is but the consequence of human frailty. . . . Likewise I declare null and void any confession which may be attributed to me from this day forth."

The blow fell on 26th December. The Cardinal was arrested and brought to trial on 3rd February, 1949.

It is not the intention here to give an account of this terrible travesty of judicial process. Many books in English, French, Italian and German have been written about it. The most sinister aspect of it was the moral wreck to which the Cardinal had been reduced by his torturers in the short space of forty days, so that he was brought before his judges broken physically and mentally to such an extent that he—like so many other strong and good men in similar circumstances—condemned himself out of his own mouth. But for the letter which, probably understanding his own human limitations more perfectly than any who knew him, he had written to the Bishops, the spectacle which the Cardinal presented in court and the words heard to issue from his mouth must have caused the greatest confusion among the clergy and the Faithful. Found guilty of treason, spying and plotting against the security of the State, and illegal trafficking in foreign exchange, the Cardinal was sentenced to life imprisonment.

The arrest of the Cardinal, though widely expected throughout the country, nevertheless caused the widest disquiet. The Government, fearing violent repercussions, took various measures to bolster their position. All priests who were considered likely to make a stand against the arrest were themselves arrested and imprisoned and many of them have never been heard of again. The Communists also went to work in schools, factories and villages and coerced workers, peasants, teachers and students to sign petitions demanding exemplary punishment for the Cardinal and the liquidation of all reactionary priests. The newspaper and radio campaigns of vilification of the Cardinal were whipped up to even greater heights.

At the end of December 1948 the Archbishop of Kalocsa, Monsignor Josef Grosz, and the Bishops of Hajdudorog, Vac and Szekesfeherva were summoned to the Ministry of the Interior and accused of being almost as responsible as the Primate for the way in which the situation had developed. They were told that they had been implicated by statements of the Cardinal and that documents proving them to be involved in illegal financial operations had been found in the Primate's palace. It was suggested that it would be better if they resigned, but when they refused to do so, fearing that to arrest them might cause a situation which they could not control, the Government was content to let them go with threats.

An exactly opposite approach was made to a number of other prelates and to the clergy. When Church property had been confiscated in 1946, the State had undertaken to provide a subsidy renewable yearly, for the payment of stipends. Two days after the Cardinal's arrest, the Archbishop of Eger was informed that the Government was prepared to renew the subsidy for another year. In addition, the Vicar-General in Budapest was invited to the Government's reception on New Year's Day, and the Press attributed to him statements about the cordial relations which existed between the Church and Government. On 4th January, 1949, negotiations between Church and Government were reopened, but, making no progress, were once more abandoned on 12th January. But perhaps strangest of all the Government's moves was the suggestion that diplomatic relations between Hungary and the Holy See, which had been broken off on 4th April, 1945, when the Apostolic Nuncio had been ordered to leave the country, should be renewed. This was merely an attempt to create the illusion that the responsibility for diplomatic relations not being renewed before this was entirely the Primate's. Naturally, the Vatican refused.

After the imprisonment of the Cardinal, the Government began to work along lines familiar in all Communist countries, in the struggle between the Church and State. From the beginning of the régime the Communists had made constant attempts to weaken the Church by splitting the clergy from the hierarchy and the clergy among themselves. Now a firm policy was introduced to make a split a demonstrable fact.

In March 1949 a number of priests were invited to attend a Peace Conference organised in Budapest by the Communists. Many of these priests attended under coercion, though there were some renegades who went of their own free will. In April Father Ferenc Varga was chosen by the Government to organise a Catholic Priests' Peace Movement. Father Varga, who was not the Communist sympathiser the Government thought him to be, could see no way out of his dilemma except by fleeing from the country. His attempt to escape failed, however, and he was caught at the frontier, and died of wounds and torture not long after. To take Father Varga's place, the Communists appointed Canon Miklos Beresztoczy, who, during a term of imprisonment, had been subjected to brain-washing. Priests were coerced into joining the Peace Movement under threat of losing their stipends or imprisonment on trumped-up charges.

On 31st May, 1949, general elections finally consolidated the Communist régime and on 20th August a new Constitution was introduced, under which Church and State were totally separated.

While professing to recognise freedom of religious practice, the State no longer guaranteed the rights of the Church; and religious instruction was no longer obligatory in schools. If parents wished to have their children instructed in religion, they had to apply to the school on or before a certain date. But many obstacles were put in the way of the children to prevent them receiving instruction. Religious classes were held after the other classes were finished; teaching was restricted to an exposition of the truths of religion with all mention of errors being forbidden; children might be assembled in church only for Confession, Confirmation and First Communion; the hours for teaching were strictly limited—for First Communion to two hours weekly for two months only; for Confirmation to one hour; and the time and place of instruction, and the date of the First Communion and of Confirmation had to be supplied to the authorities well in advance.

But besides this campaign to weaken the Church in the ranks of the Faithful, the Government aimed also at weakening the Church within itself by developing the split among the clergy by means of the Catholic Priests' Peace Movement and by destroying the religious Orders from which the Church gained invaluable support.

The attack on the Religious began through the schools. Scarcely a week went by without the police discovering a plot against the State being hatched in one or other of the colleges conducted by the Religious, and a number of Religious were arrested and deported on charges of conceiving or aiding these conspiracies. When the schools were nationalised, Religious who refused to teach in State schools worked in the ministry or charitable organisations. Such work was now regarded as subversive activity. But besides this, religious Houses to which schools and colleges had never been attached were seized under the nationalisation of schools law; chapels, retreat houses, cultural institutes, seminaries and even printing-presses were confiscated; missions, retreats and pilgrimages were forbidden, as was sick-visiting; Sisters nursing in hospitals were dismissed; the freedom of movement of Religious was restricted on the grounds that they were making collections for the Church.

But the Government had formulated its plan. On 5th June, 1950, the Minister for Popular Culture declared in a speech: "A

People's Democracy has no need of Religious for they not only do not fulfil their vocation but actually sabotage the aims of democracy. They must, therefore, be put, as soon as possible, in a position where they will be unable to harm the interests of the People's Democracy."

This speech seems to have been the signal for direct attack. During the night of 9th/10th June police served an order on 320 male Religious and between 600 and 700 nuns in southern Hungary, for immediate expulsion from their Houses and confinement in a place of detention. The police gave the Religious thirty minutes to get ready, and allowed them to take no luggage in excess of ten pounds weight. There was no appeal against the order, which was justified by the police, who declared that radio-transmitters, espionage material and writings inciting to revolt and sabotage were found in the Houses.

In view of these arrests, the Archbishop of Kalocsa, Monsignor Grosz, called a conference of the Bishops for the 20th June. To intimidate the Bishops, during the night before the conference opened, between 1,500 and 2,000 more Religious were arrested.

Faced with this position, the Bishops felt that they would be wrong to do anything to aggravate it, and asked for the reopening of discussion with the Government for finding a *modus vivendi*. The Government agreed, but feeling that they now had the upper hand, they presented the Bishops with conditions, accompanied by threats; and to underline that they meant what they said, between 10th and 12th July a new series of arrests of Religious was carried out and on 1st August the Catholic Priests' Peace Movement was officially inaugurated in Budapest.

On 30th August the Bishops signed an "agreement" with the Government under which they undertook to support the established order and constitution of the Hungarian People's Republic; deal severely with clergy who acted contrary to the legal orders and reconstructive schemes of the Republic; strongly condemn all subversive activity against the State and the social order; not to permit the religious sentiments of the Faithful and the Church to be used for political ends in opposition to the State; invite Catholics to co-operate in the realisation of the Five-Years' Plan and forbid parish priests to oppose the Co-operative Agricultural Movement; support the Peace Movement and oppose the use of the atomic bomb.

For their part, the Government guaranteed, in conformity with the Constitution, Catholic freedom of worship and the freedom of the Church to discharge its duties; agreed to six boys' schools and two girls' schools being restored to the Church and to a sufficient number of men and women Religious being maintained to staff the schools; and undertook to provide subsidies, according to prescribed descending scales, over a period of eighteen years.

It might have thought that the signing of this agreement would have led to peace between Church and State. On the contrary, the campaign against the Religious was continued, and on 1st September the Government ordered the dissolution of fifty-three Orders and Congregations. Only those Religious needed to staff the eight schools were allowed to remain, the rest being required to leave their Houses within three months and take up civilian employment. All the Houses and their property were confiscated.

The Bishops, amazed by this act of the Government, at once issued a Pastoral Letter of protest. They also asked that the disbanded Religious should be allowed to leave the country so that they might follow their vocation elsewhere. The protest was ignored, the request refused.

Peace between the Church and the Government did not last long. When the Bishops were asked to sign the Stockholm Manifesto (Appeal of the World Peace Committee—a Communist organisation), they refused. When several attempts to persuade them to sign failed, the Communists immediately cried out that the agreement had been violated.

So in spring 1951 the struggle was renewed.

This time the Government used the Priests' Peace Movement in an attempt to bring the Bishops to heel. Without consulting the Bishops, the Government announced that priests of the Movement would be appointed to vacant parishes. To try to prevent this from happening, the Bishops eventually agreed to sign the Stockholm Manifesto.

It was, indeed, a Government victory, which they did not hesitate to drive home. The priests of the Movement were now invited to discuss the matter of subsidies with the Government, and the latter agreed to double or treble the sums already being received by the clergy on condition that the clergy would take an oath of loyalty to the State. Not all the clergy—indeed, large numbers—refused to take this oath, and it became clear that there still existed a large body of opposition within the Church. This had to be removed, and the best way of doing so, in the Government's opinion, was by the arrest of Archbishop Grosz and five other priests on charges of plotting against the State. The arrests were made on 15th May, 1951.

According to the charges, the Archbishop had been entrusted by Cardinal Mindszenty in 1948, with the organisation of a plot to overthrow the Government, after which, if the Cardinal himself was "not available", he was to put himself at the head of a Provisional Government, as Regent, until the Hapsburgs had been restored to the throne. To this were added charges of organising escape-routes, illegal currency transactions, secreting arms. All these charges bore a striking resemblance to those levelled against the Primate two years earlier. On 28th June, 1951, Archbishop Grosz was sentenced to fifteen years' imprisonment, and his so-called collaborators to fourteen, thirteen, ten and eight years.

On the day that the Archbishop was arrested a State Bureau for Ecclesiastical Affairs, on the Russian model, was set up to implement the agreements between Church and State. At its head was placed one of the greatest enemies of the Church, Istvan Kossa. This was an indication of the State's unbounding enmity against the Church.

But such an indication was not needed. On 23rd June the Bishops of Vac, Szekesfehervar, Csanad and Veszprem were confined to their palaces under house arrest, and the Auxiliary Bishop of Szekesfehervar was similarly treated two days later. Pressure was then brought to bear, in his confinement, on the Bishop of Csanad, who was also Apostolic Administrator of the Archdiocese of Esztergom (and in the Primate's absence in charge of Esztergom), to nominate Vicars-General for Esztergom and Szeged. As the heavy responsibility of the charge of two Sees devolved upon him, and as he could still direct the affairs of his own and the Archdiocese, though under house arrest, fearing that refusal would mean imprisonment and deprive the two dioceses of his direction, the Bishop agreed, and appointed Miklos Beresztoczy, leader of the Priests' Peace Movement, to be Vicar-General of Esztergom, and Antal Szeczy, also a prominent member of the Movement, to be Vicar-General of Csanad. A similar attempt was made upon the Bishop of Vac to get him to replace his Vicar-General with a member of the Movement, and when he refused, his Vicar-General was compelled to replace his pro-Vicar and Chancellor with members of the Movement. The Bishop of Veszprem was forced to appoint a new Vicar-General, and the Bishop of Szekesfehervar a new Chancellor.

A conference of the Bishops who were still at liberty was now called under the leadership of the Archbishop of Eger, at which the Government demanded that they issue a declaration of loyalty to the State and condemn every act of violence. The new Vicars-General were called to the same conference, and as they out-numbered the Bishops, the conference complied with the demands. At the same time the Government issued a decree regulating the formalities to be observed in filling vacant Sees, made retroactive to 1st January, 1946. The decree stipulated the consent of the State to such appointments.

The four free Bishops, who were still recognised by the State, were placed in a serious dilemma by these events. Either they must accede to the Government's demand or be cut off from the religious life of the country. Deciding that the latter would be disastrous for the Church, the Bishops took the oath of loyalty and replaced their Vicars-General and Chancellors with members of the Priests' Peace Movement. By these moves, the Movement, scarcely a year old, was now practically governing all the dioceses, and this meant that nearly all fields of Church activity were completely under the influence of the Communists. Thus the situation remained for the next two years.

The State, however, was experiencing other troubles, and in July 1953 the Prime Minister, Imre Nagy, introduced yet another new Constitution. Since, fundamentally, the persecution of the Faith was closely bound up with the events that led to the introduction of this new Constitution, the Government of Imre Nagy was anxious to make at least a show of good relations with the Church, and certain modifications of policy were introduced.

In mid-June 1955 Cardinal Mindszenty was released from imprisonment on grounds of age and health, and confined to house arrest. Some months later the Bishop of Vac was released from house arrest and allowed to resume his episcopal duties. On 11th May, 1956, the Archbishop of Kalocsa, Monsignor Grosz, after five years in prison, was released as an "act of clemency", and permitted to take over the administration of his diocese.

But these were only acts designed to have an effect on opinion abroad. The Government still supported the Priests's Peace Movement, and through the State Bureau for Ecclesiastical Affairs to direct the activity of the Church. All attempts by priests or people to elevate the practice of the Faith to its rightful place in the life of the country were still regarded as subversive activity and ruthlessly punished.

The Hungarian people, however, were gathering their strength to throw off the yoke which had weighed them down in all aspects of their life for ten long years and more. In October 1956 they rose up in their anger against their oppressors.

The Government immediately returned the Cardinal Primate to prison, from which he was released by the Army and a group of insurgents on 31st October. Two days later the Government issued a communiqué stating that the Cardinal might once more assume his ecclesiastical functions and exercise his civil rights, since there had been no justification at all for the charges made against him.

But the uprising was short-lived, and when Soviet force had restored the Communist *status quo*, the régime of Janos Kadar returned to the persecution of the Church with renewed vigour. Fortunately, the Cardinal Primate has been able to find sanctuary in the United States' Legation in Budapest, but though he is prevented from taking part in the life of the country because of this, he is the constant centre of attack by the Communist Press.

The attitude of the régime towards the Church is still as bitter and relentless as ever it was. The general policy was stated by Kadar when he said in a public speech: "We will not allow reactionary elements to continue to exercise their influence over women and to torture our children by teaching them the knowledge of God," if, to "women" and "children" is also added "all men". But the State has not yet won the battle. It may see what men do; but it cannot look into their hearts.

CHAPTER XIV

Poland

THROUGHOUT HER long history Poland has suffered much from external pressures. Before 1919 she had experienced no fewer than three partitions, the last of which, in 1795, destroyed her as an independent power. During the Napoleonic wars the Poles made an attempt to regain independence, by fighting on the side of the French, in return for which, Napoleon, in 1807, created the Duchy of Warsaw, which was to be the nucleus of a Polish State. The defeat of Napoleon, however, dashed all hopes of resurgence, especially when the Congress of Vienna gave the greater part of Polish territory to Russia. The Russians treated the Poles so badly that in 1830 and 1863 they rose in revolt, only to be crushed after long and bloody struggles.

An independent Poland, however, was included in President Wilson's Fourteen Points, and when the Allies were victorious in 1918, the Treaty of Versailles restored Poland to the map as an independent power. Her new independence she maintained until she was attacked by both Germany and Russia, who once again partitioned her, the Russians annexing a large strip of territory some 160 miles wide and 500 miles from north to south.

The meeting of the Big Three at Yalta in February 1945, without consulting the Polish Government-in-Exile, agreed that Russia should keep this strip of territory and that Poland should be compensated on her western frontier. The same meeting also agreed that a Communist Provisional Government, which had been set up by the Russians at Lublin in July 1944, should be the recognised Government, provided that its base was broadened by the inclusion of democratic leaders from the exiled Government. Russia accepted this stipulation, knowing full well that a little political manœuvring would soon remove these democratic elements.

The boundaries of the new Poland, then, were fixed in the west on the line of the Oder-Neisse, in the south by her pre-war frontier with Czecho-Slovakia, and in the east by the Ribbentrop-Molotov line, and took in what had formerly been East Prussia. Under the arrangements, all Germans were expelled, and the large Ukrainian (4,780,000), White Ruthenian (1,500,000) and Lithuanian (90,000) minorities were absorbed by Russia, while no fewer than 3,500,000 Jews had disappeared during the War, exterminated by the Nazis. When all adjustments had been made, the total population of post-war Poland was 27,500,000, compared with 34,000,000 before the war. Of the 27,500,000 people, approximately 26,500,000 were Catholics, a fact of great significance for the post-war history of the country.

The Nazi terror during the War, the strangely arbitrary treatment by the Allies, the economic run-down of the country, the loss of large portions of the population and the addition of others who were of alien stock, faced the new Poland with vast problems of reorganisation. But if the State was faced with this situation, a situation of the same proportions and character also confronted the Church. It was, perhaps, fortunate for the Church that the State was pre-occupied, otherwise the calamity which has overtaken the Church in Poland might have been utterly disastrous in its consequences, which, in all conscience, are already bad enough.

The reorganisation of the Church took about seven years. By the end of 1951 the new position had become more or less stabilised. The hierarchy was composed of four Archbishops, twelve Ordinaries, nine Apostolic Administrators and between twenty and twenty-five Auxiliary Bishops. Of these, nine Ordinaries, five Apostolic Administrators and fifteen Auxiliary Bishops were new appointments since 1945. The clergy, whose ranks had been seriously depleted by Nazi persecution during the War, numbered about 9,000, administering just over 6,000 parishes. In seventeen senior and fifty-nine junior seminaries there were almost 10,000 students.

As has been suggested, but for the preoccupation of the State with its own gigantic troubles, this reorganisation might never have been achieved—at least, not on this scale; for although the Government were preoccupied, they nevertheless gave signs of their opposition to religion and the Church, which were portents of its future hostility and intentions. For the first two post-war years, during which the Provisional Government had wielded power, there were, at all events, formally correct relations between Church and State.

The first elections were held on 19th January, 1947. The Western Allies had insisted that these elections should be held on democratic principles, but were in no position to see that they were applied. The Red Army was still in occupation, and under its protection the Communists had things much their own way. On one pretext or another about two million voters who constituted potential opponents were disenfranchised, and arrests and threats were used to coerce others, while right of assembly and freedom of expression were suppressed. As a result, the Communists and their supporters won 383 of the 444 seats.

The new Government were not long in indicating that the former correct relations between Church and State had been merely a truce. Even under the truce the Provisional Government had not been entirely inactive. For example, nationalisation of the schools had been mooted, the Concordat with the Holy See, signed in 1925, had been abrogated by the Government, laws had been introduced making a civil marriage ceremony obligatory and introducing greater facilities for divorce, while as long ago as 1946 there had been moves to establish a Polish National Catholic Church.

As each of these new measures had been introduced, the leaders of the Church had not hesitated to protest to the Government and to warn the Faithful of the traps being prepared for them. On the 3rd and 4th October, 1945, the Bishops had met in conference at Jasna-Gora monastery, and in the middle of the month had issued a joint statement urging the Faithful to beware of resurgent materialism and to oppose those who were, by various means, attempting to provoke an attack on the Church. On 7th December they issued yet another joint statement protesting against the new marriage and divorce laws.

When the setting up of a National Catholic Church was mooted, the Primate of Poland, Cardinal Hlond, Archbishop of Warsaw, issued a statement denouncing the Government's intentions. The Government, however, were unmoved, and on 30th September official recognition was given to the National Catholic Church, and subsidies were granted it to enable it to carry on its work. It is sad that even in Poland, where the Catholic Faith was so widespread, there should have been renegade priests willing to fulfil the Government's wishes. The numbers of these "patriot" priests, as they were called, has always been small. The maximum was reached in 1953, when they numbered about 100, or 1 per cent of the entire clergy. Nevertheless, even a score or two gave the Government an instrument with which to try to undermine the Church.

The protests of the Bishops were subject to Press and radio attacks, in which they were accused of meddling in politics and working against the true interests of the people. But besides this a new wave of terrorism was directed against the lower clergy. Priests were arrested on the slimmest of pretexts and sentenced to long terms of imprisonment. Others were tortured, yet others disappeared, never to be heard of again. Between 1945 and 1947 no fewer than 100 priests were liquidated in this way by the State Security Bureau.

As has been said, the new Government, elected on 19th January, 1947, were not long in beginning to press their attack on the Church. The campaign was conducted along lines that by now are no longer novel to the reader. Little by little the Church was deprived of its sources of income; hospitals, orphanges, homes for the aged poor, kindergartens and other charitable institutions were taken over by the State; the schools were nationalised; and everything was done to create a split between Bishops and clergy. No compensation was paid to the Church for the loss of buildings and other property, and the nuns who had engaged in charitable work were driven to live entirely on alms given them by the Faithful. Nor was it only in works of charity that the Government intervened. Priests were forbidden to visit the hospitals, except twice a week for the hearing of confessions, and failure by the patients to profit by these visits for any cause whatsoever barred them from spiritual comforts, even Extreme Unction in the case of the dying.

In the face of these restrictions, Cardinal Hlond was constrained to protest yet again. "The policy of these atheists," he said, "is calculated to erase the religion of the people and to dechristianise them. The Church is attacked not only in the workshops and factories, but even in the humblest cottages. . . . The independent mission of the Church and its moral influence over men, anger the partisans of totalitarianism. By refusing to keep rigidly within the walls of its sacred buildings or to become the tool of a political party, infuriates them."

Throughout the year the measures continued to increase, and in September the Bishops issued a letter which once more put the Faithful on their guard. Its outspoken and courageous terms angered the Government to such an extent that in a speech to the Sejm on 29th October the Prime Minister declared it to be an act of open opposition to the Government. Though it could scarcely be thought possible, the propaganda campaign against the Church was even further intensified.

In February 1948 Cardinal Hlond sought, and was granted, permission to visit Rome to seek the advice of the Holy See. On his return he was accused of supporting Vatican policy, which, it was contended, supported the German claim to the former Reich territories, called the "recovered territories", east of the Oder–Neisse line. The Cardinal refuted this accusation in what was to be his last public statement. He died on 22nd October, and was succeeded by Monsignor Wyszynski as Archbishop of Warsaw and Primate.

A fresh campaign of threats and arrests was launched early in the year against the Bishops and clergy. In May the former Auxiliary Bishop of Pinsk was sentenced to six months' imprisonment on a charge so trifling that no one can recall what it was. A Father Buchala was sent to prison for three years for having "ridiculed the People's Democracy". The more usual charges against priests at this time were of immorality and secret activities directed against the State, and so fiercely was the campaign waged that by September no fewer than 400 priests were in prison or in concentration camps. Many prominent clergy were among the victims. Father Pawlina, a former director of the great charitable organisation Caritas, and three others were sentenced to penal servitude for moral complicity in the murders of three democrat agitators. Father Kacynski, who was Minister of Education in the Government-in-Exile during the War, was imprisoned for "activities detrimental to the State". Father Boleslas Stefanski was condemned to death for having "formed his pupils into a secret gang". And there were many others.

Simultaneously with these attacks on the clergy, a frontal attack on religion in schools was launched. It had begun in February, when Skrzeszewski, the Minister of Education, had announced: "The whole teaching body should belong to the Communist Party. The schools should be secular schools and there should be nothing of religion in the classrooms. Every youth organisation of a denominational character should be forbidden in schools." Naturally, the hierarchy responded at once. "The Church will never accept the principle of education based on materialist teachings." But the reorganisation of the educational system went ahead.

Teachers were required to pay "attention to the democratic line in the education of children", who were to be taught the "elements of historic Materialism". Such requirements called for the creation of a new type of teacher. Those who were already members of the Party were advanced. All teachers in elementary schools were required to take a course in political education, at the end of which they were examined as to their fitness and ability to put the theory of Marxism–Leninism into practise. The training of teachers in secondary schools was revised so that every one of them should be absolutely free of old bourgeois prejudices and pre-conceived class ideas.

All teachers were obliged to join the Professional Association of Polish Teachers, which kept a check on their work in the classroom as well as their ideological loyalty. A single youth organisation, the Union of Polish Youth, was inaugurated, in which all pupils were enrolled.

Educational centres, which replaced the former kindergartens, were set up for children between four and seven, and staffed with women trained in materialism. Nurseries for children between one and four were opened. Thus from the age of one to at least eighteen all the youth of the country were under the pressure of materialist influence.

Religious instruction in schools was drastically reduced and in the high schools completely abolished. In any event, it could be given only to those children whose parents submitted a request. Children were deflected from observing feast-days by Party demonstrations organised for the same days. Anti-religious organisations were formed to counteract religious organisations which were forbidden to carry on their activities in schools.

If the Government had lost time at the beginning, they certainly made up for it now. Within two years the whole school system of the country was brought into line, and the schools became instruments of ideological pressure more effective than any other means devised for the re-orientation of the nation.

The next stage was the usual attempt to make the Government in the eyes of the people appear reasonable and to fix upon the hierarchy the responsibility for any disagreement there might be. So in March 1949 the Government approached the Church, through the Secretary of the Episcopal Commission, with a view to establishing a *modus vivendi*. In their letter the Government pointed out—it was really a covert threat—that the clergy were engaging more and more in anti-Government propaganda which was "capable of creating anxiety and unrest in the minds of the people". In their reply the Bishops said that they were anxious to re-establish the truth. "Be sure," they said, "that it is certainly not by being traitors to God that you will build a better Poland." They also suggested that a mixed commission should be appointed to examine all problems affecting Church and State.

The Government waited until 26th July before announcing their representatives, and in the meantime the fact that the discussions were to take place did not prevent restrictive measures directly aimed at the Church and clergy from being promulgated. On 5th July a decree was published requiring the clergy to keep a strict account of all offerings made by the Faithful so that the Government might check them whenever they wished. The previous year the Minister of Education had pronounced: "Public opinion must be made to realise that Catholic morality is inferior to Socialist morality", and to bring this about more and more clergy were arrested for crimes against morals. The Press reported all such cases in lurid detail, most of which was pure invention.

During this same period all fifteen Catholic printing works were nationalised, two of the leading Catholic newspapers were suspended. The Bishops protested about these events, and about the suppression of several Catholic associations and the dismissal of large numbers of nuns from hospitals, on 18th July, 1949. But at the beginning of August two more decrees were published, one prescribing heavy penalties, including death, for anyone found guilty of making use of religion to disturb public order, and the other applying the 1932 Law of Associations to all Church associations. This law required all associations to make application for registration, and forms were sent out to all the Catholic associations. The questions asked on the forms were such, however, that the Bishops decided that application for registration was not to be made, and the associations were voluntarily closed.

By a Government definition, the religious Orders were required to fill in the forms, though the Minister of Public Administration had assured them they were not required to do so. They filled in the forms and returned them, and then heard nothing more.

A decree of 11th August demanded that all baptismal registers should be handed over to the State, and on 23rd November a Government circular interpreting a decree of 11th March, 1932, in a way in which it had never been interpreted before, forbade processions on public highways, the blessing of fields, the placing of crosses and statues on the public highways, the calling of meetings, conferences, open-air parish meetings, the performance of plays, the organisation of religious demonstrations and of pilgrimages. In fact, the activities of the Church were more or less reduced to the celebration of religious services only in churches.

This position was further emphasised when the advent of 1950 was signalised by an attack on Caritas. This immense relief organisation had under its care on 1st January, 1950, 18 workers' hostels, 17 hostels for poor children, 258 homes for the aged, 38 convalescent homes for sick children, while 16,500 children were cared for in its 334 orphanages. Nearly 100,000 meals were distributed daily by its 346 canteens, while in shattered Warsaw alone, in the space of three years 100 homes for the aged, 27 homes for small children, 19 kindergartens, 18 homes for poor students, 12 rest homes and 12 holiday camps for children had been built up out of the ruins, with the aid of American relief organisations and donations from Poles in America. On 23rd January a decree was published which closed the great majority of the diocesan headquarters of Caritas, and an administrative council composed of priests, coerced into joining, and "progressive" Catholics, was set up.

The Bishops at once protested to the Government that Caritas was an integral part of the institutions of the Church, pointing out that the action taken against the organisation was contrary to all the laws in force in Poland. A Pastoral Letter was also sent to parish priests, to be read from all pulpits on 12th February, in which the real motives for suppressing Caritas were exposed. The priests were also urged to have no part in the new organisation being sponsored by the Government. Many priests were arrested and imprisoned for reading the Letter, and for refusing to join the new organisation. A day or two later the Bishops made yet another protest complaining in general terms of the ever more open and bitter attack being made on the Church by the Government. "We feel it necessary," they said, "to emphasise that the struggle against religion long being carried on in Poland is being directed according to tactics which up to now it would have been impossible to imagine in the fight against God."

The Government remained unmoved, and in mid-March yet another decree was published which practically deprived the Church of all its sources of income by nationalising Church property not previously seized. The Government set up a Church fund "to replace the lost income", which thus gave it a stranglehold on the Church. All offerings for Masses, funerals and other religious functions were also taxed.

It is difficult to believe, but while all this was going on, negotiations between the hierarchy and the Government to find a *modus vivendi* were being held. Towards the end of March these talks had reached the stage at which a declaration could be made. The Government called the declaration an Agreement, but this the Bishops refused to do, arguing that it was in no way a Concordat, but merely the result of a statement of views on certain subjects by both sides.

The Declaration contained nineteen Articles, with a supplementary protocol of four Articles. The Preamble contained the phrases: "the possibility of working peacefully together", "the Government . . . recognises the principle of religious liberty", and "the Polish hierarchy . . . has in view the well-being of the Church and the present political interests of the Polish State". Under the terms of the Declaration the Bishops undertook to see that the clergy taught the Faithful respect for the Law and for the State authorities, and would encourage the Faithful to work with greater enthusiasm for the reconstruction of the country; they recognised that the economic, historical, cultural and religious rights of the "recovered" territories demanded that these territories should belong to Poland for ever, and this being so, would request the Holy See to raise to episcopal Sees those ecclesiastical administrative centres which at present enjoyed the privileges of resident bishoprics; that they would oppose all the revisionist manœuvres of a certain section of the German clergy and, within the limits of their powers, oppose all hostile activities directed against Poland; that they would recognise that while the Pope was the supreme and decisive authority in matters of Faith, morals and ecclesiastical jurisdiction, in all other matters the interests of the Polish State were supreme; that they would instruct the clergy not to oppose the development of the agricultural co-operatives; that they would oppose all criminal subversive activities and apply canonical sanctions to those members of the clergy participating in underground movements directed against the State.

Article 10 dealt with religious instruction in schools and was of great importance, for the Government declared that it would not apply any restrictions to the manner of imparting religious knowledge now obtaining in schools. The programmes would be drawn up by the school authorities in agreement with the Church authorities; suitable text-books would be provided; and all teachers of religion would be placed on the same footing as all other teachers. Nor would the State authorities place any restrictions on students wishing to take part in religious services outside school hours, and would arrange times for students wishing to receive Confirmation. Students who wished to recite prayers either before or after lessons would not be prevented from doing so by the school authorities. Those Catholic schools which still existed would continue to function, but they must follow the curriculum laid down by the State. The free Catholic schools would enjoy the same right as State schools, and finally, if a school was changed to a public school not providing religious education, Catholic parents would be allowed to transfer their children to schools which did.

The remaining nine Articles dealt with the University of Lublin, which was to continue to function as at present; Catholic associations which were to continue as they were; the right of the Church to direct works of charity and assistance within the framework of the existing laws; the Catholic Press and other publications, which were to have the same rights as other sections of the Press; military chaplains, who were to be appointed in accordance with special statutes to be drawn up by the military authority in agreement with the Church authority; religious ministry in prisons, and, at the request of patients, in State as well as independent hospitals; religious Orders, which were to be allowed complete freedom of action within the framework of existing laws; public worship, pilgrimages and processions, which were not to be hindered, though they must be arranged, for the maintenance of order, by agreement between the Church and the administrative authorities.

The supplementary protocol provided that Caritas should become a Catholic association, with the object of providing the poor and needy with relief. But instead of being organised according to diocesan boundaries as formerly, it was to operate in territories coinciding with the State administration of the country—that is, by districts, counties and regions. The Government undertook to examine the possibility of paying compensation for the non-movable property of Caritas which it took over, either by contributions from the Ecclesiastical Fund, or by leaving the right of property to the Church, provided the Church guaranteed never to dispose of the property left to it, in any way. The needs of Bishops and religious institutions would also be examined so as to provide them with assistance. The Ordinaries were to receive suitable sums from the Ecclesiastical Fund for the needs of their dioceses. Finally, the call-up for military service of students in ecclesiastical seminaries would be deferred until they had finished their course, and after ordination priests would not be called up, but be put on the reserve. The same applied to Religious after they had taken their vows.

There were several points in this Declaration with which the Bishops did not entirely agree, but for the sake of achieving some concessions, they felt that compromise was worthwhile. On the face of it, the Declaration could have provided a workable *modus vivendi*, and it was hoped that the friction between Church and State might now become considerably less, even if it could not be altogether overcome. These hopes, however, were doomed to disappointment.

In the spring of 1950 the Ministry for Public Administration was dissolved, and its powers and duties transferred to regional administrative bodies. Under this reorganisation, the Office for Religious Affairs was placed under the control of a special bureau, whose chief was Anton Bida, who as former Chief Press Censor had been extremely hostile to the Catholic Press.

The Party also ran into internal difficulties, in this period of what may be termed Stalinisation. The Minister for Public Education, Vladislav Volski, was expelled from the Party and imprisoned. This would have had little effect in any case, and it is mentioned here only because Volski was one of the two Government officials who had conducted the negotiations and signed the Agreement, or Declaration.

As a kind of counter-poise to these events, the Government, in complete disregard of the Agreement, continued its attack on the Church, particularly through the schools and the Catholic Press. For example, permission to teach the catechism was refused in some schools; schools conducted by nuns were nationalised; and a campaign against the teaching of religion in schools was developed, supposedly by the spontaneous request of parents and students. As a result of this campaign some 500 priests and Religious who taught religion were dismissed.

Pressure was next brought to bear on the hierarchy to obtain their signatures to the Stockholm Manifesto. At first the Bishops resisted, stating that since the Church was ever a firm supporter of peace—that support of peace was, indeed, an important part of the Church's mission—to sign the Manifesto would be superfluous. Some of the Bishops, however, believing that refusal to sign would adversely affect the working of the Agreement, agreed to put their signatures to a declaration supporting the Manifesto. The Government announced this immediately, in order to make capital out of it, and the remaining Bishops, fearing that their continued refusal might be construed as a split in the ranks of the hierarchy, also signed.

Less than two months after the Declaration had been signed, and only a few days after the Bishops had supported the Manifesto, they were accused at a Press conference, by a high Government official, of breaking Article 8 of the Declaration. (This Article bound the Church to oppose the "criminal activities of underground groups" and to apply "canonical sanctions to those members of the clergy who are guilty of participating in clandestine movements or in any movement directed against the State".) The attack signalised a new campaign of arrests and the closing of the schools and religious Houses, which continued through the summer. Though the Government declared themselves justified on the grounds that it was the Church who had broken the Agreement, it was they who ignored the terms which had been negotiated by their representatives.

By the end of the summer the position was such that when the hierarchy met in plenary session at Czestochowa in mid-September, they drew up a letter to Beirut, President of the Republic, in which they set out all the abuses, from 1945 to date, to which the Church had been subjected. It was a formidable list, beginning with the unilateral revoking of the Concordat, and including, to mention only a few of the twenty specific complaints, restrictions placed on freedom of public worship, the continued and systematic closing of Catholic schools and institutions, the nationalisation of Church property, the liquidation of Caritas, Press campaigns against the hierarchy, the setting up of anti-Christian youth organisations and anti-religious propaganda in kindergartens, schools, holiday camps. The letter drew attention to the fact that since the signing of the agreement there had been "an accelerated suppression of social institutions and other Church organisations", and went on to deal with such matters as the materialist education of youth, the curtailment of time allowed for religious instruction in schools, the mass dismissal of priests who taught catechism, the Government's support of "patriot priests", the great number of arrests and imprisonment of priests without legal reasons, and repeated violations of the Agreement by the Government. On the arrest of priests the letter said: "Many priests have been taken directly from the churches, from the Confessional, and from the midst of children awaiting confession to the bewilderment and anxiety of the Faithful. This is a singularly new occurrence in our life, for up to the present, priests have had very little contact with the penal code. Even the Bishops do not escape this supervision. During their pastoral rounds, meetings and visits they are surrounded by dozens of informers who make their presence known by their provocative behaviour. Many priests have been compelled to collaborate with the Information Service. This has been brought about by methods of intimidation which have been used even on the assistants in the episcopal Curiae." The Bishops said that they could have enumerated many more abuses than they had, and concluded: "We see no way to that peace of mind which is so indispensible, and to national unity, except by ending the struggle against religion."

The Government, it seems, had the same thoughts in mind, but differed in their ideas as to how the struggle against religion might be ended. The methods they adopted were designed either to eliminate religion altogether, or so to cow the Bishops and clergy that they would be completely submissive. To this end hundreds more clergy and Religious were arrested. The charges against them would have been fatuous had the consequences not have been so serious. The Government claimed, for example, that sensational secret dumps of arms had been discovered hidden in the Houses of the Jesuits at Cracow and the Franciscans at Radecznica.

Bishops were included in this new campaign. In January 1951 the Bishop of Kielce and his Vicar-General were arrested, and towards the end of the month a Government decree expelled the five Apostolic Administrators for the circumscriptions in the "recovered territories". In order to clarify the situation with regard to these territories, which had formerly belonged to Germany, Archbishop Wyszynski sought permission to visit Rome, which was granted. On his return he issued a circular to all the clergy in which he instructed them to refrain from all political activities and not to interfere in Party matters. All priests were, therefore, forbidden, he said, to join secret or subversive movements, or other social, economic or political movements. In an interview with a Catholic weekly newspaper, the Primate explained the attitude of the Vatican towards the former German territories. "It is a fact," he said, "that the Holy See has taken cognisance of the ecclesiastical organisation set up by the late Cardinal Hlond in the western territories (that is, the establishment of circumscriptions instead of dioceses). Furthermore, the Holy see has authorised the re-establishment of diocesan Curiae, ecclesiastical courts, seminaries, etc., all well-defined organisations which belong canonically to the independent life of a diocese. As Church life develops, so its external organisation will not fail to take on better defined forms." From which it would seem that the German Church was to be mollified by the continuance of the circumscriptions, while preparations were to be made to organise the circumscriptions as though they were dioceses, which would appear to accept the stand taken by the

Government, that the "recovered territories" would never revert to Germany.

In 1952 new general elections were held, and a new Constitution adopted, as a result of which all the junior seminaries belonging to the various Orders and religious Congregations were confiscated and closed, and the majority of students sent to labour camps. This marked the beginning of a new wave of violence in which the arrests of Bishops and priests increased to the accompaniment of as violent anti-Vatican and anti-Pope propaganda campaigns. By the end of the year it was estimated that no fewer than 1,000 priests, or 10 per cent of all Polish clergy, were in prison. Among the hierarchy arrested were the Bishop of Katowice with his Auxiliary Bishop and Coadjutor, the Archbishop of Lwow, the Apostolic Administrator of Cracow, the Auxiliary Bishop to the late Cardinal Sapieha, and the Chancellor of the Curia.

Although the Constitution of 1953 proclaimed the separation of Church and State, and freedom of religion, on 9th February, 1953, a decree was published which gave the State control over every act of ecclesiastical jurisdiction. It stated that Church offices might be held only by Polish citizens, that the appointments to all posts must be approved by the State, even when transfers only were made, that all the holders of offices must take an oath of allegiance to the Republic and that the State could remove any priest from his office if, in the opinion of the authorities, he was engaging in any activity contrary to law and public order.

A month later Archbishop Wyszynski, who had been given the Red Hat at the same Consistory at which the imprisoned Yugoslav Archbishop Stepinac had been created Cardinal, sent a letter to the President of the Council in which he denounced the Government for all the abuses and brutality which had been inflicted on the Church, and asked if the Government really intended to act on the decree, "which incidentally the Polish Constitution deprives of all juridical authority".

The Government's reply was to tighten yet further the grip of the Office for Religious Affairs upon the clergy by requiring every individual priest to apply to the Office for the wherewithal to satisfy his personal material needs. A full inquiry was made into each case, and the application might be approved if the priest proved pliable, or reduced or refused. Priests, both prelates and parish incumbents, were removed from their posts, which were then filled by priests nominated by the Government. By September no fewer than eight Bishops—the Bishops of Kielce and Katowice, the Coadjutor and Auxiliary of Katowice, the Metropolitan Archbishop of Lwow, who was also Apostolic Administrator of Cracow, the Bishop Vicar-General of Cracow and the Bishop Vicar-General of the Primate—had either been removed from their Sees or forbidden to exercise their functions, while the Bishop of Danzig had been imprisoned in 1946 for eight years for alleged collaboration with the Nazis.

The Bishop of Kielce had been arrested in 1951, and after two years and eight months in prison, he was at last brought to trial at the end of September. What had been done to him while he was in prison is not known, but in court he made a pitiful self-accusation in which he involved other Bishops, the dead Cardinals, Hlond and Sapieha, and the Pope. He was sentenced to twelve years' imprisonment. Cardinal Wyszynski protested vigorously to the Government, denying most strongly that the Vatican had ever issued political directives to the Catholic clergy in Poland.

This latest protest brought matters to a head for the courageous Cardinal Primate, and on 26th September the Government announced that he had been "forbidden to exercise the functions connected with the ecclesiastical charges devolving on him up to the present. This decision has been taken following Cardinal Stephen Wyszynski's persistent abuse of his ecclesiastical office, despite several warnings. He has violated the Protocol of Understanding, stirred up trouble and created an atmosphere favourable to subversive activities, as has been proved by the trial of Bishop Kaczmarek, activities particularly disastrous at a time when the integrity of the frontiers of the People's Republic of Poland is being threatened."

The Cardinal was not brought to trial. It was merely announced that he had been confined in "a comfortable monastery". His whereabouts were kept a strict secret.

A short time after this the Cardinal's close collaborator, Monsignor Anthony Baraniak, was also arrested. He was held in custody until 1955, when he was released, but prohibited from resuming his functions.

Two days after the Cardinal's arrest, the Bishops met in Warsaw and elected the Bishop of Lodz to be president of the episcopal conference. According to the Government, the Bishops declared themselves anxious to work in harmony with the State and in conformity with the Government's wishes. The Bishops were also stated to have taken the oath of allegiance to the State, and a delegation to have been received by President Beirut.

On 15th October the "patriot priests" held a national congress in Warsaw, and decided to set up a Central Committee of the National Front of Progressive Priests and Laymen, under the presidency of the Reverend Professor John Cruz. The objects of the Committee were to cement and strengthen the unity of the nation, to oppose the calumnious propaganda of "the enemies of our country", and to fulfil the tasks arising out of the declaration made by the Bishops at their conference on 28th September.

A year later, in October 1954, theological studies were permitted only in the University of Lublin, the theological faculties at Warsaw, Poznan and Cracow universities being closed. Even at Lublin they were permitted to continue only because five "progressive priests" nominated by the Government were accepted as professors. A month later the Government set up an Academy of Catholic Theology at Bislany, with Cruz as Rector.

During this time, so quietly as to be almost secretly, measures had been taken to liquidate the communities of nuns. Convents were closed and confiscated, and the nuns expelled. Hospitals owned by women's Orders were taken over and the Sisters replaced by Communist nurses. In Silesia alone, by August 1954, no fewer than 1,200 nuns had been expelled from their convents.

With the removal of the Primate and with nine Bishops either in prison or prohibited from exercising their duties, with "patriot priests" in many of the high positions and in control of parishes, with Religious teaching in schools almost completely suppressed, with Catholic associations forced out of existence, with every priest in the country reliant on the State for his material livelihood, with hundreds of obstreperous priests safely out of harm's way in prisons and concentrations camps, with the Catholic Press almost entirely suppressed, the Government might believe that they had broken the Church in Poland. They might also have believed that they had broken and crushed the nation until all men and women were their slaves. But the Polish people have always been proud, and in their history have suffered so much oppression that it has built up in their characters a resistance to slavery which can never be entirely broken.

This was manifested in the uprisings of October 1956 which broke out all over the country, and shook the régime to its very foundations. The people were not strong enough to throw off the Communist yoke altogether, but they were strong enough to gain an easement. When the Party had cleaned up its own house somewhat, this easement was reflected also in the relations between Church and State.

The new leaders, affixing all blame for the brutalities and abuses inflicted on the Church squarely on the shoulders of the Stalinists, released the Primate from confinement and restored him to his full duties. The Government spokesman, Michalski, referring to the Cardinal's return said: "The decision to put the Cardinal away belongs to the Stalinist period in the politics of our country. The return of the Primate proves that that period is at an end and that we have reverted, at least in the Church–State sector, to bilateral discussion of controversial matters." But he went on that this did not mean that there were no longer any matters for disagreement between Church and State. Separation of the Church from the State was a principle which could not be revoked.

In fact, the new position was merely a reversion to the status quo existing *after* the signing of the Joint Declaration in April 1950. Nevertheless, even this was preferable to the terrible conditions inflicted on the Church between 1952 and 1956. Confiscated Church property was restored, imprisoned Bishops were freed and with others who had been removed permitted to take up their episcopal duties once more.

Gomulka, realising that in a country so predominantly Catholic relations between Church and State must be satisfactory if progress were to be made, set up a Commission to settle outstanding questions between Church and Government. Under the agreement which this Commission was able to reach, the decree of February 1953 was rescinded and the State undertook not to interfere in religious appointments, though new appointments would be made by the Church in consultation with the Government. Priests expelled from the "recovered territories" were allowed to return, and nuns were allowed once more to take up their work in hospitals and other institutions. With regard to the problem of the "recovered territories" a compromise was reached—the Church agreed to raise the administrations to Sees when the peace treaty was eventually signed. Two important Catholic newspapers were permitted to resume publication. But perhaps most important of all was the re-introduction of religious instruction in schools. Admittedly, it was to be an optional subject and the teachers were to be appointed jointly by Church and State, but it was the strongest counter-poise to the monopoly enjoyed by atheistic materialism, and as such, of infinite value.

It cannot be said that the state of the Church in Poland is a happy one, even now; nor can it be foreseen how long the present situation will last. But, from all reports, the Faith in Poland is strong and vigorous, despite, or perhaps because of, the persecution of past years, and in that there is consolation and hope.

CHAPTER XV

Rumania

THE SUPPRESSION of the Catholic Church in Rumania offers a specially interesting example of Communist repressive strategy, and even a brief study demonstrates the unholy skill with which the Communists seize upon the opportunities presented to them by a variety of conditions and turn them to their advantage.

Of the twenty million inhabitants of Rumania, only three million were Catholic, the greater majority of the people belonging to the Rumanian or National Orthodox Church. The situation, therefore, which faced the Communist rulers was somewhat different from that facing the new régime in Hungary, for example, or Poland, where Catholics represented the great bulk of the population. Numerically, Rumanian Catholics presented a not insurmountable problem, the solution of which was made easier by the fact that the Catholics themselves were divided, the majority belonging to the Church of the Oriental Rite (alternatively known as the Greek-Catholic Church or Uniate Church), while the remainder worshipped according to the Latin Rite. It is not necessary here to go into the particulars of the two Rites; it is sufficient to say that both were equally members of the Church, recognising the Pope as the Supreme Pontiff.

The Rumanian Constitution of 1923 recognised freedom of worship. Because its members were more numerous than those of other Churches—with the exception, of course, of the National Orthodox Church—the Church of the Oriental Rite was given, by the Constitution, precedence next after the National Orthodox Church. This did not mean, however, that it was given preference over the Church of the Latin Rite, or any other minority Church.

The Rumanian Government was empowered by law to make subsidies to both Rites, both for the exercise of worship and for the support of Catholic schools. A Concordat, which came into force on 29th May, 1929, more precisely regulated the relations between Church and State, but since the First World War, at any rate, the Churches of both Rites had enjoyed conditions in which they could develop continuously and progressively.

The Red Army marched into Rumania on 23rd August, 1944, an unconditional surrender followed and the country was compelled to declare war on Germany, whose very reluctant ally she had previously been. King Michael, who had been held a virtual prisoner by the pro-Nazi Antonescu, took an important part in the surrender of his country, with the help of the opposition leaders Bratianu and Maniu. Unfortunately, however, the political structure was unstable, and in the immediate post-armistice period a number of coalition Governments were formed, none of which survived more than a few years.

One of the reasons for the non-survival of these Governments was the constant pressure placed upon them by the Communists. The interesting point is that the militant Communists in Rumania at this time numbered only about 1,000, most of whom were members of Petru Groza's Ploughman's Front, splintered from the Peasant Party in 1934. This extremely small minority, however, had the full backing of the Russian forces of occupation and of Vyshinsky, the Soviet Vice-Commissar for Foreign Affairs, who took up residence in Bucharest.

In March 1945 the coalition Government then in power was replaced, at Vyshinsky's insistence, by a Government of the Popular Front, which was composed of Leftist elements, with Petru Groza as Prime Minister. From this moment, under the Russian-bolstered dictatorship of Groza, the Communists gradually seized all the power. In November 1946 new elections were held, on allegedly false registers, and the Communists were returned to power with the fantastic majority of 348 seats to 29.

A peace treaty was signed by Rumania and the Allies in Paris on 10th February, 1947. Certain territories were transferred to former owners, and reparations to Russia were set at three hundred million dollars-worth of oil, timber, grain and machinery, payable within eight years from 1944.

The Government of Groza carried out a campaign of terror against all its rivals. Bratianu and other democrats were fortunate in fleeing the country in 1947, while the veteran Maniu was arrested and sentenced to solitary confinement for life. On 6th November the Government was reconstituted, and consisted thereafter entirely of Communists or fellow-travellers. On 30th December

King Michael was compelled by this Government to abdicate, and a republic was proclaimed. From this moment on the communisation of Rumania has developed along the well-known lines. This development has, however, one aspect which differentiates it from that in other countries, with the exception of Bulgaria.

Roughly thirteen million Rumanians were members of the National Orthodox Church. The Communists did not seek to destroy this Church, but instead set out to gain control of it and make it a tool against the Catholic Churches. This it did with some cunning. A decree was issued which debarred all priests of the National Orthodox Church over the age of seventy from holding any post in the administration or government of the Church. This removed several Bishops and a number of elderly priests who constituted strong opposition to the régime, and they were replaced by priests who were willing to co-operate. When the Patriarch Nicodemus died in February 1948, Bishop Justinian Marina, one of these willing collaborators, was appointed by Parliament to succeed him.

The next step was to revise the Constitution of the National Orthodox Church so that all ecclesiastical affairs were placed in the direct control of the Patriarch. This was done, and so, within less than two years, and with a minimum of difficulty, a potentially powerful opponent was transformed into an ally. The way was now clear for the extinction of the Catholic Churches, in which the Communists recognised their next greatest opponents.

The attack on the Catholic Church began with a propaganda campaign of vilification. At the time that it was started the Press of both Rites was totally suppressed, and Pastoral Letters subjected to rigorous censorship, which removed any possibility of reply by the Church.

The propaganda campaign followed the usual lines. The Catholic clergy were opposed to the democratic régime and to the interests of the nation and people. They were also subject to the Vatican, which, as everyone in the world knew, was reactionary and imperialistic. The clergy could not be permitted to follow the directives of the Vatican or make use of the Church as a means of propaganda against the democratic order.

Daily attacks, by Press and radio, were made on the Church and on the Pope. His Holiness, it was said, while being the head of Catholicism, was at the same time the director of a political and financial organisation, which made use of religion to maintain the privileges of the dominant class. Epithets hurled at the Vatican were "the protector of fascist criminals", "an espionage agency", "the fifth column of American expansion in Europe", and so on. The Pope and the hierarchy of the Church were principally responsible for the War and for all the misery after the War.

The first active measure against the Church was the publication of a series of decrees and laws, one of which summarily revoked the Concordat of 1929 and all laws ratifying later conventions and agreements, though Article 23 of the Concordat required six months' notice to be given should one side or the other wish to abrogate it. One of the declared reasons for this act was that the Concordat gave all the advantages to the Vatican and imposed all the obligations on the Rumanian State.

On 14th August, 1948, a decree governing the general regulations for religions was published, the effect of which was to bring every Church activity under State control. It formally guaranteed liberty of conscience and religion to all Rumanians, in return for adherence to the laws of the State. But it then went on to require "the organisation and functioning of any religious cult to have State recognition in the form of a decree of the National Assembly", and pointed out that recognition could be refused for sufficient reasons. It further declared that the heads of all religious organisations—metropolitans, archbishops, bishops, superintendents, apostolic administrators and administrative vicars—must be approved by the National Assembly before they could take up office. In addition, no representative of any religion could have any relations with Religious, institutions or official persons located outside the country except with the approval of the Minister for Worship, and through the intervention of the Minister for Foreign Affairs; nor could any religious cult from a foreign country exercise any jurisdiction over the Faithful of the Rumanian State.

Another measure concerned the changes made from one religion to another. It stated: "If at least ten per cent of one local community passes to another religion, that community loses its legal title to a part of its property proportional to the number of Faithful who have abandoned it, and the part lost passes officially to the community of the adopted religion. If those who change to another religion represent seventy-five per cent of the Faithful of the abandoned religion all the property becomes by law the property of the adopted religion."

Now, place by the side of this a statement made by the Minister for Worship on 24th August, 1948, and the intention of the measures becomes clear. "Some of the Catholic clergy and Faithful," the Minister said, "are turning towards the People's Republic of Rumania, and are separating themselves from their leaders. We expect all Catholics to re-examine their attitude and particularly those Rumanians of the Oriental Rite whom we remind of the example of their ancestors, who in their time knew how to be one with the people and to understand their sufferings."

The Church of the Oriental Rite had come into existence towards the end of the seventeenth century. The synods of the schismatic Church meeting in 1698 and 1700 decided once again to unite their Church with Rome. After a rather violent struggle within the hierarchy of the Church, this course was adopted, and from the moment of reunion with Rome, the Church of the Oriental Rite developed rapidly, and played a vital part in education and in the reawakening of national, political and social awareness, through its Press, its weekly and monthly journals, and the books coming from its printing houses. Through its religious Orders, its great charitable works and its organisations in every branch of Catholic Section, it exerted wide influence. Of the three million Catholics in Rumania, more than a million and a half were members of the Oriental Rite. If these members could be persuaded or coerced into transferring their religious allegiance to the National Orthodox Church, under the new decree they would reduce their Church to destitution and impotence, by causing it to lose its property.

Other decrees placed all relief work and gifts received by religious organisation under control of the State; all seminaries came under similar control; and required State approval for the administrative and academic curricula of the seminaries.

A far-reaching and implicitly antagonistic reform of the educational system was announced at the same time. All private schools and denominational schools and other educational institutions were taken over by the State, together with all their goods and property. The teachers in State schools were required to inculcate in their pupils "the political and social idea of the historic times in which we live", to "remove mysticism, prejudice and superstitions" by showing that "all phenomena come from natural causes which science either knows or will know in the future". New text-books, mostly translated from Russian, and teaching atheistic Materialism, were to be used.

A Party agent was appointed to each school, to see that the wishes of the Government were carried out. Pupils' Unions were organised, the members of which were encouraged to denounce their teachers if they thought them not to be sufficiently democratic. All religious teaching in schools was forbidden, and every difficulty was placed in the way of the children to prevent them practising religion.

On 29th July, 1949, a decree was published forbidding all religious Orders to engage in teaching or relief work. All male Religious were ordered to congregate in the Archbishop's palace at Bucharest and Alba Julia, there to carry on their religious life, while the female Religious were directed to special Houses set apart for them at Radna, Ploesti and Timisoara, for the same purpose. This done, the Government confiscated all the property of the Orders.

This decree brought to a conclusion the general measures directed against the Church of both Rites. The attack now followed another plan. First, the Church of the Oriental Rite was to be destroyed, and when this had been achieved, attention was to be turned to the Church of the Latin Rite.

In the attack on the Church of the Oriental Rite, the Communists received full support from the National Orthodox Church. In one of his very first speeches, the Government-appointed Patriarch said: "Our thoughts go out to our Brothers of the Rumanian Greek Orthodox Church (Oriental Rite). . . . To the clergy of this Church. . . . I address my paternal entreaties: do not allow yourselves to be deceived any longer by your enemies. . . . What is it that still separates us? Nothing other than the loyalty you persist in, accorded to Rome by your submission. Show now the same loyalty to the Church of our people." A similar appeal was made by the Metropolitan of Sibiu: "I address myself to you whom foreign interests have separated from your good Mother, the Orthodox Church, and invite you warmly and paternally to return to the common fold. . . . The day of our national resurrection will be that day when we can embrace you and call you brothers. Come! We await you with open arms!"

When these invitations fell on deaf ears, the Government took active measures. In September 1948 four of the six Bishops of the Oriental Rite were deposed, and on its own initiative the Government called a meeting of the Synod, the object of which was to sanction the union of the Church of the Oriental Rite with the National Orthodox Church.

Towards the end of September every priest of the Oriental Rite received an invitation to delegate two priests from his department—these delegate-priests were nominated by the Communists—to represent him at a Congress which was to meet at Cluj on 1st October, and to vote for him on a resolution which was to be put to the Synod, on the return of the Church of the Oriental Rite to the National Orthodox Church. Instead of being sent through the post, these invitations were delivered by hand by Party or Government representatives, with false explanations, threats and promises. Though some priests were deceived or coerced by threats and extreme physical torture, by far the greater number refused the invitation, the majority of whom were immediately arrested. However, thirty-eight priests were "delegated", and met at Cluj on 1st October. Now, at the Synod of Alba Julia this number of priests had passed their resolution exactly 250 years ago on 21st October. It had always been the intention of the Government to effect the return of the Church of the Oriental Rite to the bosom of the National Church before that date. The choice of thirty-eight delegates was a nicety which did not pass unnoticed.

The Congress of Cluj completed its business with some despatch. After the election of a president and secretary and the reading of the names of the delegates, there were four speeches only, and the resolution, which had been drawn up by the Minister for Worship, was read and unanimously passed. The delegates then went to Bucharest, where they were met by the Patriarch of the National Orthodox Church, five Bishops and all the Orthodox priests of Bucharest. A solemn meeting was held in the Great Hall of the Holy Synod, speeches were made, the resolution announced and the Patriarch expressed his satisfaction. The company then adjourned to St Spiridious's Church, where the "delegates" were received into the Orthodox Church. This concluded, the Church of the Oriental Rite was considered to exist no longer.

The Faithful of the former Catholic Church of the Oriental Rite were now required to sign a form stating that "voluntarily and without compulsion" they reunited themselves with the Orthodox Church. All kinds of fraud were used to obtain signatures. In one place, the form was described as an appeal for world peace; in another, that it was a mere formality devoid of significance. But if men refused to sign then they were threatened with heavy fines, deportation to Siberia, confiscation of property and summary execution.

To give the impression that the Faithful of the Oriental Rite had accepted union with the Orthodox Church with great joy, a great festival was organised at Alba Julia on the two hundred and fiftieth anniversary of the union of the Church with Rome. At this festival a resolution was read and passed by all present, declaring: "We break for ever our relations, of whatsoever kind, with the Vatican and with Papal Rome. We incorporate ourselves with our whole being into the Rumanian Orthodox Church." Within the next few days, empowered by the decree regulating changes made from one religion to another, the police began to hand over the churches and other property of the Oriental Rite to the National Orthodox Church.

The account of the liquidation of this great Church thus briefly and baldly told gives no idea of the background of resistance by the Church of the Oriental Rite to the machinations of the Communists and their Orthodox allies. As we have seen, before the attack was set in motion four of the six Bishops had been deposed, and others placed under house arrest. The lower clergy were, therefore, unable to receive any guidance from their spiritual leaders.

Among those held under house arrest was the Bishop of Cluj, Monsignor Julius Hosen. When he heard of the proposed Congress he managed to send out by stealth a circular letter to the priests of his diocese. In it, among other things, he declared: "By virtue of the power vested in me as Ordinary of Cluj, I apply the penalty of excommunication *ipso facto incurrenda* to all those who take part in the projected meeting. Those who unfortunately will attend the Congress will be excommunicated by name by our decree which will be read in all the churches of the diocese." This gave a lead to the clergy, but could not have any effect on those bent on reunion with the Orthodox Church.

The day following the Congress, the Apostolic Nuncio, an

Irish-American, Monsignor Gerald O'Hara, now Apostolic Delegate in Great Britain, sent a Note to the Rumanian Minister for Foreign Affairs, protesting against the violence done to the Church of the Oriental Rite. It recalled the solemn undertakings made by the Rumanian Government at the signing of the peace treaty and stated categorically that these undertakings had been violated by the acts against the Church of the Orthodox Rite. He underlined the responsibility of the authorities in these acts, and described how priests had been taken to police bureaux, where they were terrorised, threatened with imprisonment, deportation and death, were thrown into underground cells, ill-treated, subjected to endless interrogation and released only when they were prepared to sign the declaration of schism. The Minister for Foreign Affairs replied at once, rejecting equally categorically the protest of the Nuncio, which was an interference in the internal affairs of the Government and an act of provocation, he said.

On 7th October the Bishops of the Oriental Rite sent to the President, Petru Groza, a letter signed by all, in which they drew his attention to acts committed against their Church by the administrative organisations and the secret police. Protesting against the confiscation by the police of one of their Collective Letters, they then went on to describe how some of them had been arrested and concluded: "For reasons of prudence we do not judge it opportune to enumerate here all the vexations and acts of violence to which the archpriests and priests whose signatures they wished to obtain were subjected."

Indeed, it was refusal to sign the required "form" which plunged the Church of the Oriental Rite into martyrdom. Out of 1,810 priests only 430 could be induced to sign, even when the police used the most brutal persuasions. Those who would not sign were imprisoned without trial, packed into underground cells in conditions resembling the Black Hole of Calcutta, tortured, starved and sent to forced-labour. Within forty-eight hours between 27th and 29th October all the Bishops were arrested, together with all the professors of the seminaries and all the members of the episcopal Curiae.

Having suffered violence at the hands of the Communist police, the Bishops were transferred to the Orthodox Patriarch's summer villa, where the Patriarch visited them many times to try to persuade them to join his Church. When they consistently refused they were transferred to the monastery of Caldarusani. Nothing was then heard of them for two years, when it was discovered that they had been in underground cells at the Ministry of the Interior, and subsequently in the prison at Vacaresti. It has been impossible to discover how they have been treated, but it is known that Monsignor Basil Aftenie, Vicar of Bucharest, died on 10th May, 1950, as the result of treatment received from his captors. Later the Bishops were imprisoned at Sighet.

The parish priests were kept in prison only a short time, but when they were released they were kept under constant police supervision. Many managed to evade their surveillers and escape to the mountains, where, outlawed, they perform their ministry in secret, hidden by members of the Faithful, despite a decree of the Ministry of the Interior offering large rewards for denouncing "former priests" and the infliction of up to eight years in prison for giving hospitality to "former priests". Hundreds of the higher clergy are still in prison.

With the Church of the Oriental Rite removed, the Government next turned its attention to the Church of the Latin Rite. In dealing with the Church of the Latin Rite, different tactics had perforce to be used, because there was no Church with which it could be reunited.

The main instrument of the Government in its destruction of the Latin Rite was that part of the decree governing the General Regulations for Religions, which required all religious denominations to submit its statutes to the Government for its approval. The demand for the submission of the statutes of the Church of the Latin Rite was made at the time that the campaign against the Church of the Oriental Rite was at its height. In order to survive, therefore, the Church prepared the statutes demanded.

With the deposition of the Archbishop of Bucharest and the Bishops of Timisoara and Satu Mare, only two Bishops were now recognised by the State—the Bishops of Alba Julia and of Iasi. These two presented the statutes to the Government on 27th October, 1948. The statutes were rejected by the Government, since naturally they insisted on the right of the Pope to have spiritual jurisdiction over all the Catholics in the world, and the two Bishops were instructed to draw up new statutes omitting this. They refused and were arrested. The Government then instructed the Vicars-General to present new statutes, and they merely re-presented the statutes drawn up by the Bishops, on the grounds of lack of authority. Faced with this refusal, the Government had to find new tactics.

The new tactics were not novel. On the last day of February, 1950, the Holy Synod of the National Orthodox Church addressed a letter to all the clergy and Christian Faithful in Rumania, asking for their support for the Stockholm Manifesto. The Government also organised a Congress, to be held at Targu-Mures on 27th April, at which they hoped, by means of special preparations, that a certain number of Catholics present would demonstrate a hostility towards the authority of the Church on the grounds that the Church was not doing its utmost to work for peace; in other words, refused to support the Stockholm Manifesto.

Barely 100 attended the Congress, but numbers were not essential to the plan. Under the presidency of a Communist nominated priest, Father Andrew Agotha, who was excommunicated on 5th May for the part he played, the Congress set up a Catholic Committee of Action, whose function was to disseminate the Communist idea of peace, to persuade Catholics, and particularly priests, to sign the Stockholm Manifesto, and finally to work for a breach with Rome.

At the same time the Minister for Worship re-opened the question of the Church statutes. Copies of the statutes as drawn up by the Bishops and corrected by the Minister were sent early in June to the Episcopal Curiae of Alba Julia and Iasi, with a covering note that only the statutes as they now stood would be acceptable to the Government.

The corrections had so cunningly been made that at first reading they seemed reasonable enough. But the briefest study revealed their treachery. For example, while Article 2 recognised that "the Pope is the Supreme Authority in faith and morals, and in all matters concerning spiritual jurisdiction in the Roman Catholic Religion", Article 13 referred to the right to name the Metropolitan and Bishops as belonging to the Holy See, but went on: "These however must first be proposed by the Roman Catholic Church of the People's Republic of Rumania, and be approved by the Government", which, in effect, deprived the Pope of all initiative and would allow him to appoint only those acceptable to the Government.

Knowing that these statutes would be as unacceptable now as they had ever been, the Government decided to remove the main sources of opposition before they could act. During the night of 10th May the Vicars-General of Alba Julia and of Iasi were arrested, and a week later the Archbishop of Bucharest and the Bishop of Satu Mare. The Vicar-General of Iasi was treated so harshly that he died on 25th May, and the Bishop of Satu Mare was killed some time later.

The Bishop of Timisoara, who had been placed in retirement, was, however, still at liberty, and he at once courageously addressed to the Faithful a Pastoral Letter in which he referred to all the acts of violence committed by the Government against the Church, and deplored the signing of the Stockholm Manifesto by certain priests. The Bishop was arrested on 18th July. Ten days later the Catholic Committee of Action issued a declaration in which it urged the clergy and people to accept the revised statutes. It claimed to be acting in accordance with the laws of the Catholic Church.

But before this happened the Government had removed yet another source of possible trouble. In June an ex-chauffeur of Apostolic Nunciature was arrested on charges of espionage, together with others who at some time had been employed by the Nuncio. When brought to trial, the ex-chauffeur, Nicholas Popescu, deposed that the Nuncio, Monsignor O'Hara, and his Counsellor, Monsignor del Mestri, had persuaded him to engage in pro-American propaganda among his friends, to gather information of military importance and to engage in espionage on behalf of the "imperialists". The accused—there were seven of them—were all found guilty and given sentences ranging from seven years' forced-labour to imprisonment for life.

The Government claimed that the evidence at the trial proved without doubt that the Nuncio was leading a plot against the State, and demanded that Monsignor O'Hara and Monsignor del Mestri should leave the country within three days. In this way the Government removed what might have been embarrassing witnesses to the complete destruction of the Catholic Church in Rumania.

Another Congress was then convened at Gheorgheni on 16th September, under the presidency of Agotha, who had presided at Targu-Mures and was chief of the Catholic Committee of Action. At its conclusion the Congress expressed the desire for a meeting of a General Catholic Assembly.

This Assembly was called to meet at Cluj on 15th March, 1951. Between the meeting at Gheorgheni and this date, however, many opposing priests were arrested, and so-called Progressive priests were put in charge of parishes, with the result that "representatives" of 601 parishes gathered at the Assembly. The statutes were the main item of consideration, and a final motion concluded: ". . . the assembly confides to the directing Council of the Statutes the sacred duty of making it possible for the higher administration of the two dioceses to proceed without delay to bring the Church within the framework of the legal order, thus responding to the desires of all the Catholics of the country who love peace".

The object of all this was to create a split within the Church of the Latin Rite, and to aid the creation of the schism the Government set about creating confusion in the minds of the Faithful. By changing parish priests frequently they made it very difficult for the people to discover whether their priest was a collaborator or true to Rome.

Now the eighty-one-year-old Bishop of Timisoara and a number of priests, members of the Episcopal Curiae, were brought to trial accused of treason in that they had been involved in the Apostolic Nuncio's spy-ring. At the conclusion of the trial the aged Bishop was sentenced to eighteen years' imprisonment, and the others to sentences varying between ten and fifteen years. Among those condemned were the Vicars-General of Bucharest and Timisoara. Progressive priests were appointed in their place.

When the Faithful did find out that their priests were collaborators, they left the churches, and in an attempt to remove this distrust the Government tried all manner of propaganda tricks. The priests, for example, were instructed to declare their fidelity to the Pope in their sermons. But this and similar ruses were not successful. The main weapon of the Government was the creation of confusion.

Despite persecution and all other harsh and restrictive measures taken against the Church of the Latin Rite, however, the plans of the Government have not been entirely successful. Though many of the Faithful stay away from the churches, and though the atheistic materialism taught in the schools is having a grave effect upon the rising generations, which will rebound upon the Church, the Church is not yet completely destroyed.

CHAPTER XVI

Czecho-Slovakia

THE SAD history of Munich, the rape of their country and their embroilment in Hitler's war, is seen by some to be behind the present apparent contentment of the majority of Czecho-Slovaks with their Communist régime. Whether this is so or not —and cruel, bitter accusations have been thrown at them for their failure to rise at the time of the Polish and Hungarian revolts of October 1956—they showed themselves to be a people of great courage, a courage which has been reflected in the stand taken by the Church in Czecho-Slovakia in the face of relentless persecution over the past ten years.

During the War a Government-in-Exile in London, headed by Dr Benes, had thrown in its lot with the Allies. On 18th July, 1941, an agreement was signed in London whereby Russia recognised this Government, and a military alliance was entered into, which, two years later, developed into a twenty years' Treaty of Friendship and Mutual Assistance. Throughout the War, from the Battle of Britain onwards, sizable Czecho-Slovak formations had fought with tremendous courage on almost every front. In the country itself a gigantic resistance movement was organised which was one of the largest and most successful of all such movements. In the last weeks of the War, on instructions from London, the Movement joined battle with the Germans, and paved the way for eventual liberation by the Russians and a small body of Americans.

In April 1945, a large part of the country having been cleared of the enemy, and final clearance being only a matter of time, Dr Benes returned to Czecho-Slovakia and set up a Provisional Government at Kosice. After the fall of Prague to the Resistance, the Russians and the Americans on 10th May, this Government moved to the capital there to inaugurate the Second Republic.

In the Provisional Government Dr Benes had been compelled to include Communist and extreme Left-wing representatives, for these parties had played a prominent part in the Resistance, and could rightly claim a voice in the future of the country. But the Czecho-Slovak democrats, as elsewhere, were unprepared for the methods used by the Communists, and though the expulsion of more than two million Sudeten Germans and the nationalisation of all businesses employing more than 200 people, which were the first measures passed by the Provisional Government, should have been a grave warning of what was in the wind, the parties of the Right and Centre seemed to be blind to the danger.

The danger was not long in manifesting itself. In May 1946 the first elections were held, as a result of which the Communists and fellow-travellers won 152 seats to the Right and Centre Parties 148 and the Communist leader Gottwald became Prime Minister. In the following month Dr Benes was re-elected President, and for the next two years affairs were in a state of flux, with neither side quite strong enough to force their entire will on the other. Then on 25th February, 1948, the Communists organised a *coup d'état*. Aided by the resignations of nine democrat members of the Government, who chose this method of protest at the way the Communists were behaving, and by the presence still of the Red Army, Gottwald formed an entirely Communist Government. Dr Benes resigned, and was succeeded by Gottwald, and Czecho-Slovakia was set on the path which, by this time, all the countries of eastern and central Europe in the orbit of Soviet Russia were already following.

The more one ponders these events, the stranger they seem. The population of the Second Republic, when the adjustments had been made, which restored the territories filched by Germany and Hungary, numbered approximately twelve and a half millions. Of these, no fewer than 75 per cent were Catholics. How Catholics, who knew what to expect from a Communist régime, since the example of Soviet Russia and the newer Communist States was there to warn them, could have allowed the Czecho-Slovak Party to manœuvre itself into power, is one of those mysteries which may never be satisfactorily solved. This is not the place to attempt a post-mortem. It can only be pointed out that the Catholic Church in Czecho-Slovakia was strong and active in every sphere of educational, cultural and religious life, and in charitable work.

On his return to the country in 1945, Benes had made an early move to establish diplomatic relations with the Holy See, and in May 1946 representatives were exchanged. This led, in its turn, to the filling of the Archiepiscopal See of Prague, which had been vacant since the death of Cardinal Kaspar in 1941. The new Archbishop was Monsignor Joseph Beran, who, during the war, as Rector of the Prague seminary, had shown great courage in resisting the Nazis, for which he had spent three years in various concentration camps. On the day of his enthronement, the Military Cross in recognition of his services during the war, was bestowed upon him by the Communist Minister for the Interior. No better man could have been chosen for this post, in view of what was to come.

During the years of the Provisional and Coalition Governments, the Catholic Church in Bohemia and Moravia had enjoyed a certain amount of liberty, though the Ministry of the Interior, held by the Communists, had introduced various anti-religious measures, in particular, one reducing the hours of religious instruction in schools. A number of clergy and Catholic laymen had also been purged, having been accused of plotting against Benes. The situation in Slovakia, however, was rather different.

At the time of the seizure of Czecho-Slovakia, Hitler sought to ease the burden of suppressing a brave and proud people, by splitting the country in two. He set up a Protectorate of Bohemia and Moravia, under Baron von Neurath, but transformed Slovakia into an "Independent" State. The Slovaks, who possessed different national characteristics from the Czechs, had for some time been demanding autonomy, though within the overall framework of the Czecho-Slovak State. The movement had been started soon after the formation of the State, by Father Andrej Hlinka, leader of the Slovak Clerical Party, who had organised a semi-military formation known as the Hlinka Guard. When Hlinka died in August 1938 the leadership passed to Father Tiso, and it was he who whipped up the demand for autonomy after the Munich dismemberment of Czecho-Slovakia. Through the Hlinka Guard he organised Slovakia on Nazi lines, and it was the threat of a revolt against the Prague Government that gave Hitler his pretext to intervene. Slovakia was granted a measure of autonomy, but was absorbed completely into the Nazi war-machine.

It was Slovakia that the Russians chose for the spearhead of their designs on Czecho-Slovakia. During 1944 Russian military and political instructors were parachuted into Slovakia, who attempted to win over the Slovak Government with promises to recognise the independence of a Slovak Soviet Republic after the War. They made some headway, and a National Slovak Council was formed. As soon as parts of the country were cleared by the Red Army in the autumn of 1944, one of the first measures announced by the National Council was the nationalisation of the schools and universities, together with their staffs.

During the final stages of the military struggle the Communists treated the Church with extreme violence and cruelty. Church property was destroyed, priests' houses and Bishops' palaces were entered and searched, and Religious driven out of their Houses. Many priests were arrested and imprisoned and many others were shot out of hand, for no reasonable cause.

Under the Second Republic, Slovakia was accorded a measure of autonomy, with the National Council made up of Communists and Democrats, the latter being almost as Anti-Catholic as the former. Catholics were excluded from public life, and by a series of decrees and regulations were submitted to a policy of ruthless suppression. In April 1945 the Bishop of Spis, the Auxiliary Bishop of Trnava and the Director of the Society of St Adalbert were arrested and imprisoned. The population, however, were shocked by these arrests, and after some months the Bishops were released.

In May 1945 a series of decrees nationalised 1,800 primary and 77 secondary schools, and 30 colleges, involving a total of 40,000 pupils; confiscated all school property and all student hostels; and dissolved all youth organisations of Catholic Action and confiscated their property. Many seminaries were also compelled to hand over a large part of their buildings, which were turned into co-educational schools, and the students were made to attend public schools, and receive lessons in atheistic Materialism. Many Catholic newspapers and magazines were banned from the libraries, and a number of them were forced out of existence.

After the elections of May 1946 there was a slight improvement, but new measures hit the Church hard blows. Sundays and Holy Days were declared working days; members of Catholic Action were sent to prison for wearing a small metal cross; and in 1947 all Church property was confiscated.

The day after the seizure of power by the Communists in Prague, three of the largest Catholic weeklies were suppressed. The reason given was the scarcity of newsprint, but underlying it was the intention to deprive the Church of an important means of rebutting the anti-religious propaganda and the charges levelled against it. The suppression of the Catholic Press gained impetus throughout the rest of the year, so that by the beginning of 1949 more than sixty newspapers and periodicals had been forced to cease publication, and all religious books, including Prayer Books, were banned from the bookshops. The presses and publishing houses were taken over by the State.

Elections were held on 30th May, but before this the Government presented a Bill to Parliament for the suppression of Catholic schools and the seizure of their property. But for some reason or other, Gottwald wished a Te Deum to be sung on his forthcoming election to the Presidency, and so a clause was interpolated which said: "The Government has the power to make exceptions." Negotiations were at once started, and an agreement was reached by which those schools directly depending on ecclesiastical authority were exempt. But this, as will be seen, proved to be only a temporary respite.

A new Constitution was introduced on 9th May, which declared Czecho-Slovakia to be a Peoples' Republic. Article 15 guaranteed liberty of conscience, while Article 16 declared that "all religious denominations as well as non-adherance to any particular denomination are equal before the law". While the Constitution treated of many issues in general terms, a law was promulgated on 6th September which gave detailed information of the regulations governing relations between Church and State. Article 28 of this law was to be invoked more than any other. It stated: "Anyone who abuses his office, whether religious or other, by influencing politics in a way detrimental to the Peoples' Republic, will incur a penalty of from one to twelve months' imprisonment." Many priests were arrested under this article, in several cases for helping refugees to reach the frontier.

In June 1948 the appointment was announced of a mixed Commission to begin negotiations to find a *modus vivendi* between Church and State. On the same day it was announced that all primary and secondary schools would be nationalised on 30th September, thus breaking the former agreement. This took place, and in November all kindergartens were taken over, the nuns in charge of many of them being expelled from the country.

After the nationalisation, religious instruction was still permitted in schools. This was a clever move on the part of the Government, who were aware of the repercussions the total banning would have had on the predominantly Catholic people. It was, however, made an optional subject, and a propaganda campaign was launched to dissuade parents from allowing their children to attend religious classes.

At the same time the Catholic organisations were attacked. Catholic Action had always been divided into two parts, one serving Bohemia and Moravia, and the other Slovakia. Central Bureaux for each of these organisations were situated in Prague and Bratislava respectively. On 22nd November the Central Catholic Secretariate, through which the Slovak Bishops directed their Catholic Action, was closed, its director arrested and Catholic Action dissolved. In December Czech Catholic Youth was suppressed, and a few days later Catholic Action in Bohemia and Moravia was dissolved. All other Catholic organisations suffered the same fate "in the public interest which demands the unification of all forces in conformity with the People's Democratic Order".

A rather different procedure was used in Czecho-Slovakia from that used in similar circumstances in other countries with regard to the suppression of some associations. In Slovakia, for example, a decree issued in December ordered the *fusion* of the Slovak Catholic Women's Union with the Communist Slovak Women's League; and similarly the Catholic Youth of Bohemia was ordered to fuse with the Czech Communist Youth League. This was done, according to the Minister for External Affairs, because "the unification of youth, the formation of one single organisation, is the logical result of the political development which has taken place in Czecho-Slovakia. It is universally known that the Peoples' Democracies guarantee freedom of worship to various denominations; but we cannot permit youth associations formed on a religious basis, for these would destroy the unity of our youth and impede its efforts towards the building of a better future."

Besides the associations, charitable institutions and bodies, particularly the great organisation Caritas, were submitted to similar treatment. Hospital and kindergartens run by religious Orders were nationalised, and the nuns who worked in them expelled. In addition, all real property belonging to the Church was confiscated, which deprived the Church at one blow of one of its most important sources of income, and in itself automatically curtailed the volume of charitable work.

Against all these measures the Catholic hierarchy protested vehemently in a letter to the Government. "Despite the promises of religious liberty," the Bishops said, "and despite repeated affirmations of good-will, a campaign has been conducted which is anti-religious and anti-clerical. This campaign has developed along well established lines exactly similar to those followed in other countries where the Catholic religion and the Catholic Church have been attacked." This letter was ignored, and when the Bishops proposed acquainting the people of it and its terms in a Pastoral Letter in September, the reading of it was prohibited. In the following month the Ninth Congress of the Czech Communist Party made clear, without any equivocation, the ultimate aim of the régime—to liquidate all opposition and everything which might stand in the way of totalitarian Communism.

The negotiations between the hierarchy and the State had been going on all this time, and it is little wonder that in the atmosphere created by the Government measures they should fail. The hierarchy refused to compromise on its stand for liberty and autonomy in all ecclesiastical matters, though it was prepared to preach the duty of loyalty to the State at all times; and the Government, for its part, was determined to make of the Church an instrument of its own policy. No communiqué was issued when the discussions were finally broken off in February, but in an interview with the International News Service on 17th March, 1949, the Archbishop Primate gave three reasons for the failure. These were, he said, a demand by the Government that the Church should make a declaration of loyalty to the State, the Government intention to confiscate yet more Church property, and a Government demand that ecclesiastical sanctions which had been imposed on three Slovak priests now holding Government posts in contravention of the hierarchy's instructions should be lifted.

The breaking-off of the negotiations angered the Communists, and at once a whole series of restrictive measures were put into effect. All parish real estate was confiscated, thus depriving the Church of all its property of this kind; pilgrimages and religious functions held outside the church were banned; any religious associations that were still active were to be suppressed; priests willing to collaborate with the State were to be encouraged in every way; all religious publications of any sort were to be banned; and a watch was to be kept by "men of confidence" to discover whether priests were being supplied with clothing coupons and food by the Faithful. The police were directed to see that all these measures were carried out.

On 29th April the Bishops addressed a memorandum of protest to Gottwald, which they concluded with these words: "We know that these orders are only the first phase of the final and decisive blow." The Government merely responded by a campaign designed to separate the Bishops from the clergy and the Faithful. Blaming the Bishops for the failure to reach agreement with the State, they declared that the only way to effect conciliation was for the clergy to negotiate directly with the Government. To bring this about propaganda against the Bishops and the Vatican was intensified, a new periodical called *The Bulletin of the Catholic Clergy*, edited by renegade priests, was published by the Ministry of the Interior, a Catholic Action Committee was formed to provoke and encourage divisions within the Church, and three decrees aimed at curtailing the independence of the Bishops even in ecclesiastical affairs were promulgated. The first of these decrees required all Bishops to submit to the Ministry for Public Instruction all documents destined for priests or public, notification of all clerical meetings, whether held in public or in private to be made to the National Committee of the district at least three days in advance and declared all penalties inflicted by the hierarchy on priests for political reasons to be null and void.

The Bishops were not slow to recognise what the inevitable next step would be—the creation of a schismatic Czech National Catholic Church; and they issued warnings to the clergy. Despite these warnings, however, on 10th June a number of priests and laymen attended a meeting called by the Government in Prague for the purpose of forming the so-called Catholic Action Committee. At the end of the meeting a declaration was signed and issued by about sixty priests present, to the effect that an overwhelming majority of the Faithful were at one with them in hoping for agreement between Church and State. The Catholic Action Committee was formally inaugurated a week later, but two days before this, on 15th June, the Bishops issued a Pastoral Letter to be read from all pulpits on 19th June, warning the clergy and Faithful of the attempt to bring about a split within the Church. "A pseudo-Catholic Action is now being formed against the will of the Bishops," the Letter stated. "It aims at confusing the Faithful and to make it impossible for the Bishops to defend the Liberty and rights of the Church."

In the evening of the day on which the Letter was drawn up a number of police agents entered the Primate's Palace. Archbishop Beran was absent at the time, and when he returned he found a Government Commissar installed in his secretariate, who announced that henceforward he would control and countersign all the documents of the Curia and would supervise the whole administration of the archdiocese. In the meantime the police had searched the Curia, arrested two priests of the Curia staff and seized official notepaper and the archiepiscopal seal, which they took away with them, and with which they forged an order forbidding the reading of the Pastoral Letter.

The Commissar made every attempt to isolate the Archbishop from the people, by holding his mail and turning away visitors. Naturally, the Archbishop protested to the Government, and when his protests had no effect, on the Saturday, in the church of the Premonstratensian monastery at Strahov, he preached a courageous sermon to a vast congregation in which he described what had happened in the Palace, what the pseudo-Catholic Action's rôle was and warned all the Faithful of the intentions of the Government.

After the service the Abbot of the monastery was arrested, but the Archbishop was not touched. He was due to preach the sermon at Mass in Prague cathedral the next day. The Communists ordered their followers to fill the cathedral, which they did, and while the Primate was preaching he was constantly interrupted by cat-calls, shouts and whistles. That evening he was placed under house arrest in his Palace.

When they heard what had happened, the Bishops drew up another Pastoral Letter, which was to be read on the following Sunday. By keeping it secret, and by employing all manner of secret means, they were able to place copies in the hands of the great majority of priests throughout the country. This letter was the most outspoken denunciation of the Government up to this time. It listed all the abuses to which the Church had been subjected and concluded that the Government had set in motion "a systematic persecution of the Church in Czecho-Slovakia, well and methodically prepared".

At the inauguration of the Catholic Action Committee on 17th June it was claimed that no fewer than 1,500 priests had joined the Movement. This was soon seen to be false, for when the Vatican condemned the Committee on 20th June, the decree of the Holy Office was read in nearly every church in Czecho-Slovakia, and of the 5,780 secular priests only about 170 actually joined the Movement. On 17th July the faithful priests issued a declaration stating that the Committee was anti-Catholic and schismatic.

The next move of the Government was to post police-agents at the entrance to the palace of every Bishop so that all his movements might be checked. A Commissar was also placed in every Chancellory. These Commissars intervened in all ecclesiastical matters to a most extraordinary extent, and on 5th August the Primate, still under house arrest, wrote to the Attorney General protesting against the measures recently taken and questioning their legality. Whether the Attorney General replied—or what he replied—is not known.

The campaign to establish the Catholic Action Committee was intensified during these months. Threats were levelled against the clergy to make them join, and when these were ineffective scores of priests were arrested and imprisoned. But even this did not prevent the great majority of clergy and Faithful from resisting all the Government's efforts to create a Catholic Church separated from Rome.

In November the Government set up a State Bureau for Ecclesiastical Affairs, which, operating on the Soviet model, was to see that "ecclesiastical and religious life develops in harmony with the Constitution and the People's Democratic régime, and thereby to ensure that each citizen enjoys the liberty of conscience guaranteed by the Constitution on the basis of religious toleration and the juridical equal of all denominations". All Church activity was, therefore, to be brought under State control.

A powerful instrument in this policy was another decree published at the same time, dealing with the payment of clergy and the defraying of Church expenses and of those "religious associations recognised by the State". A stipulation of this law was that only those priests and persons approved by the State and who had taken the oath of loyalty might perform those duties "proper to the sacred character of the Church and religious associations". In order to receive remuneration from the State— and there was now no other source from which remuneration could be provided—the priest must give no cause for criticism and must fulfil the general conditions required of ordinary Civil Servants. The fact that the State held the money-bags naturally gave the Government a tremendous hold on all the priests and, through them, on all Church activities.

The Bishops at once pointed out to the Government that the setting up of the State Bureau for Ecclesiastical Affairs and this new law deprived the Church entirely of its autonomy, placed the Church outside the law and were contrary to those fundamental laws of the Republic concerning freedom of worship. The clergy of two dioceses also issued declarations in which they denounced the Bureau, renounced the "pecuniary benefits provided for in the law", and reaffirmed their loyalty to the Bishops. Both protests, the Government proclaimed, constituted a deliberate refusal by some of the clergy to carry out their civic duties, and blamed the Bishops for what was happening, as Gottwald insisted in an interview with the French Communist organ *L'Humanité*. "The conflict," he said, "is not between the Catholic Church and the Czecho-Slovak State, but between the State and certain high dignitaries of that Church. The majority of the clergy and the Faithful are in agreement with the State. The State is striving to strengthen this agreement, as is shown by our religious laws which guarantee the material existence of all the Churches, so that being free from economic worries they may devote themselves to their religious mission. The conflict between the State and certain high dignitaries of the Church has nothing to do with religion. It arises from the political activity against the State of a group of higher clergy."

So 1949 came to a close, but with this explanation of the President of the Republic, it was plain what the Government's intentions were, and it came as no surprise that the campaign against the Holy See should be intensified in the early months of 1950, and that in the early spring diplomatic relations should be finally completely broken off. Nearly a year before this happened—that is, in April 1949—the first step had been taken towards this end, when the Government requested the Vatican to recall its Chargé d'Affaires. The Vatican protested at this request, for no charges were levelled against Monsignor Verolino. To avoid making the situation worse, however, the Vatican met the request, but asked that Monsignor Verolino should be permitted to remain in Prague until a new Chargé d'Affaires could take over from him. The Secretariate appointed as Monsignor Verolino's successor the Counsellor of the Apostolic Nunciature in Berne, Monsignor Bertoli, and applied for a visa for him. The Minister for External Affairs assured the Holy See that the visa would be given immediately, but weeks passed without its being forthcoming. On 13th July, 1949, Monsignor Verolino was ordered to leave the country, and still Monsignor Bertoli had not received his visa, so the Secretary of the Inter-nunciature took over the duties of Chargé d'Affaires. Months passed, during which a Press campaign of outstanding virulence was waged against the acting Chargé d'Affaires, and the Government refused to recognise him. Finally, not by any normal means of communication, but in a broadcast from Radio Prague on 16th March, 1950, the Secretary was given three days in which to leave Czecho-Slovakia. There was nothing to do but accede, and when the Czech representative to the Vatican returned home without even taking leave of the Secretary of State, the break was absolute.

What had raised the anger of the Government had been a Vatican decree, published on the day that Monsignor Verolino left Prague, excommunicating all Catholic Communists and their collaborators. The Government proclaimed the decree to be interference in the internal affairs of the Republic and therefore constituted an offence against the State. "The aim of the Pontifical decree is clear," declared *Rudé Pravo*, the organ of the Czech Communist Party. "It obliges the Faithful to undertake subversive activity against the régime and the law." But the decree was really used as an excuse for getting rid of independent observers who could inform the world of what was happening.

Even before the final break came the Government had taken its next step. Two agents were sent to every religious House, to take over the administration and to re-educate the inhabitants, though their arrival was really a preliminary to the final taking over of the Houses by the State. The Government were aware, however, of the repercussions this measure would have on the people, and had to put up some justification, which they did by declaring that the religious Houses were centres of espionage on behalf of the Vatican. To prove this, a trial was staged in Prague of eleven Superiors and other outstanding members of Orders on charges of high treason and espionage. After a hearing which lasted from 30th March to 5th April, 1950, ten of the accused were given sentences ranging from ten years to life imprisonment. The acquitted man was sent to prison for two years, nevertheless, because, knowing of the other accuseds' treachery, he had not denounced them.

On the basis of this verdict, on the nights of 13th/14th and 21st/22nd April all the Houses of the male Orders were occupied, and the Religious sent to "concentration monasteries" or forced-labour camps. In September all women's Houses were similarly treated. It was announced that the Religious were not being arrested, but merely being concentrated in more convenient Houses, where they could more easily apply themselves to their vocation. But the people were not deceived by this, and in several places in Slovakia police had to be called out to control popular demonstrations.

Nearly 2,000 Religious were herded into the various "concentration monasteries", where, in uniforms and known only by numbers, they were compelled to follow indoctrination courses in dialectic materialism. After a time all the men, with the exception of those who were considered politically dangerous or unfit to work, were put into industrial works up and down the country, while the women were also put to work in the factories and fields. In the autumn the younger Religious were drafted into the Army.

In July a new penal code was brought into force, under which anybody who had given proof of hostility towards the Republic, and who had not changed his views while serving a prison sentence, on completion of his sentence would be sent to a forced-labour camp for a period of from three months to two years. Roughly seventy forced-labour camps had been set up by this time, and this number was to be considerably increased later.

Besides the Religious, at least 2,000 priests were serving terms in prison or in forced-labour camps by the autumn of 1950.

While the campaign against the religious Houses was being waged, a similar campaign was directed against the seminaries. First, all teachers of theology were appointed exclusively by the Bureau for Ecclesiastical Affairs. All Catholic faculties and schools of theology were then closed, and the State opened two seminaries, in Prague and Bratislava, for the preparation of potential priests according to its idea of what that preparation should be. Students who refused to attend the State seminaries were either sent to forced-labour camps or drafted into the Army. The majority of seminarists chose this fate, rather than collaborate with the Communists.

From the beginning of 1950 every priest, from the highest prelate to the lowliest parish priest, came under the strict surveillance of the police, who were required to report, not on the way in which they carried out their religious duties, but on their personal activities, and particularly on their attitude towards politics and the pseudo Catholic Action Movement. Like the attachment of agents to the religious Houses, this was a preparatory move in a campaign to break the resistance of the priests by threats and imprisonment. To give legal form to the persecution that was to follow, a new law was promulgated which made it a crime for priests to obey certain instructions of the hierarchy, as, for example, the reading of Pastoral Letters banned by the Government. Acting on this law, the Government were able literally to fill the prisons with priests.

This campaign was waged with unrelenting violence throughout the whole of 1950. Besides attempting to bring the clergy to heel, an attempt was made to separate the hierarchy and leading clerics from the corpus of lower clergy, by arrests. Between July and September two Bishops and four Auxiliaries were arrested and imprisoned, two Bishops were placed under house arrest, while another was confined in a cell in the monastery of Broumov. Vicars-General and other officials loyal to the Church were removed and replaced by "patriot" priests.

On 27th November the Auxiliary Bishop of Olumouc, Monsignor Stanislas Zela, together with Monsignor John Boukal, first secretary of the Archbishop Primate, Monsignor Joseph Cihac, Archdeacon of the Metropolitan Chapter, Monsignor

Jaroslav Kulac, of the Archiepiscopal Chancellery, Father Anthony Mandl, Secretary of Catholic Action in the Archdiocese, Monsignor Otokar Svec, former Chancellor of the Apostolic Inter-nunciature, Father Vaclav Martvy, former interpreter at the Inter-nunciature, the Abbot of the Premonstratensian monastery of Strahov and the Abbot of the Benedictine Monastery of Brevnov were brought to trial in the notorious prison at Pankrac, on charges of attempting to overthrow the régime, to destroy the economic and social order of the Republic and of spying for foreign powers. All the accused had clearly been submitted to brain-washing while awaiting trial, for all "confessed" in court to their crimes. The Auxiliary Bishop was sentenced to twenty-five years' imprisonment and fined the equivalent of slightly more than £900, while others received sentences varying from imprisonment for life to different terms of penal servitude.

A second trial began in Bratislava on 10th January, 1951, the accused being three Slovak Bishops—the aged Bishop of Spis, the Bishop of the Oriental Rite of Presov and the Auxiliary Bishop of Trnava. As in the trial at Pankrac, so now the charges were of attempting to overthrow the régime and of spying for foreign Powers, and the accused "confessed" and asked pardon for their crimes. The Bishop of Spis was sentenced to twenty-four years' imprisonment, and the Bishop of Presov and the Auxiliary of Trnava to life imprisonment.

In February a series of trials of priests was begun that continued for several months. The charges were invariably the same, the accused "confessed" and the sentences were uncomprisingly vicious. As a result of these trials many parishes were left without their priest.

While all this was in progress the Government was removing all manner of high officials, Vicars-General and Vicars-Capitular and Canons, and replacing them with "patriot" priests. Meetings of these "patriot" Ordinaries and others were held, and much publicity given to their declarations of loyalty to the State. A Sacred Congregation of the Consistory held on 17th March, however, courageously declared all these Government appointments null and void, but their act only served to intensify the persecution.

Early in March the Archbishop Primate was fined the equivalent of slightly more than £300, and moved first to the castle of Rozmital and then to Nova Rise. Under the penal code, the fine rendered the Archbishop incapable of holding office, and the Archiepiscopal See was declared vacant.

By the middle of the year the replacement of high officials by "patriot" priests had created an almost entirely new hierarchy of Government collaborators. Only Bishops did the Government not appoint, but since the Vicars-General and Vicars-Capitular took over the administration of the dioceses, this did not really worry the régime, though every kind of pressure was brought to bear on the Bishops, without success, to make them take the oath of loyalty to the State.

For the remainder of 1951 and throughout 1952 the Government continued to crush the loyal clergy and Bishops and to encourage the collaborators. From time to time they made so-called gestures of "good-will", as when they began once more to pay the stipends of all the clergy still at liberty, and make grants for repairs to churches. But this was done more for its propaganda value abroad than for any motives of compassion.

In 1953 the Bishop of Brno was arrested on the grounds that he had made arrangements for the observance of the Marian Year, which, because it had been decreed by the Vatican, fell foul of the law which prohibited loyalty to a foreign Power. The Vicar-Capitular of Roznava was also arrested and imprisoned. In the following year the Bishop of Litomerice, who had been prohibited from exercising his episcopal functions in 1951, was arrested together with his Vicar-General and a Father Francis Vlak, on charges of spying for the Vatican. All were sentenced to twenty-five years' imprisonment. The Archbishop of Olomouc was also said to have been arrested in a general round-up of clerics and laymen. This cannot be stated categorically, for the Government had now stopped publishing the news of arrests and trials. But the Archbishop certainly disappeared for a long time, and when he at last returned to his diocese, weary and ill, he gave no indication of what had happened to him.

By 1955 no fewer than thirteen of the Bishops were in prison or confined in some unknown place. Even as late as March 1957 the whereabouts of the Archbishop Primate was unknown. Without their leaders it is small wonder that the clergy were confused, and though many still resisted, many gave way in the hope that by doing so they were doing what best served the interests of the Faithful. Now and again the Government has made moves to relax tension. In October 1956, for example, it was announced that the Bishop of Spis and the Auxiliary Bishop of Trnava had been released, and though forbidden to return to their dioceses, were permitted to travel freely throughout the country. Liberty has also been offered to the Religious held in concentration monasteries if they would undertake not to wear the habit or try to get in touch with their former Superiors. There has not been reported a single case of these offers being accepted. On the other hand, secret trials of Jesuits and Salesians have been held, the victims being accused of having escaped from their place of confinement and secretly exercised their ministry.

In none of the other People's Democracies has the Church been so completely broken as in Czecho-Slovakia. The Government here have not been content to wait for time to bring about the dissolution of the Catholic Church. They have dealt the Church such a blow that now only a miracle can revive it. Perhaps the age of miracles has not yet passed.

CHAPTER XVII

The Technique

"THE PHILOSOPHICAL basis of Marxism," wrote Lenin, "is dialectical materialism . . . materialism that is absolutely atheistic and resolutely opposed to all religion."

In these words lies the *raison d'être* of all the Communist persecution of all the Churches, not the Catholic Church alone. Though we have dealt in the foregoing pages with the terrible suffering inflicted only on the Roman Catholic Church, it will be well to remember that equal suffering has been inflicted on all Churches and all religions which have not found themselves able to align themselves with Communist ideology.

Now, if it is true to say that materialism is resolutely opposed to all religion, it is no less true that all religions which are jealous of their integrity, and which have as their basis the belief that Man is inferior to some Supreme Being, are equally opposed to materialism. Particularly is this true of all religion based on Christian principles. Religion and Communism must, therefore, always find themselves in violent collision with one another.

Communism has much to fear from Christianity, apart from the fact that it is a "jealous god" which insists upon its devotees giving themselves wholly and entirely to it. It is this which makes it impossible for it to permit a rival to take the field as well, even though that rival may confine itself to a part of Man for which Communism has no use—the soul. Indeed, to recognise the existence of the soul would be to recognise something completely at variance with dialectic materialism. But in order not to stray into the realms of philosophical or religious argument, let us accept, once and for all, that Communism dare not accept a rival, so vulnerable is it to the goodness that there is in all men.

Lenin may have had his ideals, and may have been an idealist, in the sense that he desired the great mass of men to enjoy the full fruits of labour both of the hands and the mind. There is no doubt that the proletariat had been exploited and depressed by the comparatively small ruling class, and to change this was a laudable wish and intention. But, as it has turned out, the Communist régimes that have developed have not produced the Lenin ideal. A recent visit to Russia has convinced this writer that the great mass of the proletariat is still being exploited for the benefit of the few. Indeed, there is more class distinction in Soviet Russia today than there is in England. The ruling class is not an aristocracy of birth, but an aristocracy of money, and, therefore, of power. The Communist maxim that in order that the State may be exploited for the good of all, all must be exploited for the State, is just not being applied. The State and 99 per cent of the people are both being exploited for the welfare of the remaining 1 per cent. If, in the course of this being achieved, many of the workers find themselves better off than they were, this is fortuitous, and though it may make them happier, the improvement of their lot is entirely comparative. They live constantly the victims of a great delusion. Besides, the number of such people accounts still for only a very small proportion of the whole population.

For a nation to be exploited in this way, it must be entirely subservient to the directions of the small body of rulers. In such circumstances it would be fatal for the individual to be allowed freedom of thought or action in any sphere. To be able to worship as one wishes demands freedom of conscience as well as of thought and action; and if you have these freedoms in one sphere you cannot deny them in others, such as politics, which would automatically permit opposition to, as well as support for, a Government. It is this which makes Communism the resolute enemy of religion.

And religion is made the resolute enemy of Communism by its demands not only for the free exercise of conscience, thought and action, but because it recognises that there is something higher than the State, and that very often what the State proposes to do or even does, is diametrically opposed to the fundamental teaching of goodness, truth and honesty, which is the basic teaching of all religions. The Christian religion, no matter what denomination is involved, is based on the doctrine of Free-Will. The Communists deny this doctrine. For these reasons, among others, there can be no compromise between religion and Communism, or between Communism and religion.

Since the State bases its power upon physical strength, whereas the strength of a religion is based on morality, the State has the instruments for imposing its will on the minds of the people through their bodies. That is to say, a bludgeoning with a length of lead piping can be much more effectively persuasive with the majority of men than moral argument, talk of sin and damnation, or of goodness and salvation. The Church, in any encounter with the State, is, therefore, bound to lose—until such time, of course, as moral strength reasserts itself and provides a physical strength which can withstand beatings, even though death may result from the beatings. So deeply implanted are goodness and honesty and rightness of conscience in the souls of men that they cannot be destroyed, and sooner or later they must achieve the ascendancy. In this lies the future triumph of Christianity and the Church. For though the new generations may be brought up *not* to know about any religion but dialectic materialism, sooner or later the serious flaws in the new religion must become apparent, and there is only one way to remove the flaws—by a return to God. The Communists in several countries are believed to be content for time to bring about the final utter suppression of the Churches in their country—once they have been smashed into relative ineffectiveness by persecution—but they do not see how time must work against them. Communism may be able to fool some of the people some of the time, but it will never be able to fool all, all of the time.

Communist leaders have realised, however, that in order to establish a régime at all, the Church, which they rightly recognise to be their chief enemy, must be made as ineffective as possible, as soon as possible. There were many ways in which this could be done, and the Great Prototype worked out a technique which all the satellites have faithfully followed. There have, naturally, been slight variants to suit special conditions, but by and large, the overall technique has remained constant.

One strange thing, however, emerges from all the measures enacted to suppress the Church: this is the insistence of all the régimes to do whatever they proposed doing under a cloak of legality. That is to say, schools and property were not seized and confiscated until *laws* had been introduced to allow this to be done *legally*. Even the suppression of the Catholic Press has been brought about by the passing of censorship laws, though "shortage of newsprint supplies" has in fact, more often than not, been quicker and more effective in reducing the size of the Press. It was when the back of the Press had been broken by the with-holding of newsprint that censorship delivered the coup de grâce.

Why should the Communists set so much store by the law? Two reasons suggest themselves. One, the effect on foreign opinion of their action against the Church might, in the Com-munist view, have been much more devastating if the sup-pression of the Church had been carried out without the backing of the law. In actual fact, this belief of the Communists has been proved false, for the simple and foreseeable reasons that the action was not taken under existing laws, but under laws specific-ally decreed to meet the situation, and that the majority of people, especially in the Western democracies, have no respect for laws which permit persecution. But the second reason for making persecution legal has perhaps even more importance in the Communist mind. Most people in twentieth-century Europe are instinctively law-abiding. To obey the law has become so ingrained in practically all national characters that even bad laws tend to be obeyed as automatically as good laws. On the other hand, any bad act which has not the cloak of law is bound to be resisted even to the point of physical resistance. The Communist insistence on introducing repressive laws may, therefore, have a strong psychological basis, the rightness of which seems to be borne out by the fact that even in predominantly Catholic countries the vast majority of the people have made no attempt to bring pressure on the Government to stop the persecution of the Church. The uprisings in Poland and Hungary and East Germany, for example, were revolts against tyranny which affected the private and domestic lives of the man in the street; by which is meant that the Poles and Hungarians and East Ger-mans rebelled not because their religious life had been made impossible and their Church suppressed, but because they were oppressed in their secular day-to-day existence. Though one must admit that religious persecution added to the sum of their oppression, religious persecution was not the main cause of rebellion.

The first two acts of all the new Communist régimes were the nationalisation of land and of schools. If the laws affecting this were not promulgated simultaneously, they followed one another with only a short space of time in between. It cannot be said that the nationalisation of land was aimed specifically at the Church, but since the Church almost invariably derived a large part of its essential income from land, it was viciously hit by the earliest decree of the new Government. On the other hand, the nationalisation of schools was a blow aimed directly at the Church. In the first place, the Church had always been one of the pioneers of education, and owned a number of schools. In State schools under the old régimes in predominantly Catholic countries, two or three hours a week of religious instruction was always included in the curriculum.

As we have already pointed out, the Communists believe that by suppressing the religious education of the young and replacing it by lessons in dialectic materialism and atheism, they are tackling the problem at its roots. There is a good deal of justification for this belief, for it had been a similar belief in the reverse process which had prompted the Church to organise schools of their own, and to teach religion in all schools. "Give us a child up to twelve years old," the Jesuits are supposed to have said, "and we care not what happens after that"; implying that they can so form the child in its early years that no contact with any other religion, or atheism, can seduce the adult from the Church.

All the Constitutions of the People's Democracies contain clauses or articles guaranteeing liberty of conscience and liberty of worship. Here again we have an indication of the psychological understanding of the situation by the Government and of its two-facedness. To have suppressed the Church at a single blow, to have refused all practice of the religion in which they had been brought up, would have undoubtedly resulted in revolt. If this had happened before the régime had consolidated itself in other spheres, it could—in fact, would—have dealt a death-blow to the régime. If, on the other hand, no brake had been put on the Church from the beginning, the result could have been equally fatal for the régime, since, its activity unimpaired, the Church could have brought great moral pressure to bear on the Faithful to make them discard the new régime.

The régime, then, could not afford either to suppress the Church at one blow, or to permit the Church to function unhindered. At the same time that it guaranteed freedom of religion, however, it interpreted the Church's function to be merely the exercise of its activities in the churches; that is, the celebration of religious rites. This was where it was two-faced. Only the Constitution of Yugoslavia uses the specific phrase "liberty of *worship*", which is not at all the same thing as "liberty of *religion*". All Churches, all religions, are involved not merely in the celebration of religious rites in churches. The practice of religion is carried into many spheres of the daily life of the Faithful: through schools, through charitable organisations, through youth organisations, through literature, and so on. To curtail the function of a priest merely to the celebration of the Sacraments is to deprive him of 80 or 90 per cent, or even more, of his ministry, which is the Church's ministry. But this was what the régime always retorted that it meant by "freedom of religion", whenever the hierarchy protested that the régime was acting contrary to the Constitution. "We don't mind a priest celebrating Mass," they have said, "nor do we mind people hearing Mass. But in every other sphere of life the responsibility is the State's for seeing that old people and orphans are looked after, that the youth is provided with leisure activities, that the children are educated, that the sick are tended and comforted." Though they did not add that they could not afford to allow the Church to do these things for the people, since through them much influence accrues to the provider.

The Constitution was always one of the first acts of the new régime. The inclusion of the phrase "Liberty of religion" was obligatory, therefore, for reasons already quoted. To have suppressed freedom of religion would have automatically meant the immediate and total suppression of the Church. To have made it clear, without any possibility of ambiguity, that "freedom of religion" merely meant "individual liberty to go to church", might well have had results equally disastrous to the régime as the total suppression of the Church. It was natural, perhaps, that the Church should interpret "freedom of religion" to mean the right to carry on all the activities of the Church as hitherto. Perhaps it was just as natural that the Church in Yugoslavia should interpret "Liberty of worship and the free exercise of religion" to mean the same thing as "freedom of religion" always meant. There is as little doubt that the Communists meant the Church to interpret the phrase in this way in the early days of the régime. It provides, however, another example of the insistence of the Communists to cloak everything with legality.

But the Church and the Faithful must have been somewhat gullible if they really believed that the régime would allow the full exercise of a Christian ministry. The régime could no more do this than allow the Church to keep its schools and to provide religious instruction. For, while it took over schools and eventually made religious instruction impossible as a long-term policy, it had to reduce the influence of the Church in all other ways, if only because through its organisations and extra-ecclesiastical activities it could wage war on the régime.

The régime was alive to the dangers with which the Church confronted it in its outside activities, and made no bones about admitting it. It demanded the complete separation of Church and State, and explicitly prohibited all political organisations with religious backgrounds. It feared the influence of the Church on the political thought and actions of the people with an honest fear, a fear which, moreover, was justified however much the Church might reject the suggestion that none of its functions was political. The Church has always had great political influence, which it has yielded through Catholic Action. It has been thrust to the forefront of attention only recently by the case of the Bishop of Prato, in connection with which it has been admitted openly on all sides that the Christian-Democrats owe their predominance on the Italian political scene to the support of the Church.

Of almost equal danger with the organisations, of course, were the Catholic Press and Catholic printing-houses; for the Church is a propagandist *par excellence*. There is no doubt that there was a genuine shortage of newsprint in the years immediately following the War in eastern as well as in western Europe. This automatically reduced the effectiveness of the Catholic Press, by reducing circulation; but if there had been fair rationing the Church would not have objected. But there was not fair rationing. The State-owned Press had almost all the newsprint it needed—at the expense of the Press owned by the various denominations. Censorship could do the rest.

Censorship was used in every possible sphere of the dissemination of Church propaganda. But it was a logical extension when it was applied to Pastoral Letters, however much the Church might protest that this was interference in purely ecclesiastical matters. The Pastoral Letter can be a very effective instrument in influencing the Faithful.

Do not let it be thought from these remarks that the actions of the régime are condoned. Attention is being drawn to these things merely to underline the ruthless campaign by which the Church was attacked. The State had to have all the weapons if it was to vanquish the Church.

Thus we have, so far, these steps in the technique:

1. Nationalisation of Church real estate.
2. Nationalisation of schools and restrictions on religious education in schools.
3. Suppression of Catholic organisations and religious Orders.
4. Suppression of the Catholic Press.
5. A ban on all extra-ecclesiastical religious manifestations such as processions, pilgrimages, meetings, etc.

By the time stage 5 has been reached the Church has been severely wounded. But as each wound has been received, the more courageous have the Church leaders become and the more outspoken in their protests. Yet though, from its point of view, the régime has every right to deliver the quietus with one final blow, it does not deliver it.

Faced with intransigeant Primates and prelates, naturally it strikes at them. Admittedly a Church deprived of leaders is a weakened Church; but it is not a dead Church. While the lower clergy and their congregations still have Faith, the Church will not succumb. Yet, at this stage, it would have been so very easy for the State to have suppressed the Church; but still it does not.

When the reason for this is sought, it would seem that the régime has not at this point been sure of its position and its strength. For some reason, it still believes that the adult population which has not embraced Communism still needs the solace of some sort of religion. But while providing for this, it takes the weakening process of the Church still further by attempting to set up a National Church, separating the lower clergy from the Bishops and by causing a schism within their ranks.

This attempt to split the Church, and to set up a National

Church, is, to our minds, one of the strangest manifestations of the entire campaign. If dialectic materialism, as defined by Lenin, is "absolutely atheistic and resolutely opposed to all religion", why this attempt to set up a National Church? If the organisers of the campaign, on being asked, gave an honest answer, it is likely that they would offer some such explanation as this: "So long as people brought up in religion constitute a formidable proportion of the population, they must have the opportunity of letting off religious steam. A National Church would not only provide the requisite safety-valve, but would have the advantage for us of being a Church entirely subservient to the State. Not only that, it would ease the conscience of the more religious to have the régime supported by a Church. Of course, the creation of a National Church, particularly if composed of former elements of the Catholic Church would weaken the Catholic Church in two ways: the actual splintering would drain off much of its strength, and a powerful rival would even further reduce its influence. In time, of course, the need for even a National Church will disappear as the present younger generations brought up in atheism reach adulthood and the present religion-bound adults die off. So it is only a temporary expediency, and in no way opposed to the tenets of Communism as expounded by our great founder, Lenin."

The various steps taken to split the Church and to found a National Church follow a definite pattern. Fortunately for the régime, and unfortunately for the Church, in every country where the attempt to found a National Church has been made—and in only Estonia, Latvia and Bulgaria, where Catholics were in the minority, has no attempt been made—priests have been found willing to co-operate with the régime. They have never been numerous, but always enough to form an effective nucleus. Some of them no doubt honestly believed that they could reconcile the Faith with the tenets of Communism; a few others believed that by collaborating they could avoid the complete denial of their ministry to their flock; but the majority of them were utter opportunists, without any moral or spiritual values.

With the co-operation of these so-called "patriotic" or "progressive" priests a Movement would be founded, which priests loyal to the Faith were invited to join, and if they refused, were coerced by economic pressure or by threats of torture and imprisonment. Many priests chose martyrdom rather than compromise with their consciences.

These steps were accompanied by three other steps, all of which were directly aimed at the formation of a National Church. Naturally, the Bishops warned their clergy not to become involved in the Movement; the counter to which was the imprisonment of the Bishops, either preceded or closely followed by the arrest and confinement of the Primate. With the Bishops, Auxiliaries and high administrative prelates—the Vicars-General and Vicars-Capitular—unable to perform their functions, the State proceeded to appoint "patriot" priests to the administration of the dioceses. The State never appointed Bishops, for the simple reason that Bishops must be consecrated, and the Faithful would have been horrified if the occupants of *sedilia* were not in the Apostolic Succession. Vicars-General and Capitular, however, are not consecrated, and could be appointed.

These appointments were, again, made under the cloak of legality. Laws were introduced which gave the State power to make such appointments, at the same time that it required all other appointments, even of parish priests, to be submitted to the State authorities for approval. Thus the State claimed the best of both worlds: the separation of Church and State, and the control of ecclesiastical appointments.

The third step, though generally taken simultaneously with the others, was the breaking-off of diplomatic relations with the Holy See. Only Poland and the East German Republic had no Nuncio or Apostolic Delegate; Poland because the Vatican had never recognised the Lublin Government, the East German Republic because it was a new State and had no Concordat with the Vatican. There are one or two variations in the order of events. Hungary, for example, broke off relations as early as 1945, though the arrest of the Primate did not take place until 1948 and the imprisonment of the Bishops until three years after that; while Yugoslavia maintained relations until 1952, though Archbishop Stepinac had been arrested and confined in 1946. The supposed aim of this step was to remove the political influence of the Vatican, which the Communists pretend to see as a temporal Power on a par with any other hostile Power. Thus "spying for the Vatican" has been made a capital charge and the one most often preferred against the higher clergy as a means of removing them. The true aim, however, most certainly seems to be the removal of uncomfortably influential independent witnesses of the measures being taken against the Church.

With the National Church functioning in some degree or another, with the State control of high appointments, with the hierarchy *hors de combat*, with relations with the Vatican broken off, with the clergy dependent for material necessities on the State, with the youth of the country practically unable to receive any religious instruction and with the religious experience of adults restricted to the attendance of church services—and only those adults who are not directly dependent on the State for a living dare to go to church—the way has been cleared for further restrictive measures against the Church. Among these is continued pressure on the lower clergy, accompanied by arrests and imprisonment or forced-labour. Religious Orders, which have been attacked in various ways earlier on, now come under the full weight of the State's crushing-power. The Religious are forced into civilian life, their Houses closed and confiscated. Seminaries, which are the nurseries of the clergy of the future, are also greatly reduced in numbers, if not totally suppressed. In several countries entry to a seminary is forbidden before fifteen, so that in the formative years of seven to fourteen potential priests come under the influence of atheistic materialist teaching. By these measures, the future of the Ministry is being attacked.

As the accompanying chart shows, the Technique has been followed on twelve broad lines by all the People's Republics. There have been variants or "refinements" employed to meet local circumstances, as the foregoing accounts have illustrated; but the general picture is the same for all. This suggests that the countries we have considered have all followed the same "blue print"; and it does not require deep thought or a long search to find the architect who has drawn this blue print.

In one of his protests to the Polish Government, Cardinal Hlond commented: "Since the persecutions of Nero, the Church has not experienced an attack that can be compared with the present one." We would suggest that, terrible though the sufferings of prelates, clergy and Faithful have been and are, hope can spring from the horror of the persecution; for the attack made by Nero produced in the end, not the extinction of the Church, but a Church revivified, stronger and greater than ever before.

If there is a God—and the Church could not have found the tenacious strength which has preserved it from complete extinction were this strength not of Divine Origin—then the time must come when the Powers of Evil will recoil, retreat and finally disappear before a Church resurgent in greater glory than it is within our capabilities to conceive.

CHART SHOWING MAIN DEVELOPMENTS IN TECHNIQUE OF PERSECUTION

	Schools nationalised and religious inst. restricted	Church property nationalised	Economic blockade	Attempt to split Church	Catholic orgs. suppressed	Laws for State appointment of officials	Arrest of Primate	Break with the Vatican	Imprisonment of bishops	Public meetings etc. prohibited	Orders and seminaries suppressed	Catholic Press suppressed	*Modus vivendi* discussed
Yugoslavia (P.D.R. 1945)	1946	1945	1952	1949	1948	1945	1946	1952	1945–1953	1945	1946 1950 1952	1945	1953
Bulgaria (P.D.R. 1945)	1948	1948 1950	—	—	1949	1949	—	1948	1950–1952	1949	1950 1952	1948	None
Albania (P.D.R. 1945)	1945	1945	—	1951	1945	1951	1948	1945	1948	—	1945	1944	None
East Germany (P.D.R. 1945)	1948	1946	1953	1950	Partial 1953	—	—	No representation	—	1946 1953	Partial 1953	Partial 1953	None
Hungary (P.D.R. 1946)	1946	1945	1951	1949	1946	1948	1948	1945	1951	1957	1950	1948	1950
Poland (P.D.R. 1947)	1945	1946–1947	1950	1950	1950	1951	1953	No post-war relations	1948 1952	1949	1949 1950 1952	1950	1950
Rumania (P.D.R. 1948)	1948	1948	1949	1948	1949	1948	1950	1950	1948 1950	1949	1950	1948	None
Czecho-Slovakia (P.D.R. 1948)	1948	1948	1949	1949	1948	1948	1949	1949	1950	1949	1950	1948	None
Baltic States: Estonia Latvia Lithuania (All Soviets 1940)	1940	1940	— 1940	— — 1946	1940	1940	— — 1945	1940	— 1947 1946	— 1940	1940	1940	None

Bibliography

THE CHURCH AND THE CROOKED CROSS

Religious Resistance in Holland—H. S. Boas.
Le Cardinal van Roey et l'Occupation Allemande en Belgique.
Martyrologe 40–45—Josse Alzin.
L'Episcopat Français—A. Deroo.
Cahiers Clandestins du Témoinage Chrétien.
Quatre Années de Resistance à Albertville—L'Abbé Ploton.
Aufbau im Widerstand—K. Rudolf.
Christus im Dachau—P. Lenz.
Church and State in Fascist Italy—D. A. Binchy.
Rossano—Gordon Lett.
Race and Reich—J. Tenenbaum.

COMMUNIST PERSECUTION OF THE CHURCH

La Documentation Catholique.
La Civiltà Cattolica.
L'Osservatore Romano.
FIDES (International News Agency).
Neues Deutschland.
Informationsbüro West.
Otescstven Front (Sofia).
La Bulgarie Nouvelle (Sofia).
Magyar Kurir (Budapest).
Szabad Nép (Budapest).
PAP (Polish News Agency).
Trybuna Ludu (Warsaw).
Monitorul Oficial (Bucharest).
Telegraful Roman (Bucharest).
Lidova Demokracie (Prague).
Obrana Ludu (Prague).
Rudé Pravo (Prague).
CTK (Czecho-Slovakian News Agency).
Borba (Belgrade).
Politika (Belgrade).
The Soviets against the Church—Persecution in Soviet Latvia—Latvian Central Committee, Germany.
La Situation de l'Eglise Catholique en Lithuanie—J. Manclere.
Le Drame Hongrois—F. Honti.
Il Cardinale Mindszenty—S. Péterffy.

245

BIBLIOGRAPHY

Il Cardinale Mindszenty—N. Boer.
La Lotta dietro la cortina di ferro—F. Nagy.
"Le Procès des évêques hongrois"—*Esprit*, September 1951.
"The Case of Archbishop Grösz"—*Clergy Review*, August 1951.
"Recent Events in Hungary"—*Clergy Review*, October 1950.
White Paper on the Persecution of the Church in Poland (London, 1954).
Dieu contre Dieu?—C. Naurois.
New Moves in the Communist Struggle against the Church in Poland (London, 1955).
Le Calvaire des Catholiques en Roumanie—G. Stefanescu.
L'Ame Roumaine Ecartelée—P. Gherman.
Kirche unter Hammer und Sichel—N. Pop.
Problèmes Religieux dans un Pays sous Régime Communiste—A. Michel.
The Church of Silence in Slovakia—T. Zubek.
Governo comunisto e Chiesa cattolica in Cecosloacchia—F. Cavelli.
Collection of Laws and Regulations of the Czecho-Slovak Republic.
Church and State in Czecho-Slovakia—Ludvik Nemec.
Une Eglise du Silence—Catholiques de Yougoslavie (Bruges), 1954).
The Case of Cardinal Aloysius Stepinac—R. Patee.
Die rechtliche Lage der Kirche in der Ostzonen Republik.
Die Verfassung der Deutschen Demokratischen Republik.
Gibt es Glaubens und Gewissensfreiheit in der Deutschen Demokratischen Republik?—Cardinal von Preysing.
Communism and the Church—J. B. Barron and H. M. Waddams.